SAIL THE INDIAN SEA

ABOUT THE BOOK

An adventure story (which happens to be true) of the remarkable Portuguese breakthrough in the science of navigation and ship design in the fifteenth century, leading to the discovery of the sea route to India.

The leader of this expedition, Vasco da Gama, was an outstanding navigator, a great commander, ruthless, intrepid and incorruptible, under near-intolerable conditions in cramped 200-ton ships often out of sight of land for as much as 100 days.

Vincent Jones explains why the Portuguese needed to find India, what happened when they got there and how their achievements shifted the economic balance of Europe.

Less than half the crew who left Lisbon in 1497 returned in 1499. He tells a tale of endurance, skill and heroism.

ABOUT THE AUTHOR

Vincent Jones was born in 1912 and educated at Reading University. He served in Tunisia and Europe during the War and afterwards became a Director of the International Institute for Peace in Vienna. His books include a biography of John Milton, and an exciting account of the Tunisian landing *Operation Torch*.

Thank you Tessa

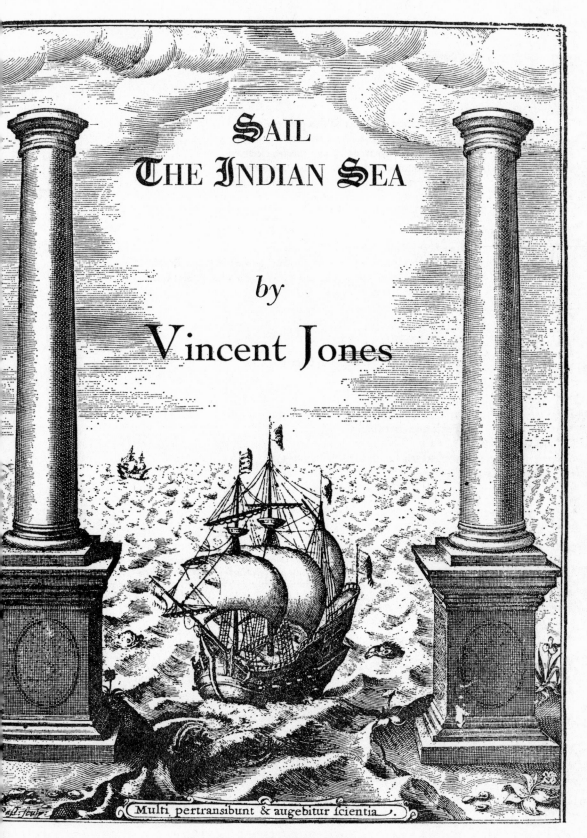

SAIL
THE INDIAN SEA

by

Vincent Jones

Multi pertransibunt & augebitur scientia.

Gordon & Cremonesi

Designed by Heather Gordon
Set in 11pt on 13pt Monotype Bembo and printed in Great Britain
by The Anchor Press Ltd and bound by Wm Brendon & Son Ltd
both of Tiptree, Essex

British Library Cataloguing in Publication Data

Jones, Vincent
    Sail the India Sea
    1. Gama, Vasco da   2. Indian Ocean –
    Exploring expeditions
    1. Title
    910'.09'164   G370.G/   77-30498

LCCN: 77-030498
ISBN: 0-86033-021-4

The publishers wish to thank the following for their assistance and permission to use illustrations included in
this work: (Navigation Section) Mansell Collection (a), Cambridge University Press (b,j,k,l,n), Junta de
Investigações do Ultramar – Lisboa (c), Bodel Nijenhuis Collection of Leiden University Library (d,e),
Bibliothèque Albert I Brussels (f), National Maritime Museum Greenwich (g,h,m,o,p), Dundee Museum
and Art Galleries (q). British Library (1-6, 10, 14-17), Biblioteca Estense di Moderna (7).

Gordon & Cremonesi Publishers
London and New York
New River House
34 Seymour Road
London N8 0BE

At the beginning of the tenth century of the Hegira among the extraordinary and terrible events of those times was the arrival in India of the accursed Portuguese, one of the accursed Frankish peoples. One of their gangs embarked at the Ceuta straits and made their way into the Sea of Darkness passing behind the White Mountains in the region where the Nile has its source. They journeyed to the east passing a strait where one side is a mountain the other the tumultuous Sea of Shadows: their ships could not anchor there and were wrecked. None of them escaped. A long time the Portuguese persisted stubbornly and were wrecked at this place, none of them able to get through to the Indian Sea until at length a caravel arrived in India. Before reaching India, when on the east coast of Africa they sought for information about the India Sea until they secured the services of an able Arab seaman, Ahman Ibn Majid, with whom the head of the Franks named Almilandi negotiated and who got drunk with the Portuguese admiral. Being drunk this seaman showed the admiral the route. 'Do not keep to this coast but sail out to sea. At the other side keep to the coast for shelter from the waves.' Following this guidance a large number of Portuguese vessels avoided shipwreck and many reached the Indian sea. At Gowwa, which is the name of a place on the coast of Deccan—this Deccan town is now in the power of the Franks—they built a fort. Later they seized and fortified Hormuz. Unceasing support reached them from Portugal; they engaged in privateering, taking prisoners and plunder. They took every ship by force so that they wrought great damage to the musulmen and to seafarers in general. Then Nyzzaffar Sah bin Mahmud Sah bin Muhammad Sah, sultan of Gujarat, sent an ambassador to Sultan Al-Asraf Kansuh Al-Guri to ask for help against the Franks.

> Kuth ad-din an-Nahrawali, in
> *Al-bark al-yamani fi al-fath al-Otmani*
> (Conquest of Yemen by the Turks),
> after Gabriel Ferrand

I, Vasco da Gama, now going out at your bidding, most high and mighty king, my master, to discover the seas and lands of India and the regions of the east, swear on the sign of this cross, on which I lay my hands, that I shall hold it high in service of God and of you and shall not let it fall in sight of Moor, heathen or any race of people wherever it may be, and through every danger of water, fire or sword shall ever guard and defend it even to death. And I further swear that in the execution and accomplishment of this discovery which you, my king and master, have ordered me to achieve, I shall serve with all faith, devotion, watchfulness and diligence, and shall fulfil the orders which you have given me at this time, until such time as through the grace of God, to serve whom you are sending me, I come back to the place in which I now stand, and see again your royal majesty.

Barros, *Decadas da India*, liv. iv, cap. 1 (Author's translation)

Contents

Foreword

A new approach

Sail the Indian Sea is a new approach to the understanding of Portugal's historic incursion into the Indian Ocean to grab the spice trade, the men who achieved it and the captain who led them—an attempt to tell the story of why and how it happened. Why did this small nation on the Atlantic lead Europe in the science of navigation? What social, economic and spiritual forces impelled the Portuguese in their dogged search to open the way to the east? Why was Vasco da Gama chosen to command the crucial expedition? What sort of man was he? What was life like for him and his small force as they ventured into the Sea of Darkness? What sort of ships did they sail in and how were they equipped? And what did it all signify for the future of Europe and Asia?

There are big gaps in the records. Vasco da Gama's instructions, his charts, his logbooks and his reports have disappeared, possibly lost in the Lisbon earthquake, possibly destroyed for reasons of state secrecy. It seems that returning captains were required to restore their charts to the royal archives under pain of death. Contemporary chronicles often become vague or fall silent where details of what happened could be too revealing to competitors or perhaps reflect badly on the King. (An instance is the sudden falling off of Pacheco Pereira's *Esmaraldo di Situ Orbis* just where details of Gama's geographical discoveries should follow.) The official histories were written a generation and more after the events—and were official.

Luckily, descriptions of the actual voyages by men who took part in them have survived. They give many vivid details of critical events and of the impressions made on the Portuguese by a civilisation outside their experience, for which they had no reference points apart from their hatred of 'Moors'. These reports give the invaluable living basis for the story. But much is missing. For example, three months at sea—months of critical interest in the history of navigation—are passed over in a hundred words. It becomes necessary to fill in from the official historians (who will have had access to the archives), from scraps of Gama's advice to later navigators and from secondary sources, such as reports by other voyagers of those times which show what life was like in such ships.

To set the scene for what Gama accomplished other questions have also to be asked. What were the scientific and technological bases for his venture? What was the context of the European economy and west–east trade within which the Portuguese organised their expansion? What were the existing trade networks which they wanted to supersede? What was the nature of the society into which they burst with such energy? How did things look from the other side of the fence?

In the narrative which results from all this I have invented nothing. Where a speech or a conversation is quoted I have taken the words from a contemporary account. My principal sources are discussed and all are listed at the end of the book. As I do not want to interrupt the story by citing in detail a great many references I give here the main texts which I have used for quotation. Those from the anonymous *Roteiro* of the first voyage are from Ravenstein's translation; those from Thomé Lopes' account of the second voyage are my own; for the third voyage I have used Stanley's translation from Correa's *Lendas da India*. Supplementary quotations from Barros' *Decadas da India* and Castanheda's *History of the discovery of the East Indies* are mainly from translations by Stanley, supplemented or modified by some of my own. For Osorio's history of the reign of Emanuel I have used mainly the Gibbs translation, supplemented by my own where the Gibbs text has gaps. For the racy tang of his language I have sometimes used passages from Astley's *Voyages and Travels*.

For ease of reading, and following the precedent set by Stanley and other translators and editors, I have adopted the style 'Gama' in preference to 'da Gama'. And to avoid confusion throughout the book I use the term 'Moor' in the sense it was used by the Portuguese (and by Shakespeare) to signify any moslem, whether Arab, Turk, Tuareg, Gujerati or East African. Also in the interests of simplicity I have transliterated the Portuguese nasal ending 'ão' as 'an', *eg* Estefan da Gama.

With this concept of setting the Gama achievement in its living context of history I have tried to let the story tell itself without putting between reader and the facts a screen of moral judgment. There is much cruelty among the dour heroism. But I doubt whether the sixteenth century has a lot to teach the twentieth in that respect.

One

Commission

'I have chosen him for this journey'

On a hot july day in 1497, Emanuel 'the Fortunate' of Portugal held an audience at his summer retreat from Lisbon's close and unhealthy heat, the hill castle of Montemór o Novo. He had summoned this assembly to witness his formal commissioning of the men he had chosen to find the way by sea to India. Their orders had already been gone through many times; their instructions had long been drafted, examined, discussed and put into final form. The leaders of the expedition knew well what they had to do; all their preparations were made. But the young King, just twenty-two with less than two years on the throne, judged it essential to impress on his court and people the full significance of what he was doing, the breadth and daring of his enterprise.

He made it a solemn and splendid ceremony in the castle hall. When he took his seat the private secretary took place beside him, supporting a massive furled standard. In front of him the crowding prelates, nobles, state officials and court gentlemen had left a space for the man who had been chosen leader and his three captains. There Vasco da Gama stood forward. He was of not more than middle height but stood tall, a man of presence, his solid frame supported by strong calves and short thighs. Broad shoulders and a deep chest were enhanced by his slashed, square-cut tunic. He wore a full, square-cut beard. His dark hair curled closely over his collar at the back and nearly hid his broad forehead in front, falling low above his dark eyes, which were deep-set and wide apart. His long nose was straight from brow to tip, emphasised by two strong vertical lines above it. He was richly dressed, a gentleman of the court, in his hand a square cap of dark velvet. Behind him were his brother Paulo, taller and grey-haired, Nicholas Coelho, a young mariner and close friend, and a sea captain, Gonçalo Gomez, who was a member of Gama's household. These were the four men chosen for the India voyage.

When all was ready and the clarions had sounded their fanfare, the King spoke to the commanders and to the assembly. He recalled the long preparations which had been made for that event, stressing the great achievements of his uncle and predecessor, Dom John II, the 'Perfect Prince'. Seamen sent out by him had sailed the coast of Africa from equator to Table Mountain and had even rounded the dread Cape of Storms, which he had renamed Good Hope. (It was the Perfect Prince who in his fourteen-year reign had broken the strength of the great feudal lords and restored the authority and revenues of the Crown. But that Emanuel passed over in silence.) Rather he went on to speak of his great desire to increase the patrimony of his kingdom. Much had already been gained by his precursors. Praise to God, he said, the Moors had been expelled from Europe and from the principal ports of the kingdom of Fez. New titles, new profits, new revenues had been found on the coasts of Africa, where nearly the whole route had been discovered. This success should surely be pursued. Could they not hope for much more by carrying this quest further? Could they not hope to secure those riches of the east which ancient writers had described, and which had made powerful states great through trade – Venice, Genoa and Florence among them?

All these things, he said, all the nation's experience, had been taken into account. He stressed his words: it would be ingratitude to God to reject what He so propitiously offered; it would be an insult to the memory of his predecessor, who had bequeathed to him the search.

Emanuel's careful phrases reflected the long battles which there had been in council, where many had opposed his wish to carry on the search for India and the lands of the east. These debates were described by Jerome Osorio, Bishop of Sylves, in his history of Emanuel's reign. Many had contended that it would be highly imprudent to run headlong into so many certain dangers upon such uncertain hopes. What advantages, they asked, were to be gained to balance the hardships of so long and perilous a voyage? Such an affair would surely bring on war with the Egyptian sultan, so powerful in the east. Even success, it was said, would draw on Portugal the envy of other princes in Christendom, perhaps with dangerous consequences. And, the King's critics added, the war in Africa, carried through with spirit and resolution, would bring greater glory; while if his concern were wealth he might gain more in numberless places of Ethiopia.

Osorio had little sympathy with these fears. The King, he wrote, 'looked upon despair as the mark of a low and grovelling mind, whereas he accounted hope to be the quality of a noble and aspiring soul'. But those fears and those debates were part of the background to this solemn audience and among the reasons for calling it.

Having made his point the King went on to describe how he had ordered four sailing vessels to be prepared; had assembled them at Lisbon; and had 'provided them with all things to pursue this voyage', which was so rich in expectations. Finally, the official annalist Barros reports him saying, 'Since I well remember that Vasco da Gama, who is present here, has admirably carried out all things that I have entrusted to him, I have chosen him to be captain-major for this journey, as a loyal and valiant gentleman, worthy of so honourable an undertaking. May God grant that he accomplish it, doing himself and me such a service that his honours, and those of all who support him in the hardships of his journey, will ever be remembered. In this confidence, and in accordance with the knowledge which I have of all of them, I have chosen them as his assistants, intending that they obey him in all things which concern my service.

'I commend them to you, Vasco da Gama, and you to them; may you be in peace and harmony, which are so powerful to overcome and transcend all dangers and difficulties, making the greatest adversities of life easy to bear: I hope God will allow that these be less for you than for those who have gone before you and that through you this my kingdom may gain the fruits of them.'

When the trumpets had sounded again all present kissed the King's hand—a slow proceeding, a ceremonial rite of acceptance and thanks. Silence followed and Vasco da Gama knelt before the King. The secretary unfurled the great banner which he had been holding, a banner of white silk decorated with the red Maltese cross of the Order of Christ. He held it out to the captain-major as he swore his oath to the King on the symbol of that cross. And, when the vow was made, he gave the banner into Gama's keeping and handed him his written orders. With these there were also letters for various kings and princes who were believed to reign in the far places of his search. There were messages of special weight for Prester John of the Indies and for the King of Calicut. When all was done Emanuel stood, wished Gama and his captains good fortune and with his guard left the hall. In the silence after the King had gone, Gama turned from the chair of state. He raised the great banner and led his captains through the assembly, out of the hall and into the hot sun.

It is astounding that almost nothing is known about Portugal's most famous conquistador before he was given this great command. Later, when his name had become a legend in the land, many stories were told. His brother Paulo, some said, had been the King's first choice as commander but had pleaded ill health and asked the post for his brother. Others had it that Vasco had a claim because John II had intended to appoint his father; or that Vasco, when chosen, had asked the King to appoint his elder brother instead. Most probably Vasco da Gama was chosen by John II, for at the time of the King's death, plans for a voyage to find the sea passage to India were nearly ready. But all is uncertain.

At the time of his commissioning Gama was thirty-five or thirty-six years old and unmarried. He had been born at Sines in Baixo Alentejo. This small coast town south of Lisbon, set between high cliffs, lived by fishing; its men were sailors, as the Moors who were there before the reconquest had been; and the design of their boats and their seamen's skills owed much to these predecessors. His father had been civil governor of Sines and he spent his childhood there. Perhaps he went to school at Evora, but no one knows. At some time, perhaps in the mid-1480s, he was accepted among the gentlemen of his court by the Perfect Prince. After he had become famous one annalist (Pedro de Mariz quoted by Ravenstein) recalled 'a young man, high spirited and indefatigable, his knowledge of navigation so thorough that he could have held his own with Europe's most experienced pilots'. Castanheda wrote that he was 'a man experimented in matters of the sea, and of navigation, wherein he had done to this kingdom much service . . . a man of great courage and valour, and therefore very apt and likely to attain and achieve the end, that was by the King desired'.

Such snippets of gossip apart, only one clear incident of Gama's earlier days is known. It happened in 1492, when he was about thirty. In that year a caravel returning laden from the royal mines on the Guinea coast was seized by a privateer of France, 'though at that time there was peace between the two countries'. When this report reached Lisbon, leading counsellors at court advised a diplomatic gesture, as counsellors often do. Send an envoy to the King of France, they said. This did not suit King John at all. 'I have just the contrary mind from every one of you,' he said. 'I have no wish to see a messenger of mine ill received or made to kick his heels in ante-rooms—a fate more grievous to me than would be the loss of the gold.'

He left the council and sent for Gama to his private quarters, for Gama was 'a man in whom he had confidence, who had seen service in the fleets and in the affairs of the sea'. With secret orders Gama crossed over the Tagus lagoon for Setubal, twenty miles south. There is no record of whether he took men with him from Lisbon or whether he requisitioned them from the port commander when he arrived, nor whether he acted in the dark that night or next morning. With fast horses ridden hard the journey from Lisbon to Setubal would have been some four hours' travel. Time was needed to form a posse. Sudden and secret action was essential.

It seems probable that Gama had his men deployed by daybreak on the quay, where ten French ships freighted with fine merchandise lay berthed. Whatever means he may have used, the outcome was certain and abrupt: each ship was arrested; its cargo was taken and sealed in bond; tillers and yards were locked away; the men were put ashore; and an armed guard was put aboard.

The result justified John's judgment: 'All the owners presented themselves to the King of France making complaint and petitioning him that he act that they might regain their ships. And the King of France at once so ordered things that the matter was settled and accomplished; and he sent King John his caravel with all his gold without a piece missing. So it came about without discussion;

the King of France sent his apologies; and the King ordered all things to be given back to those shipowners just as they had been taken away with nothing missing.'

After this event nothing more is recorded of Gama until Dom Emanuel sent for him.

Two

Preparation

*'It was not by chance that the Portuguese
found the sea route to India'*

Was Ptolemy right?

They stayed that night at Montemór, for there was to be a dedicatory high mass
next morning, celebrated by a man well known to Gama, Ortiz de Vilhagas,
who had for many years been chairman of John II's group known as the
'mathematical commission', the back-room experts for his 'discoveries'.
Approval and blessing from the church was as necessary to these men as the
King's commission. It was an essential spiritual stimulant to carry them on their
way; to be repeated in a different form that evening when they arrived, hot and
dusty from the long ride to where their crews were waiting for them, in hope
or trepidation. Their ships had already been moved from the lading quays of
Lisbon to anchor off Restello village where the Tagus lagoon narrowed towards
the sea. On the nearby sands stood an austere chapel, provided by Henry the
Navigator for the prayers of questing seamen. And that night Gama with his
officers there made their final spiritual preparation for their journey, dedicating
themselves for a daunting task.

There is no record of how they passed their dark vigil. There can be small
doubt that on that hot July night the air in the chapel was heavy with the
smoke of tapers and of incense. Each man will have knelt enclosed in his own
thoughts, as so many an other had done before him, seeking to strengthen his
soul before venturing into the Sea of Darkness. At least one of the men assembled
there had been there before, chosen this time to be pilot for the commander's
own ship: he was Pero d'Alenquer, who had been with Bartolomeu Dias nine
years earlier, when they were the first men from Europe to sail round the Cape
of Good Hope into the Indian Sea. Possibly old Bartolomeu was also one of

the men in the chapel, since he was to be their companion part of the way. His brother Diogo was sailing as clerk to the commander.

Sixty years earlier, before he built his chapel, the Navigator had sent out from Sagres men in small craft to sail round Cape Bojador into the dread Saharan seas. Year by year each one failed to overcome terrors that for generation after generation had gripped Iberian mariners. It was well known to mankind that beyond Bojador there was no race of men, no place for habitation; the land was sandy as the deserts of Libya, without water, tree or green herb; so shallow was the sea, men said, that it had no more than a fathom depth a whole league out from shore; currents so fierce raced down that coast that no ship which passed that way could ever return; and in those dark and ever storm-tossed seas were monsters yet unknown. These powerful fears gripped men of learning just as strongly as they did unlettered mariners. Such sages as Pomponius Mela and Master John Sacrobosco, skilled astronomer of England, warned men that the country on the equator was uninhabitable from the sun's great heat, and being uninhabitable could not admit of navigation. To foster such fears there were the Moors of Ceuta and Granada, and earlier those of the Algarve, who were among the first teachers of Portuguese mariners and fishermen. They had reason to protect their coasts with fables. For they knew of good fishing further down the shores of Africa and wanted no intruders. It may be that it was owing to reports of their voyages that it became possible to record Cape Bojador on a Catalan atlas of about 1375.

Fear was not unreasonable in the hearts of those first Portuguese who crept down past the Canaries, which were themselves still only half explored. The low coastline, where fogs are common, has ever-beating surf the rumble of which is heard many miles off. Currents do flow past that coast south-east into the limitless ocean. For much of the year the winds blow with the stream; but during the rains they drive in from the sea.

Year after year for twelve years, hardy seamen, unnerved by what they saw and feared, turned back. At last, in 1434, Gil Eannes doubled the cape. He found the sea navigable, reached a sandy shore where no signs of men were seen, and brought back to his master a plant of 'Mary's Roses'—the 'Resurrection Plant' (*Anastatica hierochuntina*) which he had found. His little vessel was a *barca*, perhaps thirty tons burden, not more. Such craft were three-quarter decked, with one big mast and square sail forward and a small mast aft to carry a lateen sail when needed; the crew would have numbered about fifteen. A year later he went again, with him this time Afonso Gonçalvez Baldaya in a *barinel*, rigged in the same way but larger and oared as well. They sailed 200 miles beyond Bojador to a shore on which they found footprints of men and camels.

The progress down the coasts of Africa had begun. Step by step, at times with speed and vigour, at times static or slow-moving, it led to a world-changing goal—a goal unconjectured at the start.

Henry, called the Navigator, who started the invasion down the shores of Africa, was not a superman, a saint or a scientist. A grandson of John of Gaunt, Duke of Lancaster, he was a Renaissance prince of wide interests, seeing further than many. When he was twenty-one he made a name for valour at the taking of Ceuta in 1415. He was a main inspirer of that scheme to seize for Portugal— or for Christendom—this stronghold in Barbary. It was a historic leap out from the Algarve (al-Gharb, the west of the Moorish world from early in the eighth century of Christendom, the first of Islam), the last part of Portugal to be cleared of the Moors. This assault on Ceuta, just across the narrows from Gibraltar—and from the kingdom of Granada, where Islam still reigned—was invested with all the trappings of a crusade. And so it was, in part, for the men of the Renaissance were not the ones to act from simple, clear-cut or wholly conscious motives. Portugal had been formed as a kingdom in a contest of 200 years against the infidel. It had been a long, hard struggle against the eager swordsmen who had brought learning, invention—and even some toleration— to Iberia; and in that struggle the quest for power, land and wealth was fortified by the strength which comes from serving the will of God. It worked on both sides. God's will had made all-powerful the forces from Syria and the Maghreb that in the space of just ten years had swept through from Algeciras to Poitiers. During a rule of 200 years these forces had brought civilisation to the Iberian peninsula. But in Galicia a few unconquered groups survived in their wild hills, and gradually adventuring nobles from France joined with them to start the long fight to drive the Moors back. For, as it turned out, it was also God's will that the Moors should go.

Experience taught the christians that men of Islam were little open to conversion, except by force. It was thus for the glory of God to conquer, kill and enslave those who were condemned in any event to eternal fires: a notable moral strength when other necessities urged expansion.

After the thunderclap of Ceuta, the Navigator left the Iberian peninsula only twice—twenty-two years later, for the disaster of the failed assault on Tangier; and, when an old man near his death, to seize Alcacer Ceguer (Ksar es Seghir), on the Morocco coast. He settled on his lands in the Algarve and rarely left Lagos or Sagres, a new town founded close by Cape St Vincent. There he collected men of learning, seamen, inventors—and through them gathered information, ever more information: knowledge of coasts, knowledge of navigation, ideas on the construction of ships, news of the sources of gold and of slaves. As lord of the Algarve he had important revenues from tuna and coral fishing monopolies, and from tithes on fishing too; so he was drawn close to the men in small craft who sailed ever more daring in the wake of their Arab forerunners, into the ocean, to the coasts of Morocco, to the islands of the Atlantic. For generations before the rape of Ceuta, from ports and coves of the Algarve and Alentejo, from such small harbours as Sines, where the boy Vasco grew up, these men learnt the ways of the seas and bit by bit improved their vessels. These, too, helped towards the science of navigation, Portugal's great gift to Europe for some eighty fruitful, audacious years.

Need was the spur: Prince Henry had need of greater revenue; Portugal needed grain, had to find ways to expand the static economies of Crown and nobility and to grasp its own trade (not least for spices) out of the hands of the Italians, needed gold (all Europe was short of gold) and manpower. Europe at the time of Ceuta still suffered from the effects of the Black Death; the number of its people was still less than it had been in 1340. Portugal had also lost those moslems who had migrated to southern Spain or Africa in the decades after the reconquest. There were too few working hands.

Between Europe and the sources of gold and the riches of Asia stood the broad belt of Islam, to be penetrated, conquered or outflanked. Penetration was the monopoly of Italian merchants and bankers, principally those of Genoa and Venice, who traded at great cost, one group through Constantinople and the Black Sea, the other mainly through Alexandria. As for conquest, even the vast cost in lives, wealth and morality of the Crusades had not been able to achieve it. Ceuta, and later a few towns on the Moroccan coast, held a few decades and then ceded, represented the only military successes. As Europe's promontory in the Atlantic, hanging over Africa, Portugal was placed by geography for a flank manoeuvre; and more than any country of Europe Portugal had the experience and had gathered the knowledge to bring it off.

Portugal's relationship with the Moors of the Maghreb had two faces. During the long reconquest with its many setbacks and many battles there was also constant commercial and intellectual interchange between the advancing Portuguese and the retreating moslems. When the expulsion of the Moors from Portugal was accomplished (it was to be another 250 years before Spain was wholly freed), trade with the Barbary coast became important; and it grew continuously in importance not only for Portugal but also for the rest of Europe. Islam also had its needs—above all silver, the main money metal, of which there was a famine in north Africa in the fourteenth century. Silver came from south-east Germany, Hungary, Tyrol, and principally Bohemia, which, as the Black Death had passed it by, was rich in workmen.

Safi, Ceuta, Oran, Algiers and Tunis were the chief outlets for the riches—principally salt, gold and slaves—brought by caravan across the desert from the kingdoms of black Africa, from Mandinga to Nubia. Great prices had to be paid for those cargoes from Cantor, Genni, Timbuktu, Goa, Kano, the lakes of Kanem—as was not surprising: to carry one ton across the Sahara took twenty dromedaries about two and half months. Furthermore, by the opening of the fifteenth century, the goods brought in this fashion were not enough to meet the needs (starting in the fourteenth century there was a gold famine in Europe, and for nearly ninety years from 1380 gold coin practically disappeared from the Iberian peninsula). Exhausting efforts at conquest could not have increased the supply, and, indeed, it was a benefit to Portugal that Barbary was too hard to overcome. It was necessary to find a way to the sources themselves.

Ever present in the background was a misty, ancient story that somewhere in the east there was a great christian empire ruled by a priest king. Travellers' tales had placed Prester John, as he was called, in Cathay, in the Indies, in realms beyond Persia. At last it became settled thought that he reigned somewhere in mid-Africa, and this raised hope of a potent ally against Islam, could a link with him be found.

Yet in the beginning expeditions were not conducted according to any consciously formed long-term plan. King, nobles and merchants simply sent out ships from time to time. The Navigator, who was responsible for about a third of the voyages in the forty-five years between Ceuta's fall and his death, in 1460, was the most persistent. He did most to collect and study the resultant knowledge; and he gained most from the resultant wealth. Gradually he gave purpose and direction to discovery. Unmarried, ascetic, governor of the military Order of Christ, which gave him both revenue and forces, governor of the Algarve and of Ceuta, he was able to put the weight and resources of the state into colonising the Atlantic islands and exploiting west Africa. At the time of his death Africa remained his main concern, and there is no evidence that he had turned his thoughts to India. He showed no interest in the great question of proving wrong the school of Ptolemy and revealing the Indian Ocean to be an open sea.

Perhaps his most positive achievement was his work of collecting in Sagres charts, reports, navigational data, skilled pilots, mathematicians and astronomers, and there starting the work of teaching traditional seafarers the first steps in navigational science. As they searched for fabled islands in the Atlantic—and for fish—they discovered that in the Forties (latitude) the currents of the mid-Atlantic flow east towards the Lisbon coast. This was perhaps their most valuable find for the success of their ventures west and south towards equatorial Africa. They could use this knowledge to escape the currents which flow southward down the African shore, to sail west, then north and so home. They recorded the circuit of the Atlantic winds and currents, and they kept this knowledge to themselves for so long as they could.

When the Navigator died, his whole collection was transferred to the Guinea House (later known as the House of Mines) at Lisbon. Originally this was the government office for regulating the revenues from the Guinea trade and then for organising it. John II made it also a centre for scientific study and for training. There can be little doubt that Gama, who showed himself not only a rare commander but also a navigator equipped with the newest scientific knowledge, was associated in some way with the work of the House of Mines; it is probable that this was one element of his contact with John and a factor which led to his appointment.

That is speculation. It is virtually certain that the first conscious planning for seeking out the sea-route to India began a full fifteen years after the Navigator's death, when King Afonso gave the nineteen-year-old Prince John control of exploration. When John became king himself, in 1481, much was already in train. The means and the men were found and were set to a comprehensive plan directing all discovery to his great purpose. Within seven years Dias had rounded the Cape of Good Hope and sailed into the Indian Ocean.

Nine more years were needed to prepare the consummation. In the seven years after the return of Dias in 1488 John II mounted no further recorded voyages. Apparently everything was directed towards laying the basis for the final effort—design of ships, perfection of information, choice of men. All this was carried through under direction of the Perfect Prince before he died— chiefly by his 'mathematical commission'. Its members listened carefully to the harangues of a prolix Genoese who tried to convince them that Cathay could be found by sailing due west a thousand leagues without putting into port. They refused him, knowing already that this was impossible. (When eight years later Columbus sailed due west with the aid of the credulous sovereigns of Castile, he did indeed strike the Antilles without stop on the way; and he thought Cuba to be Japan. His navigation was faulty; his mathematics were shaky; his vision-ary obsession brought him by accident to the threshold of a new world.)

Meticulous in gathering information, in 1484 (probably at about the time when Columbus applied to him), John II sent the Jewish astronomer Master John Vizinho to Guinea to establish latitudes through accurate astronomical observations. In the same year that he sent Dias to round the southernmost cape of Africa he commissioned two men of his personal staff to travel overland through the realms of Islam to Ethiopia to search out Prester John (who it had at last been concluded must be the Emperor of Ethiopia), and to India. In May 1487 Pero da Covilhan and Afonso de Paiva, chosen for their fluent Arabic, among other qualities, left Lisbon as merchants, well supplied with money and with banker's drafts. They took with them 'a sea-card, taken out of a general map of the world, at the making whereof was the licentiate Calzadilla, bishop of Visco, and the doctor Master Roderigo . . . and the doctor master Moyses, which at that time was a Jew; and all this worke was done very secretly in the house of Peter de Alcazova, and all the fore named persons showed the utter-most of their knowledge, as though they should have been commanders in the discoverie, of finding out the countries from whence the spices come . . . as though in those seas there had been some knowledge of passage into our westerne seas; because the said doctors said, they had found some memoriall of the matter.' Purchas has some of the names muddled but he gives the essence.

It was one of history's great reconnaissances, espionage on a grand scale. Together the two journeyed through Spain, Italy, Rhodes and Egypt to Aden. There they separated. Soon Paiva, whose mission was to make his way to Ethiopia, obscurely died. Covilhan, in the dress of a Moorish merchant, took ship from Aden to Cannanore on the Malabar coast, where he stayed and probably traded, the first Portuguese known to reach India. From there he moved south to Calicut, then north to Goa. Crossing the Arabian Sea and the Gulf of Oman he followed the trade lines of the Moors to Hormuz, and from there back to Zeila on the Somali coast and down to Sofala in the Mozambique channel, the southernmost Moorish trading post in Africa and chief outlet for gold from the inland mines. At length he turned to find his way back, passing through Aden again *en route* for Alexandria and expecting to meet Paiva in Cairo. Possibly by some prearranged sign, since John was a methodical prince with a care for detail, he met there two emissaries from Portugal, Rabbi Abraham of Beja and Joseph 'the shoemaker' of Lamego. These brought him new orders from the King—to take up the quest of the dead Paiva and carry his embassy to Ethiopia. So the dauntless man turned back and never saw Portugal again. He did reach Ethiopia, and there met the Emperor, was detained by him, lived at his court some thirty years, and married; and he was there still in 1520 when Rodrigo de Lima came with great ceremony as ambassador from King Emanuel, and when Francisco Alvarez recorded what he told of his adventures.

Joseph of Lamego took back to Lisbon a letter from Covilhan and with it 'ill written and disfigured' but filled up and corrected, the 'sea-card' which had been provided by the mathematical commission. In this Covilhan reported that at Cannanore and Calicut were to be found cloves and cinnamon, pepper and ginger; that the Moors traded from there to Persia and to Africa; that Sofala was the outlet for rich mines of gold. He wrote of the temper and disposition of the princes of Malabar, a country very populous, full of cities both powerful and rich. They could certainly be reached, he said, by the passage round Africa: 'the ships which sailed down the coast of Guinea might be sure of reaching the termination of the continent, by persisting in a course to the south; and when they should arrive in the eastern ocean, their best direction must be to enquire for Sofala, and the Island of the Moon'. From each one of these lands one could set a course for Calicut, '*for there was sea everywhere*'.

How many years Covilhan spent on these wanderings is uncertain: it is also uncertain when his priceless despatch reached King John. But indirect evidence shows that this essential intelligence was used in preparing Gama's voyage, as was the report made by Bartolomeu Dias when he returned after doubling the Cape of Good Hope.

Why John, and following his decision Emanuel, did not call on Dias to command the Indian expedition is a difficult question. He was a greatly experienced navigator; he had already succeeded in reaching the Indian Ocean;

and he was still active—he sailed with Gama as far as Guinea, and three years
later he was sent in charge of three ships with Cabral's Indian armada. He was a
man of knowledge and of courage; yet Vasco da Gama was chosen in his place.
The reason may be partly one of social standing. For this was to be both a
discovery and an embassy; its leader had to be both commander and envoy:
Gama was a gentleman of the court.

There may be a further reason, as is argued well by Armando Cortesão in
his book *The Mystery of Vasco da Gama*. He examines the contemporary
accounts, Arab as well as Portuguese, and the evidence provided by carto-
graphical data, figures for the annual production of ship's biscuit, and the like.
This leads him to suggest that during the apparently inactive seven last years of
his reign John II probably sent out several secret voyages, including at least one
round the Cape and north to Sofala; and he believes that at least one such
voyage was commanded by Gama. Such a conclusion helps explain the report
that Gama had 'done good service in the time of King John, [and was] a man
experienced in the affairs of the sea'.

Gama, furthermore, had shown himself a man of resolution and sudden
energy when called on in a sharp moment; whereas in the crisis of a tempest
Dias had not been able to carry his men with him and had had to turn
back.

Resource, determination, the force of character to drive through to the end
must be among the qualities sought for the leadership of such a mission. Perhaps
they were to be found in the thick frame kneeling the night through in the
Restello chapel to prepare his spirit for directing the long search. He had chosen
to take his brother with him, and his other captains and some also among his
crew were friends of his: *perhaps to be some relief to him* in the essential loneliness
of command.

In the ships as they rode at anchor, those men not at vigil took what rest
they could; and in Restello the priests and friars prepared processions for the
next day.

Under the banner of Christ

Great crowds gathered by Restello beach on the day of the feast of Our Lady,
8 July 1497, a Saturday. They came from Lisbon and the country round about—
from Estoril, Almada and Barreiro across the river, Montijo perhaps: kinsmen
and intimates of the sailors; officials and others concerned with the preparations
—customs men, fishermen, boatbuilders, sailmakers, coopers, armourers,
harbour officers, merchants and journeymen; the curious, the wealthy and the

hungry, beggars, and, no doubt, the whores and pilferers. Equipping this journey had taken many months.

For more than two years men had been at work building new ships for the voyage. The trees had been cut in the royal woods of Leiria and Alcacer during the last year of John II and hauled down to the Lisbon shipyards. Pacheco says in his *Esmeraldo* that 'they were built by excellent masters and workmen, with strong nails and wood; each ship had three sets of sails and anchors and three or four times as much tackle and rigging as was usual'. In the coopers' shops new barrels for water, wine, vinegar and oil were strengthened with many additional hoops of iron. Provisions were brought from the markets, royal estates, farms and gardens of the Alentejo—according to Ravenstein these were enough for a daily ration of one and a half pounds of biscuit, a pound of salt beef or half a pound of salt pork, two and a half pints of water, one and a quarter pints of wine, one-third of a gill of vinegar, and one-sixth of a gill of oil—for each man, for three and a half years. For fast days there was, in place of meat, half a pound of rice or salt codfish or cheese for each man. To supplement the basic diet there were also lentils, sardines, plums, almonds, onions, garlic, mustard, flour, salt, sugar and honey—the whole stock of provisions amounting to about 5,700 pounds' weight for each crew member. 'Arms and ammunition were also in excess of what was needed for such a voyage.'

The same source says that arms and ammunition for each ship included eight cannon made from wrought-iron staves held together by hoops; twelve bombards, half mounted forward and half aft; and an uncertain number of falconets and swivel guns. There were no small firearms for the men. Personal arms included crossbows, spears, javelins, boarding pikes, axes and swords. Such a fitting-out signalled a more than ordinary enterprise. Its importance could not be concealed. It was commissioned by royal command, supported by the King's authority, largely backed by exchequer funds and royal borrowings. All the world—not only the world of Lisbon, but also the spies of Castile, Genoa, Florence, Venice, London and Antwerp, and no doubt also of Fez, Tunis, Alexandria and the Porte—would have known that the discovery of a sea passage to the Indies was the aim.

With a sure eye for effect, and with a feeling for morale, the church designed that Vasco da Gama, his officers and men should go in solemn procession from Restello to where the ships' boats lay ready to take them off. Officers and men were about 170 in number and rare in quality; Gama had been able to take his choice from among 'the best and most skilful pilots and mariners in Portugal' (Pacheco). During the months of preparation and recruitment he spent much time with the men, pressing them to learn the elements of carpentry, ropemaking, caulking, blacksmithing and plankmaking; and for those who did he increased their pay by two-fifths, and himself bought the necessary tools. 'They received, besides other favours,' Pacheco says, 'pay higher than that of any seamen of other countries.' His crew on the flagship was probably approximately as follows: master, pilot and under-pilot, mate, boatswain, twenty able seamen or mariners, ten ordinary seamen, two boys, a master gunner, eight bombardiers, four trumpeters, a clerk or purser, a storekeeper, a master-at-arms, a barber–surgeon, two interpreters, a chaplain, six artificers (carpenter, caulker, cooper, ropemaker, armourer and cook) and ten servants. Divided among the ships were also ten reprieved convicts to be dropped ashore for exploration.

Some thirty of all the men are known by name. In the S. *Gabriel* with Gama and his pilot, d'Alenquer, were Gonçalo Alvares, master, and Diogo Dias, purser. Paulo da Gama's pilot in the S. *Raphael* was Joan de Coimbra, his clerk Joan de Sá. In the *Berrio* with Nicholas Coelho were Pero Escolar as pilot and Alvaro de Braga as clerk. The two interpreters were Martin Affonso, who had lived in the Congo, and Fernan Martins, possibly of African origin, who spoke Arabic and perhaps Malayalam. Only two priests are mentioned, one of them so dimly that many deny his existence. He was Joan Figueiro, who was said to have written a diary of the expedition. Chaplain of the fleet and father confessor was Pedro de Covilhan, prior of a monastery of the Order of Trinity at Lisbon. Sailors and soldiers whose names are known were Joan d'Ameixoeira, Petro de Faria e Figueirido; his brother Francisco de Faria e Figueirido, who 'wrote Latin verses'; Sancho Mexia; Joan Palha; Gonçal Pirez, who was a seaman retainer of Gama and formerly master of a new caravel at Oporto; Leonardo Ribeyro; Damian Rodriguez; Joan de Setubal; Alvahro Velho, who perhaps had spent some years at Sierra Leone and Fernan Veloso. From the names it would seem that some of those who served as seamen and soldiers were of gentle birth. Convicts named were Pedro Dias, nicknamed 'North-easterling'; Pero Esteves; Joan Machado, a friend of the seaman Damian Rodriguez; and Joan Nunez, a converted Jew who spoke a little Arabic and Hebrew.

Under the banner of the Order of Christ, probably with the royal standard furled, with crucifix and the fragrant swirl of censers, Vasco da Gama led his men down to the beach. They were already a group set apart, shut in to a common destiny. Each carried a candle as they marched through streets to shore; behind them followed priests and friars, and many onlookers, the priests calling the Litany, the people giving the responses.

Waiting by the boats was the 'vicar of the monastery', probably confessor Pedro de Covilhan. There is nothing to show that the church thought this the occasion for any higher dignitary. With all kneeling on the shore, the padre read the general confession and then gave them general absolution for all the acts to which they might be led, calling on the authority of a papal Bull which the thoughtful Navigator had secured in the early days of his raiding missions, called discoveries.

That Bull had justified and given moral right to men sent or licensed by

Prince Henry and all who followed to foray along the coasts and among the islands from Bojador to the south. They brought back valuable knowledge of wind, tide, coast and latitude, slowly opening to the power of Atlantic Europe the riches to be gained from Africa and Asia. The first gain was slaves, product of reckless slaughter and seizure of survivors, 1441 the historic year. Gold followed soon; and in due time the supply of slaves was no longer won by capture but secured by trade with chieftains and merchants of west Africa, who sold their own people. So began the centuries of a commerce which robbed Africa of its people, destroying its potential of evolution.

In his Bull, 'Eugenius the Bishop' (Pope Eugenius), writing from his concern 'for those things that may destroy the errors and wickedness of the infidels and by which the souls of good and catholic christians may the more speedily come to salvation' granted 'by apostolic authority', to Henry, Duke of Viseu and governor in spirituals and temporals of the Knighthood of the Order of Christ and the knights and brethren of the said order, and to 'all other faithful christians who purpose to make war under the banner of the said order against the Moors and other enemies of the faith . . . complete forgiveness of all their sins, of which they shall be truly penitent at heart and here made confession by their mouth. And let no one break or contradict this letter of mandate, and whoever presumeth to do so let him lie under the curse of Almighty God.'

The power of this spiritual backing is made clear by the Navigator's historian and panegyrist, Azurara, in his account of an attack in which fifty-seven Africans were taken for slaves, others were killed 'and again others escaped'. 'Oh if only among those who fled', he wrote, 'there had been some little understanding of higher things. Of a surety I believe, that the same haste they showed in flying, they would then have made in coming to where they might have saved their souls and restored their affairs in this life. For although it might appear to them that, living as they were, they were living in freedom, their bodies really lay in much greater captivity, considering the nature of the country and the bestiality of their life, than if they were living among us under an alien rule, and this all the more because of the perdition of their souls, a matter which above all others should have been perceived by them.' Enslavement is the soul's salvation: so, early on, was the civilising mission of christian Europe understood. There is little reason to doubt that these men and those who came after, not least Gama and his followers, were deeply imbued with this conviction of their moral right.

Fortified by a sense of divine sanction, the captain-major and his men got into the boats, which then were shoved off by eager, perhaps envious, hands and floated free. Oars dipped; the sunlight sparkled in their wake. As the crews rowed to the ships, which bobbed at anchor in the deeper water, perhaps they needed such spiritual strength to support their inner convictions and hopes, and suppress their fears. For from the mass of souls they left behind they heard not cheers and salutations but cries of distress and sound of weeping. By the account of Bishop Osorio, 'not the priests and monks alone, but all the concourse prayed aloud to God with tears that this perilous navigation might turn out well for them all, and that all having well performed the undertaking might return safely. This weeping and lamentation was made by so many that it seemed that funeral rites were being performed. For some spoke thus: "See whither covetousness and ambition are carrying away these wretched men! Could a more severe punishment be found for these men, even had they confessed the most horrible crime? For they have to cross over the immense ocean, and to overcome with most perilous hardships the enormous waves, and in innumerable places meet with risk to their lives. Would it not have been far more tolerable to be carried off by any kind of death on shore, rather than to be buried in the sea waves so far from home?" Such, and many like discourses they held, since fear compelled them to imagine everything sadder than it was.'

But the captain-major was not the man to let cries, groans or fears take effect. He knew his men and they him through many weeks of preparation, lading, stowing, shaping their ships for sea. When they had climbed the sides and joined the watch aboard, they may have needed time to change from their best clothes, worn for the send-off, but the whistles were soon piping; the sails were untied, shaken loose, sheeted back to bear the ships against the ebb so that the men on the peak deck could haul the anchors. The prevailing wind blew from the north. As the sails filled, the great Maltese cross of the Order of Christ glowed red against their bleached white. Leading the fleet, the flagship S. Gabriel flew the banner of the Order of Christ from her maintopmast. As the S. Raphael gathered way in her wake, Paulo da Gama broke the royal standard of King Emanuel. The smaller Berrio, commanded by Nicholas Coelho, and the storeship, commanded by Gonçalo Nunes, followed on, and with them the caravel of Bartolomeu Dias on voyage to Guinea.

'And when the sails were cast loose, all the crowd of spectators redoubled their tears and commended them to God'—Barros confirms Osorio's account.

Ships for the ocean sea

As the ships stood down the river through the narrow opening past Alges, towards Cascais and the Atlantic, the fall of land round them, the sound of the wind, the creak of masts and hull, their own movements and the voices of the men could blanket the sounds and sorrows which held them to the past. Slowly the prows began to rise and fall to the ocean. Below Cabo Raso they set course south, the tide still with them, making perhaps five knots.

Two of the ships were of special build and making their maiden voyage. Bartolomeu Dias had designed them specifically with the needs of the India voyage in mind; they were born of his experience of sailing by caravel in the seas round southern Africa. That famous craft the caravel was a precise tool created by the Portuguese during the fifteenth century to serve their expansion; it made possible the advance from port-to-port navigation to exploration in the open sea. Its origin was threefold: the fishing boat of the Moors, which contributed the liberating, manoeuvrable lateen sail; the galley of the Italian merchants, long and fast; and the slow, solid 'round ship' of northern Europe.

Three technical innovations of the thirteenth and fourteenth centuries made possible the generation of the caravel as a vessel for long voyages. The first of these—apparently developed by Baltic traders about AD 1200 or soon after, in response to the needs of broad-beamed wind-driven vessels navigating in shallow seas—was the replacement of the steering oar by the rudder hung on a stern post. This had reached Spain before the end of the century. The second innovation was to have more than one mast; the third, to find means to use several sails. The North Sea and the Atlantic were the essential influences. In the Mediterranean the galley had become the chief transport. It was fast, sure, suited to a tideless sea, and as a ship of war was capable of defence against privateer or infidel. Oarsmen became soldiers at need. From the thirteenth century the galley was the only form of trading vessel permitted by the government of Venice, which forbade the carriage of spices in ships. Though masted and equipped with sails, the galley was driven mainly by oars and thus largely independent of wind. But it was not an efficient vessel of general commerce. By 1400 the typical commercial galley, with twenty-five benches of three oarsmen each, was 130 feet stem to stern with a beam of sixteen feet (ratio of eight to one) and rather more than six feet draught. It could carry rather less than 100 tons at a speed of about five knots (when rowing). When the need for new outlets caused Venice to search for trade into the Atlantic and up the English Channel to London, Bruges and Antwerp, it was still galleys that were used. The round trip to Flanders took from April to December.

For such work and in such seas the galley could not compete with the strong ship of the north, built heavy with a hull of ratio about two to one, strongly cambered and capacious. In its earlier forms a single mast carried one great sail, with high tractive power but easily torn, the strength of its material being a limit on its size. Gradually additions were made: bonnets at the foot of the mainsail; above the 'basket' (crow's-nest) a diminutive square sail; and a short mast aft carrying a small, triangular or square sail, to aid manoeuvrability. At the stern, the castle was built up higher and higher, giving greater space for captain, pilot, officers, guns, and assault or defence in battle. Forward, the peak grew also, giving more room below and free space above for working the anchors, there being then no capstan. By the fifteenth century this was a powerful craft able to carry a large cargo, its shape well suited to the short chop of shallow seas and to tidal estuaries; but it was slow and needed a wind abaft the beam. It served well enough for trade across narrow seas and along coasts, but its greatest range was scarcely 600 miles and it was not fit to venture out in 'the ocean sea'.

Their Moorish heritage, their ever more daring search for fish (taking them further and further out into the Atlantic), the vessels of the English and Flemish trade, and the need for a ship able to sail long distances without having to call at a port were all influences on the Portuguese as they evolved their new craft. This turned out to have the long line of a galley; the bluff bow, cambered hull and raised stern of the northern ship; and the easily shifted lateen sail of Barbary, on two, three or, later, even four masts, raked forwards. The sails had long tapering yards so balanced that they could be hung either side the mast, and the total sail area was large. Such was the caravel that made possible the great leaps to the Madeira Islands, the Canaries, the Azores, and the 6,000 miles and more down to and round the Cape of Good Hope, by way of Cape Blanco, Cape Verde, Sierra Leone, Guinea, the Congo, Angola and Cape Cross. It was not the least of Henry the Navigator's services that he helped and encouraged this evolution.

Osorio described the caravel thus: 'They have no topsails; the yardarms are fixed not at a right angle to the mast but hang obliquely held to the masthead. The sails are triangular in form, with the lower edge reaching deck level. The lower ends of the yards, where they are by the ship's side, are as thick as a mast and thence taper towards the peak. Moreover because of their very great speed the Portuguese use ships of this kind in battle. The yards can easily be moved towards prow or towards poop or made fast amidships and can be shifted very quickly from starboard to port or port to starboard. The sails, which can be gathered in from the corner opposite the yard, are easily let out or shortened just as the course of sailing requires. From whatever quarter the wind blows the sails are filled without delay and they take all winds. Thus as often times the wind blows on the beam they hold the right course most perfectly and if with the same wind the course has suddenly to be changed they can bear away in the opposite direction with unbelievable speed.' (Author's translation.)

With the wind on the quarter caravels came close in speed to the nineteenth-century clipper. Their proportion of length to beam was three and a half, or even four, to one. To windward they were less good: having no keel they lost a lot in leeway. They needed a large crew to handle their sails, even for normal service: fifteen men for a thirty-tonner, who with their provisions and other needs took up seven and a half tons of lading. On a voyage of discovery, with the need to allow for landing parties and for loss by death, a sixty-tonner would require a crew of thirty-five. A discovery caravel of 100 tons had only five tons stowage space after allowing for its fifty men, supplies and spares. The longer the voyage to be made, the greater was the problem of capacity, eventually making it necessary to provide an extra ship solely for carrying stores (as in the expedition when Dias became the first European captain to double the Cape of Good Hope).

This problem of space was one of the reasons why the mathematical commission rejected Columbus. For they knew from years of study and calculation that it would not be possible to reach Asia without putting in to port. Misled by the Italian geographer Paulo Toscanelli and by his own faulty calculations, Columbus was convinced that he could reach the Isle of Cypangu—Japan—by sailing a thousand leagues due west with the trade winds. When eventually he sailed, he loaded food for fifteen months and water for six. But the Perfect Prince and his advisers were nearer the mark in calculating that the distance from Portugal to Cypangu, travelling west, was at least 4,000 leagues, or 12,000 miles.

For finding the sea route to India—almost as far again as any ship had so far travelled—the graceful darting caravel was by itself no longer enough. So Dias advised when he arrived home at Lisbon in 1488. A new model was needed. John II approved, and gave it to Dias to oversee the design and construction, commanding choice trees to be felled in the royal forests. These ships were already being built when he died. They were finished by order of Emanuel.

Dias devised a vessel closer to the earlier 'round' ship, but keeping some characteristics of the caravel. What he sought was a stouter, roomier craft, standing higher in the water and able successfully to navigate in coastal waters, better able to stand long periods in the ocean, safer in the tempests of the tropics, and with better quarters for the crew. He designed the vessel to have a foremast and mainmast, square rigged with mainsail and topsail, a square spritsail at the bow and a small lateen-rigged mizzen stepped right aft on the castle. These probably provided a sail area, without bonnets, of about 4,000 square feet. The foremast rose up through the forward castle almost directly above the stem: the mainmast was stepped somewhat aft of midship. Main and fore each had a crow's nest or fighting top. Length of hull was probably slightly under seventy-five feet, with beam about a third of that, or a little less. The hull, with some tumble-home to the gunwales and strengthened by three of four wales along its length, was almost certainly curved aft under the castle much like the bow; the square-cut transom shown in the dramatic picture of Portuguese carracks which hangs in the National Maritime Museum, Greenwich, probably belongs to the succeeding generation of ships, some ten years later. The after-castle had probably both quarterdeck and poop. Forward, the high, flat castle projected well beyond the stem, with bowsprit either piercing the prow or stepped just below.

Such, or nearly so, were the two new craft *S. Gabriel* and *S. Raphael* (the Portuguese called them 'ships' to distinguish them from caravels) commanded by Vasco da Gama and his brother, with probably about sixty men in each. Not all of these necessarily were official crew, since it seems that some officers and senior men took with them their own slaves. Contemporary accounts rate the ships at about 100 tons, perhaps equivalent to about 200 tons register in present-day terms. They were slower and less easy to handle, but steadier and roomier than the caravel. Coelho's *Berrio*, named after the pilot from whom she was bought for the voyage, was a caravel rated at fifty tons (say something under 100 tons register), with a complement of about thirty-five men.

With supplies for about three and a half years to carry, there was also need for a storeship. This was probably a so-called 'round' caravel, broader on the beam than the usual type, with square sails on the forward mast. She is likely to have been of 200–400 tons register, with a crew of perhaps fifteen. It was planned that at some point in the voyage she would transfer her stores to the other craft and then be broken up.

In the two ships the forward section of the hold was used for storing spare sails, anchors and other ship's requisites; amidships were water casks and cables; aft was the powder magazine and armoury. Bulkheads divided the lower deck into three compartments, of which two housed provisions, presents and articles for barter. Beneath gang boards which ran along the topsides from castle to castle were quarters—rough cabins—for mariners and seamen, and with them lockers for personal belongings. It was not unusual in these times for seamen's chests to be left standing on the hatches in danger of going, or being thrown, overboard in a bad storm; but it is unlikely that this happened in a fleet under Gama's discipline.

How duties were allotted in a ship of the time was described by Linschoten in the next century. The captain had the top gallery of the after-castle, his cabin lying behind it—his main duty in many ships, though not in Gama's, being command of the soldiers. The pilot had his cabins below the captain's, on the starboard side, never going down into the waist when under way; he 'standeth and commandeth the master of the ship to hoist or let fall the sails, and to look unto his course, how they shall steer, to take the height of the sun, and every day to write and mark what passeth'. (In Portuguese discovery ships it was normal for several people to take astronomical readings as a mutual check and for practice.) The master's cabins were at the same place as the pilot's but on the port side. He had command of the guns and was responsible for the care of the whole ship, including repair to sails and inspection for and rectification of any faults; he also stood and commanded 'with a silver whistle' the mainmast and its sails and everything aft.

Supplies such as sailcloth, nails or rope had to be requested from the clerk or purser and be signed for. The boatswain had his cabin in the forecastle and 'commandment and government' over the foremast and sails. Outward from the mainmast on the port side was the quartermaster's cabin and, close by, the cooking place. The quartermaster, too, sported a silver whistle, having in charge the seamen at the pump, inspection and repair of ropes, and one of the two ship's boats, which were carried amidships. 'Hard by the rudder' above the hold was the cabin of the chief gunner, who must 'always sit by the main mast looking upon the master that as the master whistleth to will the gunners to draw in their pieces or thrust them out he may be ready to do so'. The under-pilot (unclear where his cabin is) does 'nothing but help the chief pilot and relieve his quarter'; also there are two or three of the best sailors to 'do nothing else but command in the pilot's room when he sleepeth'.

The ships sailed out from Lisbon in formation, the flagship leading. In normal weather the other ships were required to conform to the commander, keeping in sight by day, navigating according to the flagship's masthead lights by night. Regulations proposed by Gama for the voyage of Pedro Alvarez Cabral, who commanded the second Indian expedition, show that the fleet was guided by gunshots from the flagship. For change of course the captain-major would fire two guns; each other ship would answer with two guns; when all had answered the fleet would turn to conform. Other signals, each of which had to be confirmed by the other ships with corresponding shots, were one to make sail, three to 'draw the bonnet', four to lower sails (no ship to turn, draw bonnet or lower sails until the flagship made signal). After sails had been lowered none were to hoist again without three guns from the flagship. A ship losing contact was to lower sail till daylight so as not to be carried so far as to be out of view the day after. Any ship with rigging down was to fire guns for help from the other ships. Other simple means of signalling available were smoke from a brazier fire hanging at the stern, or, at night, flame signals from brazier and torches.

If ships became separated by bad weather, fog, or other hazard, the fleet was to meet at the Canaries or at the Cape Verde islands. What the arrangements were once the fleet had passed Cape Verde is not known, but with such a long voyage with no port of call presumably some contingency plans had been laid.

When the ships left Lisbon the rainy season, with its frequent fogs, had already started on the African coast, but they had a fair wind and the north equatorial current, flowing south-south-west, helped them along. Seven days out, after setting course almost due south and making sometimes 110 miles a day, they sighted the Canaries. During the night of 15 July they passed to the west of Lanzarote. Cape Bojador's strand of red sand with long low profile the roar of its breakers and the cliffs beyond its bay—no longer a dark horror to seamen of Portugal—was passed at night. At daybreak the next morning the fleet reached the Terra Alta at the Tropic of Capricorn, where the crews spent some time fishing, and at dusk that evening the ships were off the 'Rio d'Oro' (which is not a river at all but a deep bay). A dense Saharan fog then closed down on them. With it came a storm from the south-west, violent but short. By the morning of 7 July the fleet was divided. Coelho's *Berrio*, the caravel of Dias and the storeship were still in touch, but neither the *S. Gabriel* nor the *S. Raphael* could be seen.

All made sail for the Cape Verde islands, the three which had stayed in touch meeting the *S. Raphael* soon after sighting Sal, the most north-easterly of the group, fourteen days and 1,600 miles out from Lisbon. With slackening winds they moved on together but fell into a calm, drifting south-west with the current for two days, lifting and falling to the rollers common in those seas in the summer months.

Under way again with an early morning breeze on 26 July they sighted Gama's ship, the *S. Gabriel*, some twenty miles ahead. Perhaps the captain-major reduced his sail on seeing them; for by evening the rest of the fleet was up within hail of him. All sounded their trumpets in joyful gereting, and saluted the flagship by 'firing off their bombards'. Bombards in northern Europe were essentially large-mouthed mortars lobbing stone balls, but the Portuguese used screw guns. These were loaded at the breech, which was closed with a screw fitting; they had screw chambers which could be taken out and used for firing blanks in salute. It was also a device that could raise the rate of fire in battle, each gun having a spare chamber in which a new charge could be prepared. They were loaded 'with cartridges or little bags of stuff'.

United once more, the next day the fleet could see through the thick haze the peak of Mount Antonio, nearly 5,000 feet high, announcing the largest of the Cape Verde islands, S. Thiago. In good spirits they anchored in Santa Maria bay, the Porto da Praia. There they rested seven days, taking on meat, water and firewood, and giving the *S. Raphael* time for much needed repairs to yards damaged in the storm. On 3 August they set out again, sailing east, then south-east for several days. Such a course keeps east of the Doldrums but leads to the east-flowing equatorial counter-current and the vacillating winds and currents off the Guinea coast. Somewhere west of Sierra Leone, Dias dipped his standard to the flagship and left the fleet on his way to sail due east, with the Guinea current, to S. Jorge da Mina. He was to take command of that fortress which John II, almost as the first act of his reign, had ordered to be built.

The Portuguese had been exploring the northern side of the Gulf of Guinea since the 1460s, marauding and trading on the Grain Coast (Liberia), Ivory Coast, Gold Coast (Ghana), and the Coast of Slaves (Togo and Dahomey). They had opened the back door to the lands which supplied the Barbary caravans. The fortress of S. Jorge da Mina (St George of the Mine), on the coast of Ghana west of Accra, stood guard where they could now trade direct with the powerful kingdoms of Melli and Benin.

On the upper Niger stood Genni (Djenne), more powerful and wealthy a city than the fabled moslem centre Timbuktu. It was capital of the great king-dom of Melli whose northern borders with the Sahara were the salt lakes of Tagaza. Guarded by six watch towers, at the extreme limit of human endurance, the black slaves who were marched down with the caravans worked for the season and such as survived that hell marched back with the last caravan to leave. Benin City, stood fifty miles inland on the lower Niger, circled by a high wall, a broad street striding through its centre crowded either side with traders. Here the Oba presided over medieval Africa's most powerful empire. From his palace with its great gate towers topped by gigantic emblematic pythons, he ruled from the borders of Nubia to the frontier of Melli.

From these rulers, or from their vassal chieftains closer by, the Portuguese bought principally gold and slaves, red pepper, cotton, ivory, civets and palm oil. This was the wealth which helped promote the ultimate leap to India; and it was buying from the rulers and merchants of Melli and Benin their unwanted or criminal subjects, or their captives, that the Portuguese began that inhuman traffic which, especially in the hands of the Dutch, French and English, was to deprive Africa of so many of its people.

For Dias this visit was a return. Five years before he rounded the Cape he had been a captain in the force, under Diogo d'Azambuja, which built the fort —not by force of conquest but as a result of cajolery and bribery. His appointment as commander of the post was a reward for his long services, perhaps a consolation for his being denied command of the expedition to India.

As the smoke of their parting salute drifted out over the water, Dias's caravel and the main fleet moved further apart from each other. The four vessels of the main fleet made course slightly more southerly, across the set of the south equatorial current; they were moving into an area where the winds are variable both in force and direction, and for a time could expect chiefly headwinds as they gradually worked their way further out into the ocean.

'To take the summer in the open sea'

With winds intermittent and changeable—sometimes contrary, sometimes cross—the small fleet plugged across the drag of the current, south-east and then south and west of south, into that disturbed ocean region where the opposing influences of the winds and tides either side of the equator cause confusion and turmoil. Thus, Gama put to practical test the great advances that the Portuguese, by dint of doggedness, audacity, careful observation and organisation, an enlightened royal policy and general state finance, had made in the art of navigation. By gathering and applying knowledge from all sources —Italians and Catalans, traders, fishermen and astrologers, Jewish and Moorish astronomers—they created nautical astronomy, converted lore into science.

Up till about the thirteenth century, sounding line and local and general knowledge were almost all the equipment that seamen had to assist them in navigation. Among some people shore-sighting birds were carried (the Norsemen for instance used ravens as did Noah), but it was on his knowledge of coasts, landmarks, currents and tides, the flight-paths of birds, the directions of the winds, and the relative positions of the stars, of how to interpret the colour and smell of the sea and tell the nature of the sea-bed, that the pilot then chiefly relied. In those days before the compass, the points of the horizon were distinguished by the winds, and seamen learnt to speak of direction in terms of the line of the wind, its rhumb.

Pilotage began to pass into navigation when the magnetised needle was taken from its home in temple and observatory, from the necromancer and astrologer, and used at sea. Whether this was first done by the Chinese, or the Arabs, or by mariners of Amalfi on the Tyrrhenian sea (who in the eleventh century shipped magnetic iron ore from mines on the island of Elba) is uncertain and not important. In the course of a hundred years, more or less, the direction-finding sliver of magnetic ore carried on a piece of wood afloat in a bowl of water and used in emergency (for instance, on starless nights or in thick fog) was supplanted by a needle balanced at right angles to a non-magnetic pin mounted in a bowl, and then by a compass card, mounted on a non-magnetic pin and with magnetised wire glued to the underside, in a wooden box.

While northern astronomer philosophers such as Roger Bacon wrote learnedly on the theory of such things, in the Mediterranean they became a necessary part of developing commerce. Practical needs of trade, assisted by rediscoveries of Greek learning (through contact with Arab and Jew), and by the liberating effect of Hindu mathematics (developed in a society in which the merchant had an honoured place), helped bring into being mathematical navigation.

In the twelfth and thirteenth centuries the Italians principally, but also the Massillians and Catalans, created charts and books of sailing directions. With these the mariner suitably equipped could sail not simply coastwise port to port, but also across and from end to end of the Mediterranean. On his chart were drawn wind-roses, giving rhumb directions (based on observed compass readings) for all prevailing winds, and a scale of distances. To the modern eye it seems an amazing confusion of lines; to him it was an essential tool. His sailing manual, or 'Compass of Navigation', later to be known as a roteiro, routier, or rutter, listed the distances and bearings between ports; shoals and other hazards; buoys and marks; tides, depths and anchorages; and the effects of different winds. Charts were not new: the Romans certainly had had them, and they probably date back still further. Written pilots were not new either: the Greeks had had them—one such being the *Periplus of the Erythrean Sea*, a first-century AD trader's guide to the Red Sea and the Gulf of Aden. What was new was the degree of scientific accuracy being brought to navigation, through the use of the compass and, in due course, ruler, dividers and sandglass. These enabled sailors to proceed by dead reckoning: calculating position, at each turn of the half-hour glass, by compass course kept and estimated distance and speed travelled.

The Portuguese learned what they could from the Mediterranean sailors, but their seacoast bordered the north Atlantic, which, with its turbulence, strong currents, and large tide movements posed far greater problems of navigation than did the Mediterranean. The influence of the moon on the tides showed the importance of astronomy in improving navigation in these waters, and one result of this was that it became deemed essential to possess an almanac of the tides, which were seen to follow a cyclical pattern.

The further the Portuguese ventured, the greater became their needs. From practical experience they learned (and kept to themselves) how to use the equatorial currents and the north Atlantic winds to make a north-west circuit up to the latitude of Lisbon and so get home; but knowledge of this type could not assist them when it came to exploring the unknown waters of the south Atlantic and the Indian Ocean. What was needed was a higher level of knowledge and a new technique. Mariners had to be taught how to apply scientifically their knowledge of the movements of the stars.

For at least 200 years European astrologer–astronomers, not least the Iberians, had known how to calculate latitude by means of the angles of the stars. They had complex instruments devised for the purpose; their conclusions and speculations were stored in voluminous tables of astro-mathematical data. The Portuguese state, first of all the Navigator, took the astronomer out of his atelier and put him to work in the ports, or on board ship, to turn the grizzled pilot into a technologist armed with a new science. Better maps, new astronomical information, new instruments, new ways of figuring were needed. Laboratory mystique had to be simplified for common understanding.

Five years after the fall of Ceuta, the Navigator invited to Lagos a certain Master James of Majorca, an elderly man, now thought to have been a converted Jew known as Jafuda Cresques, a cosmographer, cartographer and nautical instrument maker. (His father, Abraham, was creator of the famous Catalan atlas that as early as 1375 recorded part of the coast of Africa south of Cape Bojador and showed also the sources which supplied the Saharan caravans.) By about 1420 he and other experts were ready to help the Portuguese pilot take his first steps towards becoming a true navigator.

In the first stage the pilot had to learn how to establish his position by measuring the angle between his line of sight to the Pole Star and the horizon. For this he had to master a simplified form of the astronomer's quadrant—essentially a quarter-circle of wood or brass graduated from nought to ninety degrees along its arc. At either end of one of the straight edges stood out a small square piece pierced with a pinhole; and from the apex of the instrument hung a plumbline of fine silk thread. To find the elevation of the Pole Star, the observer held the quadrant apex uppermost and sighted the star through the two pinholes (that is, along the edge). The plumbline, hanging perpendicularly from the apex, across the scale of degrees, showed the elevation.

The Pole Star, however, is not fixed at true north, but circles around it; and this circle itself varies. Whereas in Gama's time the discrepancy with true north was about four degrees, now it is less than one. To deal with the problem, the experts devised a method based on observation of the two stars of the Little Dipper known as the Two Brothers or Guards, which circle around the Pole Star. A similar scheme was already in use among mariners as a way of telling the time by night. This involved imagining a human figure in the sky. Modified to help the tyro navigator make corrections for true north when he measured the elevation of the Pole Star, this became what was known as the 'Regiment of the North Star'.

Fixing position by reference to the elevation of the Pole Star led the Portuguese to develop 'latitude navigation'. This meant that when, for instance, a sailor on his way back to Lisbon through the Atlantic measured the elevation of the Pole Star (corrected for true north) as thirty-eight degrees, the latitude of Lisbon, he would turn and sail due east, along that parallel of latitude, in the expectation of reaching the port thus.

Such simplicity, however, could last only for a while. The further afield explorers went, the more latitudes were established, and in course of time charts carrying a latitude scale were drawn up; but it was difficult to take an accurate reading from a quadrant aboard a moving ship, and south of the equator (which the Portuguese first reached and passed in 1474) the Pole Star was not visible above the horizon, making it necessary to learn how to navigate by the sun. To do this one must observe the noonday height of the sun on several days in succession. This height, however, varies by latitude, days, and also (since the earth takes $365\frac{1}{4}$ days to circle the sun) year, over a four-year cycle.

To tackle these, problems, John II, following his accession in 1482, brought together a new team of experts, including one of his chaplains, Bishop Diego Ortiz; his physician, Master Rodrigo; and the Jewish astronomer Master John Vizinho. These three led the work of training a new generation of navigators, supplying them with astronomical tables and instruments with the aid of which they might sail anywhere at any time. These three formed the 'mathematical commission' that rejected Columbus. Ortiz—a Spaniard, a skilled cosmographer, and professor of astrology at Salamanca University from 1469 till 1475, when he became a political refugee in Portugal—worked out the directions and routes to be taken by Pedro de Covilhan on his spy-journey to India. Vizinho, who was the astronomer whom John sent to Guinea to establish the latitudes, was a pupil of the eminent Jewish scholar Abraham Zacuto (also of Salamanca University), who in the years 1473 to 1478 compiled his *Almanach Perpetuum*, for which, taking 1473 as the basis of his calculations, he worked out the position of the sun on each day of the solar cycle, in each latitude. This historic work, intended for astronomers, Vizinho simplified into a table to be used by mariners at sea. He and his colleagues also compiled tables for the latitudes of different places and the 'rule to raise or lay a degree'—that is, the distance to be sailed to gain or lose a degree of latitude according to the 'direction of the wind', the course on which the ship is moving.

With these tables, rules on how to use them, and for taking the height of the sun, the navigator could establish his latitude anywhere upon the ocean. Thus was created the 'Regiment of the Sun'. To learn the ways of the heavens and how the earth curves, student navigators were also given a celebrated book, *De Sphaera* ('Concerning the Spheres'), written in about 1250 by John Holywood, an English astronomer known as Sacrobosco. *De Sphaera* was highly regarded throughout Europe. Not long before Gama's expedition was set up, Zacuto himself left Spain as a religious refugee and settled in Lisbon, where his presence was highly valued by King Emanuel. He, too, therefore, became one of the tutors of the Portuguese navigators, and it would seem probable that Gama himself studied with him.

Sixty years later Gaspar de Correa described King Emanuel's many consultations with Zacuto. In his *Lendas da India* he has the astronomer explain, 'I have well ascertained, and laid it down in a kind of formula, how much the sun removes itself each day, both in its going away and in its return; in suchwise that in any part where navigators may have sighted the sun at midday, or the north star at night, and making their reckoning of the sun's declination, they may know what distance they have gone, and will know how to navigate all the seas in the world.' Correa further explains that Zacuto 'made rules for the sun's declination, separating the years, each one by itself, and the months and the days, from one bisextile year to another, which are exactly four years, and how much the sun progresses each day, reckoning from midday to midday, both in the northern and the southern region, all this with much arrangement and good order'.

In such ways Portuguese seamen were taught the new navigation, latitude sailing. To use this knowledge a new instrument was needed. This, too, was found from the astronomers' equipment: the astrolabe, used by astrologers for 'taking stars'. With it they observed the movement of the heavenly bodies, plotted their positions and tracked their movements. Much simplified, refined to its essentials, it became the sea astrolabe. In this form it was a heavy ring (for stability), usually of brass (to prevent corrosion), with four spokes (open work to reduce wind resistance). Despite its design, however, it was still difficult to use in a sea-tossed ship. One quadrant of one face of the ring was marked in degrees from nought at horizontal, to ninety, at vertical. Against this face turned a movable arm with a straight-edged point at either end, mounted on a swivel, and known as the *al'idādah* or alidade. On the alidade stood two sighting vanes (probably about three inches apart for an astrolabe six inches across), each with two apertures, a pinhole and a needle-hole. This instrument made it possible to take the noonday height without blinding onself from peering into the sun. The pilot held the astrolabe by a thread passed through a thumb ring at the top, letting it hang away from his body in the full sun. He, or more often his assistant, turned the alidade until a line of light from the sun passing through the pinhole in one vane struck through the needle-hole in the other on to a plane surface, of wood or metal, held below it. The straight edge of the point of the alidade lying against the scale of degrees gave a reading of the altitude of the sun. At night the astrolabe could also be used for taking the elevation of a star, as with a quadrant.

Also of crucial importance was the mariner's compass, but, again, its use had its problems. Portuguese mariners had learnt from experience that the compass needle varies from true north, that it 'north-easts' or 'north-wests'. Though they did not know why it did so, they had learnt to allow for this.

As the theory and practice of navigation advanced, with the help of new knowledge, charts, tables and instruments, the Portuguese seamen adventurers advanced further and further down the coast of Africa until at last they reached and passed the Cape of Good Hope. But Gama, whose mission it was to sail right round Africa to India, followed new advice, new calculations from Zacuto—who, according to Correa, said to the King, 'Sire, the sea which your ships traverse is very large; in some parts of it it is summer, in others winter, and all in one course; and two ships may go, one after the other, and both by the same course; one will arrive in a region where it is then winter and will meet with storms; and when the other arrives there it will be summer, and it will not meet with the storms which the other one found. . . . And the reason why the winters and summers are not fixed in any certain spot, is because the sea is very wide and desert, remote from the land, and the storms and calms take their course in many uncertain parts. But when the navigators shall have more experience in making their course, and they know how to take the summer which there is in the open sea between here and the Cape of Good Hope . . . they will go and come without labour and in safety, if they are prudent in their navigation.'

Three

Sailing

Through the Equinoctiall

Through his discussions with the astronomers and mathematicians Gama formed a new navigational plan, which he followed out from the Cape Verde islands. His object was to avoid the contrary currents, uncertain winds and sudden storms which his predecessors had met in sailing close to the coast of west Africa. 'To take the summer which there is in the open sea' meant to use the westward-flowing equatorial current and the westward-blowing trades, in order to catch in the south-west Atlantic a southward-flowing current and the westerly winds that were believed to blow towards south Africa.

On about 18 August, some 700 miles south-east of S. Thiago, the fleet, then sailing south, ran into foul weather such as a later traveller in this latitude described as with 'much thunder [and] lightning, which passe swiftly over, and yet fall with such force, that at every shower we are forced to strike sayle, and let the maine yeard fall to the middle of the mast, and many times cleane down'. After one such squall the captain-major fired the signal to heave to: the mainyard of the *S. Gabriel* had broken. For two days and a night the ships of the fleet lay to under foresail and mainsail while the crew of the *S. Gabriel* worked in replacing the broken yard. The pause gave time for the masters of all ships to check their rigging, make secure everything in the holds, and pump. It was a chance, too, for captains and pilots to be rowed across to the flagship for a commanders' conference.

When the commander's three guns signalled 'hoist sails' had been answered with three each from the other ships, and the slowly filling canvas gave steering way once more, the helmsmen took up a new course, the ships pointing half into the sun as it sank to the horizon.

Below the poop the helmsman at his tiller could see little more than the lower part of the mainmast, the foot of the mainsail and his compass, which was fixed to the deck in front of him in its wooden binnacle. It was aligned to the axis of the ship; and he could watch the instrument mounted in the two brass rings of the gimbals through an opening in the rearward panel. The binnacle protected from the weather both the compass and the lantern which lit it up at night. When moving with a steady breeze the helmsman's main duty was to hold the course given to him, keeping the sails full and pulling their best, and watching the lift of the mainsail foot; but he would also glance from time to time at the compass card, to judge the main course steered, and at the sand-glass which hung beside it. At each half-hour his duty boy turned the glass and struck the watch bell, once for each half-hour of the watch. He was the timekeeper; on him the rule of the ship's day and the accuracy of the pilot's calculations depended.

On the deck above was fastened the pilot's compass, also in gimbals and binnacle, and beside it was an open hatch through which the pilot or his assistant could look below to check the helmsman. For the helmsman steered mainly by feel; but the pilot could see whether the ship was keeping course or whether the sails needed trimming. According to Sir Richard Hawkins, writing a hundred years later, 'the Spaniards and Portingalls doe exceede all that I have seene, I mean for their care, which is chiefest in navigation . . in every ship of moment, upon halfe decke, or quarter-decke, they have a chayre or seat; out of which whilst they navigate, the pilot or his adjutants . . . never depart, day nor night, from the sight of the compasse; and have another before them, whereby they see what they doe, and are ever witnesses of the good or bad steeridge of all men that take the helme.'

In his cabin nearby, Pero d'Alenquer would have had his instruments and his charts, with the decorated brass locket containing his lodestone (used to 'feed' the compass hanging against the wall. Probably in convenient racks were dividers, spare compass needles, and half-hour and minute glasses, and by the chart-table a slate or board with some chalk. Place had to be found for spare compasses for abacus and quadrant (perhaps more than one) and perhaps for more than one brass astrolabe. There was also on board a big wooden astrolabe of something over two feet across; this had been specially made for the voyage, and probably was stored in Gama's own cabin, since it was not meant for use at sea. It is possible that Gama also had with him a small globe such as had been made by Martin Behaim in Nuremberg five years earlier. This globe recorded for the first time the results of Dias' voyage round the Cape two years earlier; it was a demonstration of what Portuguese navigation had achieved, one of its purposes being to impress those Nuremberg bankers from whom John II was seeking loans for his explorations. The commander would have had brass astrolabe, quadrant and compass in his own quarters for his personal use, since he undoubtedly also made his own observations and took the altitudes.

Sailing along the great arc of the course that Gama had set, and meeting different winds and currents, the fleet eventually reached 'the Equinoctiall', where as Linschoten wrote ships met a 'most extreme heat, so that all the water in the ship stinketh, whereby men are forced to stop their noses when they drink'. As had been foreseen and calculated in the shaded cloisters of Lisbon, at this time, when the merciless sun stood straight above by day, and the Little Dipper had finally dropped below the horizon, the set of the sea too began to change; the wind steadied, blowing on the port beam; and the course of the ships, to west of south, became more consistent and easier to hold.

This course Pero d'Alenquer would have recorded on the chart which, though it has not survived, certainly had been specially prepared to give the latest information from the African explorations, with the most recently established latitudes; it would also have included such information on east Africa, Arabia and India as Pero de Covilhan had supplied. The pilot book, also, would have given the latest information on the tides, winds and hazards of the south Atlantic, perhaps with profile sketches of important stretches of coast and entrances to harbours in regions already surveyed.

To plot the course on his chart, the pilot needed to know the distance covered in each watch, and to calculate that he had to know, first of all, the speed of the ship through the water. This he would be able to gauge from experience, but he may have checked his estimate by throwing overboard forward a billet of wood and pacing it to the stern (perhaps also asking for confirmation from his assistant or the commander). Speed through the water— four to five and a half miles in an hour—was, however, only the starting point. The ships with which Gama sailed, broad-beamed and without significant keels, made much leeway in a cross wind. A pilot of those times could calculate an allowance for this by means of a *catena a poppa*, though whether this device was used by the Portuguese is uncertain. It consisted of a line towed out astern, with a piece of lead-weighted wood carrying a vertical pole attached to the end of it. The pilot measured the angle of the line, using a compass from the poop, to give him his leeway. If he were tacking into a contrary wind he would need also to record the time travelled upon each point, which could be simply done by a device known as a traverse board—a round piece of wood with eight holes arranged along each of thirty-two rays of a compass rose, one hole for each bell of the watch. To the centre of the rose were attached ten or a dozen cords, each with a peg at its end. The pegs were pushed into holes along the rhumb being sailed. At the end of the watch the pilot recorded on a slate the mean course steered, judging this by sighting the pegs, which could then be pulled out for use by the next watch.

All this information, observed and calculated, enabled the pilot to work out the distance covered, and each day at noon he, and others with him, took the ship's latitude. With the latitude established he would go to the chart with two pairs of dividers to mark out the ship's new position. Within its limitations and carried through with care the system gave surprisingly accurate results. Better could not be done without means of finding a ship's longitude; but for that an accurate time-piece was needed, and the chronometer did not appear until 1760.

A disciplined routine such as this was observed on all four vessels, so that each could carry on should it become separated from the others. Probably when winds were slack the captains or pilots of the *S. Raphael*, the *Berrio* and the storeship would put out in boats to visit the flagship. There may have been a special routine for this purpose. Also it would seem that periodically the chaplain (or chaplains, since it is possible that there were two) visited each of the ships in the fleet. Such must have seemed a necessity for the spirits of men bred in the church, and mightily superstitious.

Daily life was framed in ceremony. Each action in the day's round had its prayer or psalm, many actions also their song or catch. Some fifteen years earlier, Brother Faber, on pilgrimage to the Holy Land, had noted how at night the man watching the compass 'sings out a sweet tune, telling that all goes safely, and with the same chant directs the man at the helm how to turn the rudder'. The helmsman's boy when he turned the glass and struck the bell, sang a snatch of doggerel suited to the time of day, and at night called to the lookout to keep good watch.

At sunset all the company—the captain and his officers from the poop; mariners, artificers, gunners and musicians in the waist; boatswain and seamen at the prow—led by the chaplain or, if he were not aboard, the captain, said together the *Pater Noster*, *Credo* and *Ave Maria*, made general confession, and sang, in a medley of voices from creaking bass to cracking nasal treble, the Litany and at the end *Salve Regina*—a raucous sound no doubt, as it carried from ship to ship across the water, but still a human bond and a benediction for men in loneliness. The binnacle lamps were set in their places, trimmed and lit. The boatswain or his mate put out the galley fire. The boy by the helm, as he turned the glass, sang out, 'The watch is called. Blessed be the hour in which God was born.' And the seaman's day started at eight in the evening as the men of the first watch took up their duty with a psalm and a prayer. Those of the next, the second watch, could go to their customary sleeping places (for the seamen below deck, on the bare boards; for under-officers and artificers, in rough bunks; for officers, in their cabins) for a four-hour nap, or stay on deck for a song, a gossip, a dance, or perhaps a game of cards or dice, if that were allowed.

Sebastian Cabot, Genoese in origin, who, after a spell as pilot-major of Spain the following century, returned to England and became first governor of the Company of Merchant Adventurers, wrote in ordinances for the fleet of Sir Hugh Willoughby 'that no blaspheming of God, or detestable swearing be used in any ship, nor communication of ribaldrie, filthy tales, or ungodly talke to be suffered in the company of any ship, neither dicing, carding, tabling, nor other divelish games to be frequented, whereby ensueth not only povertie to the players, but also strife, variance, brauling, fighting, and oftentimes murther. Ribaldry, filthy tales and ungodly talk are scarcely to be controlled in any enclosed body of men. Dicing, card-playing and other 'devilish games' can be. Since Gama kept a firm hand on discipline and a close eye on his men, he may well have had such rules for his own fleet. He was stern and aloof in demeanour; but he could joke and join in dancing.

Watches were kept as they are today, except that the names were slightly different. First watch was from 8 p.m. to midnight; the second from midnight to 4 a.m.; day or morning watch, from 4 a.m. to 8 a.m.; the forenoon, from 8 a.m. to noon; and the afternoon from noon to 4 p.m. Then came the two half-watches (the first and second dog watches, the first being known in Gama's time as the lookout watch) the purpose of which was to vary the rota so that men did not have the same watch each day. Each watch was divided into two parts, for port and starboard, with the men taking turns at the helm, at trimming the sails, and at pumping. On a quiet night, with the ship on a steady course, those keeping the watches had time on their hands. The officer of the watch remained at the poop, keeping an eye on the compass, the set of the sails, and the direction indicated by the windsock or burgee; and at every hour the helmsman and the lookouts at top and bow would be changed. All the rest had leisure to chat, lean on the rails, watch the moving waters, think of home, speculate how long it would be till land were sighted, and half-listen to the 'sweet tunes' at each bell, and the recurrent prayer 'Let us pray to God to give us a good voyage'.

But, if a strong wind got up, there was work to do: sheets and bowlines to be trimmed; any movable gear to be made fast; the topsails, perhaps, to be taken down. If the sea got fierce, throwing the ship about, two men (sometimes more) had to help the steersman, who would be unable to control the helm on his own: two lines and tackles would be fastened to the end of the tiller and run out to eye-bolts on either side of the room, so as to keep it steady as the stern lifted and the rudder banged and shuddered. Should it rise to a storm then all hands were called, not least to keep the pumps going hour after hour; there could be no rest for man or boy till all were safe again. All must 'stand to their tackelings' for Linschoten tells us 'there is no dallying or excuses with stormes, gusts, overgroune seas and leyshores'. There were no oilskins or sou'westers with which to keep out the wet and cold, to withstand the lash of the wind; in fear of death, with clothing soaked and hands and feet perished, without hot food or drink, slipping and sliding in vomit, their own or others', the men had to carry on sometimes for days. Some called aloud for help to Mary mother of God, and vowed offering to their tutelar saints. If the corposant hovered on the yards they called upon St Elmo, and watched to see whether it would rise up through the rigging in sign that the weather would turn fair.

When the storm passed, they would give thanks that they had been brought out of darkness and the shadow of death. With the sun came the blessing of relief; even that unremitting sun could be a benison, healing to the spirit. There would be psalms and thanksgiving; billets of wood would be set to dry, so that the fire might be relit; men could draw a ration of wine, with a piece of biscuit or some pickled fish, to keep them going till the fire was ready. Master, purser, carpenter and caulker would inspect the ship for damage, then report to the captain and collect their parties to set things right. Routine would take hold again.

At daybreak each day a ship's boy or a young seaman of the watch sang a benediction for the new day and called out the *Pater Noster* and *Ave Maria*. When the chaplin was aboard this was the time for Lauds and the *Laus Domine*: 'Praise God in his sanctuary; praise him in the firmament of his power . . . let everything that hath breath praise the Lord.' Before they were relieved, men of the second watch swilled down the decks and scrubbed them with besoms of stiff twigs. At the eighth bell the new watch would scramble up from the lower deck, having already drawn some 'breakfast'—a piece of biscuit, maybe some cheese and a pickled onion, and some water, perhaps half a mug. As the commander of the new watch (probably the pilot) took over, the offgoing helmsman would give his course to the commander of his own watch (probably the master or the mate), who would tell it to the new commander, who would pass it on to the new helmsman, who would confirm the order by repeating it to his commander.

Before going off duty, the master wrote the reckoning of his watch in the log book, cleared the traverse board if it had been used, and wiped the slate. Lookouts at bow and foretop were relieved. This was the time when a trumpet would sound to announce the captain-major, a man who believed in the value of some state and ceremony. Wearing his square cap, he would leave his cabin for the poop, there, in the company of his chaplain and officers, to pray publicly, '*Jam lucis orto sidere*' ('Now that the daylight fills the sky'). Then he was ready for the routine business of the day, to make his formal visit to the pilot's cabin, check the log, scan the chart, and discuss with the pilot the ship's progress and the course to set. Day after day, however, the course remained unchanged, at west of south.

Master, purser and artificer would then make their reports, and the master-at-arms could bring up defaulters. If it were the day for the captain to make his inspection, the musicians would play, master and boatswain would whistle for stations, and, attended by his principal officers, the captain would make his tour of the ship, inspect the guns, the hold and the stores, see how much drinking water remained and how much water there was in the bilge, and, as he went, question the mariners, seamen and artificers on their work, ask for complaints, comment, criticise and perhaps commend.

On other days, during the forenoon and afternoon watches there were the usual daily tasks to be carried out: scrubbing rails, clearing and cleaning decks, checking the rigging, making taut shroud lanyards, mending and making sails, ropes and casks, cleaning guns, pumping, and preparing food. One hot meal was taken at noon—shortly before by the afternoon watch, shortly after by those coming off the forenoon watch—with a psalm and a prayer. Commander and chief officers were served by the pages (who probably had also to cook the stew) in the main cabin. For the men there was neither mess nor cook: on a single small open grate, apparently, they prepared their food in groups. It was usually stew made from salt meat, garlic and lentils; but on fast days the meal was prepared from rice and salt fish (or fresh, if some had been caught). This they ate from wooden bowls, squatting out of the way in the lee of the forecastle, or some other place away from spray and direct blast of the wind. For jakes there were the 'gardens', stools hung over the leeside, where, as like as not, the sweep of the water as the ship heeled would wash your arse.

With the lookout watch at four o'clock the day would be drawing to its end. There was still time for men to wash their clothes and mend, search for lice and talk, sup sour wine and chew some biscuit with sardines or cheese, before the four bells struck for second dog watch and prayers. 'Be sober be vigilant; for your adversary the devil, as a roaring lion, walketh about, seeking whom he may devour' was the lesson of Compline, and the hymn was *Te lucis ante terminum*.

For sixty-five days life was much like that. Sometimes it rains in these sub-equatorial latitudes; sometimes the winds are light and fitful. During this time the fleet made about fifty miles a day or slightly less. Castanheda, but no other writer, says that in these weeks 'they sustained many and great tempests, or rather torments of outrageous winds and rain, so that they expected nothing but present death'.

On 22 October, when they had sailed nearly 3,500 miles from S. Thiago, their course by then turning east of south, they saw flights of large birds. At nightfall these birds flew vigorously to the south as if making for land. Not yet known to the sailors of Portugal, Tristan da Cunha lay some 400 miles away in that direction. The fleet was no longer with the south-east trades. Winds had begun to blow strong from the north-west and a definite current was setting eastward. The south Atlantic drift was being felt. At some point there would have been a signal of two guns from the flagship, and at the answers from the others Gama would have altered course to south-east or east-south-east. Thereafter, day by day, the wind moved against the sun: the fleet was passing into the path of the westerlies. The wind and current were carrying them on to Africa.

Without labour and in safety

Five days after the passage of the birds they sighted a large school of whales and many seals. With a strong wind on the starboard quarter, to drive them at five knots or more, they would make nearly 130 miles in a day. Sailing east at about thirty-two degrees south, the ships quivered. They heeled slightly to the steady breeze, pressing forward and sinking back to the following seas. In their surging motion they seemed to be eager, scenting the land. Every man and boy in the fleet would have felt an answering eagerness. Life was less comfortable with the strong movement, the pressure on the helm, the sudden squalls making handling of the sails hard; but the listless monotony had gone. There was a feeling of expectation in the air; men's spirits forged ahead of the ships, avid to see at last a break in the horizon.

On All Saints Day (1 November), nine days after the sighting of the birds, eel-grass (*Zostera*), a weed of shallow coastal waters, was seen floating on the sea. Double the usual number of lookouts were posted, to watch for breakers. Sail was shortened at night so that the ships should not drive on to the coast during the darkness; and the leadsman continuously took soundings from the bow. Two more days passed, and another night. Towards the end of the second watch the lead struck at 110 fathoms. When daybreak came two hours later, the horizon was still clear.

At nine o'clock on 4 November straining eyes saw a change at the meeting of sea and sky. It was land—ninety-eight days and 6,800 miles from the chapel of Restello; for eighty-four days from S. Thiago they had sailed out of sight of land.

Saluting the captain-major with their bombards, trumpets screaming, seamen and boys hanging in the shrouds, their rolling cheers answering the guns, the *S. Raphel*, the *Berrio* and the storeship closed up to the flagship. Every officer, man and boy had put on his finest clothes, as for a gala. The ships were dressed with flags and standards. They were within hail of one another, able to receive direct orders from the captain-major.

During the day the fleet tacked, moving in cautiously for a closer view; but on seeing it clearly Gama's pilot, Pero d'Alenquer, who had sailed down this coast with Dias nine years before, could not identify it. The coast was low without definite landmarks; the inland hills were long ridges without peaks; up to a mile from the shore were sunken rocks with breaking seas. A change of course was signalled. The fleet put out to sea. For two days and nights they sailed somewhat west of south, then south, moving slowly across wind and current to gain height. On the third day, heading east again with the wind and current, they could see hills with a high peak. As they closed in, they could see, on the port bow, a bold sea-cliff. Ahead the shore fell back indistinctly; but to starboard, closer to, was another headland, low, with hills behind it. Slowly a broad bay opened out to view. Sent in by Gama to take soundings, Coelho found a clean bottom of sand and mud and, in the southern part, good anchorage, with protection from most winds at about 3,000 yards from shore.

Late on the following day the fleet anchored in the bay, which Gama named S. Helena. Orders were given for cleaning ships and overhauling sails and rigging. At last, on the morning of the next day, Thursday 9 November 1497, boats were sent ashore; on the ninetieth day out from S. Thiago, men of Gama's fleet stepped on to land.

With them landed the captain-major and his pilots, and for the first time since leaving Lisbon, Gama set up his wooden astrolabe 'three spans in diameter'. This 'they mounted on three poles, in the manner of shears, the better to make sure of and ascertain the solar line'. While Gama and his staff were making ready for the noon observation, some seamen of the party sent out to find wood reported to him that they had seen two men behind a sand dune 'walking and stooping in the manner of persons gathering herbs'. Alert to any chance of gaining information, Gama ordered them to surround the men quietly and take them without using force.

Then the investigation of the sun's height absorbed him again and he turned back to his pilots and their servants. They twisted the great wheel on its cord to present its edge to the sun. While others held it steady, Gama turned the alidade until a ray from the sun struck through the holes in both sights. Once this had happened, he moved the alidade in line with the sun's ascent until at the point of noon the sun had reached its zenith. His readings showed the latitude 'to be 76°20', making the zenith distance 13°40' (Markham). From the pilot-book tables he made the allowance for declination. So 'they were able to distinctly know the true latitude of that spot', wrote Barros sixty years later, adding, 'so rudely did this art commence, which was given such results to navigation', Gama made the latitude 33°5' and so it was shown four years later on the chart of Canerio. Today's exact instruments give 32°30'—a difference of only half a degree.

It happened that the two Hottentots (as they were), burning sticks in their hands, were collecting honey from holes at the base of shrubs among the dunes. So intent were they on this that the Portuguese surrounded them unnoticed. One they took without difficulty, owing to his surprise; and they were themselves surprised—and in varying degrees shocked or amused—to see that these men wore 'sheaths over their virile members'. They tried to communicate as they led their captive, a young man, to Gama; but being terrified he 'did not take readily to signs'. Nor could any of Gama's interpreters make head with him when he was taken aboard. Clearly he was in a state of idiocy from alarm. So Gama sent for two ship's boys, one of whom was African, set them down with the youth with food and drink and took everyone else away. Food and young company calmed him down so effectively that when Gama came back the young captive was ready to join in an energetic exchange of signs, through which he appeared to indicate that his home was about ten miles away, in the mountains.

Imagining no better messenger possible, Gama gave him some little bells, beads and a cap, then suggested by signs that he go off and bring back some of his fellows, who would also be given presents. This worked to such effect that in the afternoon a dozen or so men came back with him. These Gama met on shore; each was given trinkets and finery; but, when the Portuguese showed them merchandise from the ships, gold and silver, cinnamon, cloves and seed-pearls—all those things which were the prime object of their quest, that their souls coveted—the simple men gave no hint of interest, no recognition of such things. The next day some fourteen or fifteen more came, received presents and chatted by means of signs; and the day after forty or more turned up. These chaffered with the seamen and soldiers, giving them, in return for small copper coins, shell ornaments from their ears, fox-tail whisks, and sheaths such as they used to cover their private parts. Out of all this arose an incident that has written in history the name of Fernan Veloso, one of the men-at-arms.

Being a man of some bounce he badgered the commander for leave to go off with the blacks to their village, to find out how they lived and what they ate. Gama was reluctant, but Paulo took the man's part, pressing his brother to give permission; for the Africans seemed friendly and first-hand information was always to be valued. So leave was given and Veloso went while the rest went aboard for their hot meal. Apparently all took their meal in the flagship that day perhaps because the other ships had been careened for cleaning.

Ashore again in the afternoon, the duty men under Coelho gathered wood and collected lobsters in large numbers. Paulo da Gama in the meantime went after some young whales that had swum into the bay and were chasing small fry among the ships at anchor. With two boats he got near enough to attack one of the creatures. Two harpoons struck home. Great excitement was followed by great consternation: the seamen had made the harpoon lines fast to the bow of the boat, and the whale in its leaps and plunges dragged the boat with it. Luckily the lines were long and the whale, swimming close to the shore, ran against the bottom and became stranded, 'which served to cool it'.

By this time it was late afternoon. Coelho's party were putting off from the shore with their wood and their lobsters. Paulo was making his chastened way back from his whaling. Gama, aboard the *S. Gabriel*, gave a sudden order to signal Coelho to turn back, and himself put out for the shore in haste in the ship's cutter. He had seen that Veloso was running down through the sand hills, and that some Africans were hidden in the scrub. Veloso reached the beach calling out and waving; but, to take a rise out of their bragging shipmate, Coelho's men eased their oars and held off as he reached the water's edge. As he tried to get to the boat, two Africans running down the beach tried to grab him.

They were promptly knocked back with bloody noses; and that brought others out from the bushes, throwing stones and short wooden javelins tipped with fire-hardened bone.

Jumping ashore, Gama went in trying to calm them, but the brawl warmed up. The Portuguese had got into the habit of landing without arms and had to fight off the Hottentots with fists, oars and firewood. Gama was pinked in the leg by a spear; his master, Gonçalo Alvares, and two seamen were also wounded before the whole party could scramble into the boats. What had caused it all never really became clear. Veloso told contradictory stories. It seemed that when he went off with the Africans they caught a seal; and that when they came to a clearing they roasted it, giving him a piece to eat with some roots. But then they told him by signs not to follow them any further but to go back to the beach—which he did. But why then had he been running? Well, he said, he felt some danger. When he left the Africans to go to the beach they blocked him; when he moved round they held him back; he thought they wanted to make him a hostage or a decoy. So he broke away from them and ran. He was a boaster, full of wind and vanity. But there is no record that Gama punished him.

It had been a strange day, as though men had become light-headed with the joy of having land beneath their feet. For two more days the fleet stayed in the bay—to finish work on the careened ships and to finish loading wood and filling the water-casks. Good water had been found in the river S. Thiago (now known as the Berg river), twelve miles south-east of the anchorage.

At daybreak on Thursday 16 November they left the bay, standing out towards the south-south-west. Pero d'Alenquer was uncertain how far they were from the Cape of Good Hope, which Zacuto had said 'advances much into the sea in the southern region', but he estimated the distance at about 120 miles (just a dozen or so out). Gama therefore chose to sail well out from the land. Not long before dark two days later, they saw the Cape, but as the wind blew on shore they again stood out to sea, tacking back during the night. The Cape loomed up before them again on Sunday morning. Still the wind blew from the south-south-west, driving on to the Cape; and once more the fleet turned its back on the land, making a wider cast this time and turning east again during Monday night. Yet still the great headland stood out ahead of them. With one more effort, at noon on Wednesday 22 November, with the wind astern at last they succeeded in doubling the Cape. And trumpets sounded from all the ships.

They had had strong and difficult winds but 'met less storms and perils than the sailors expected'. In the afternoon, with a good wind on the starboard quarter, they were sailing east past 'a vast bay six leagues broad at its mouth'.

This wind held steady, driving the ships forward against the westward-flowing current, so that they made about 240 miles in the next three days. Late on St Catherine's day (25 November) they entered a bay that Bartolomeu Dias had named Bahia de los Vaqueiros (Bay of the Cowboys), but that Gama named the Bay of S. Braz. It was about five and a half miles wide with a sandy beach along its west side. At the northern end of the beach, near the mouth of a river, there were ten fathoms of water a thousand yards from the shore. There they stayed for thirteen days, one of their first jobs being to unload the storeship and distribute her cargo and crew among the other three. This done, she was run up on the beach and burnt. Meanwhile the usual shore parties filled casks, from a spring near the river-mouth, and collected wood.

On the seventh day a group of about ninety men was seen, some on prominent sand-hills behind the beach, others walking down to the shore. Most of the fleet's complement, it so happened, were then at a meeting in the flagship with Gama. He led them at once into the boats, this time armed, and when close in shore he threw little bells on to the beach. Some of the Africans picked them up; some came to the boats to take the bells from Gama's hand—to the surprise of those who had sailed with Dias: for, when he had been in this bay, the people had run off refusing contact, and there was later a skirmish, with one killed by a quarrel from a crossbow when the Africans tried to prevent the Portuguese from taking water.

This unexpected friendliness prompted Gama to move the boats further down the shore to a more open part of the beach. There he landed, with his other captains and a guard of halberds and crossbows. As the Africans caught up with them he made signs to them to come to him in ones or twos. To each he gave bells and a cap; they in turn offered ivory bracelets. In colour, build, dress and ornament these men resembled those the Portuguese had met in S. Helena Bay. Next day more than 200, young and old, came to the beach, bringing with them a dozen oxen and a few sheep. When the Portuguese joined them on shore four or five of them started playing on pipes, some high, some low, 'making a pretty harmony for negroes who are not expected to be musicians'; and to this music they danced. In reponse Gama ordered the trumpets to play and the men in the boats danced too, Gama with them.

When they had danced enough, some men, sent ashore to chaffer for food, succeeded in securing a black ox in exchange for three bracelets. Next day all dined off it, finding it very fat and its meat as 'toothsome as the beef of Portugal'. Next day too—Sunday 3 December—there were again many visitors, this time including women and children. While the women hung back in the dunes the rest came down driving oxen and cows—oxen as large as those of Alentejo, fat, tame, gelded and without horns. 'Upon the fattest among them the negroes place a pack saddle made of reeds, as is done in Castile, and upon this saddle they place a kind of litter made of sticks, upon which they ride.'

Divided into two parties, the visitors again played and danced. But these were mainly the older men; the younger stayed among the bushes up the beach, where they seemed to the Portuguese to be keeping under cover with their weapons. Gama sent one of his interpreters, Martin Affonso, who had lived in the Congo, to exchange some bracelets for an ox. But he had to rely on signs, for he had not the language of these men, who 'when they spoke seemed to sob' —Osorio's not inapt words to describe Nama, the click language of the Hottentots. The men took the bracelets but led him to the waterhole, where they asked by signs why the Portuguese were taking away their water; at the same time they drove off their cattle. Cautious and suspicious, Gama called Martin Affonso back and ordered all on shore into the boats; with these he moved further along the beach, giving his men time to put on breastplates and arm themselves with lances, javelins and crossbows. When, with this show of force, he landed again, the Africans all scattered back to the scrub, where they sat on the ground watching. To make his point the captain-major ordered blank shot to be fired from two bombards on the poop of the longboat. That was enough; all ran off into the hills, dropping the skins that covered them, and letting their weapons fall and driving their cattle into the hills. The interlopers had the bay to themselves, apart from the many seals on a nearby island and the braying jackass-penguins, of which they killed great numbers.

Before the fleet left, the men set up a stone pillar surmounted by a cross and bearing the arms of Portugal, an engraving of a pelican, and an inscription giving the date—a practice invented by John II to mark all those points reached and claimed for Portugal by his captains. Beside the pillar they also raised a tall wooden cross made from a broken mizzenmast; but on the next day, 7 December, as they were preparing to sail, ten or twelve men came down from the dunes and knocked down and broke up both pillar and cross. That day the ships made less than ten miles before the wind failed and they anchored. Thereafter for three days they made only slow and fitful progress. They were close to the area in which Dias had been forced back by his crew in a violent tempest. On the fourth morning there was calm warm weather. In the almost clear sky some cloud could be seen over the south-east and a strange curtain of haze covered the horizon. The heat became more oppressive; a breeze sprang up from the east, freshened to a gale, turned northward of east. The great storm came down on them and they ran before the wind, under foresails much lowered.

'River of Good Tokens'

Gradually the wind backed to north-west, with great violence and driving, heavy rain. Carried away from land before the tempest, the ships were hurled forward, battered and soused by immense following waves. Groups of men were needed for bracing the tillers to prevent the ships from falling broadside to the wind. Gunners stood by to see to the lashings, lest any gun break loose, to become a lethal missile. Relays of men had to keep the pumps going. The wind would drop suddenly for a time leaving the ships rolling, lurching in the batter of the seas, unrestrainably shipping water over the sides. Then it would come again with greater force from a new direction, driving now across, now into the current, whipping the sea ever higher. In the darkness the only link between the ships was the rare one of a sight of lights from the crest of a great sea.

Men thrown against sides or bulkheads, or across a gun as they tried to move between decks from one duty to another lay stunned, bleeding, drenched with spume, spattered with the piss, vomit, shit of reeling shipmates, thrown uncontrollably about as they relieved themselves. Food was impossible. Only in the rare half calms could some grab a mug of water or a piece of biscuit.

Some accounts say that in all this turmoil and horror men pleaded with da Gama to run for shelter and for home, just as had happned with Dias years before. It started in the *Berrio*, the story goes. One of the boys of his crew brought to Coelho a tale of plans among the men and petty officers to seize the captain, find some way to join with the men of the other ships, turn back from death in unknown seas and make for Portugal. Coelhoe warned the boy to keep his mouth shut among the men, to wait, watch, listen. Gama, ever vigilant, learnt from his servants of trouble in the flagship: 'They had heard the sailors say that they were many, and the captains only a few single men, that they would rather die where their wives and children and fathers were, and in their native country, not in the sea to be eaten by fishes.'

In a lull from the horror of wind and rain and thunder, the fury and crash of seas on the shuddering craft, the ships closed to one another hove-to; Coelho called to the flagship with veiled words, that it would be well to put about, for 'so many men who went in their company were so piteously begging to put back the ships and if the captains did not choose to do so it would be well if they should kill or arrest us, then they could put back or go where they could save their lives—which we ought to do and if we do not let each one look out for himself'. As the *Berrio* was blown away again, Gama shouted that he would consult and would signal his answer.

To his crew gathered in the waist below the poop Gama said that he feared death as they did. He was not so cruel that he did not feel their griefs; but he had no wish to be accountable to God for their lives: 'Work for your lives and safety,' he shouted, 'and if the bad weather comes again I will put back; but to make me right with the King I shall write a paper of our reasons and you must sign it.' 'All raised their hands to heaven, saying that its mercy was already descending upon them, and that all would sign.' But the captain-major said that it was not necessary for all to do so; so the master and pilot named three seamen as delegates.

This agreed, the captain-major went to his cabin, posted his servants at the door and took in with him the clerk. Calling in the delegates, he asked them about a plan for turning back to port; the clerk made a record, and the men signed it. Gama then ordered them into his store-cabin below and sent down to them the master and pilot that they also should sign. Then he called them in to him one by one, each to be seized by his waiting servants, bound and put in irons—'heavy irons for the master and pilot'. As they were hauled out on to the poop for the others to see, Vasco da Gama took the pilot's instruments of navigation from his cabin and threw them overboard. 'See, men,' he called out, 'you have neither master nor pilot nor anyone to show you the way forward, for these men whom I have arrested will return to Portugal below deck unless they die sooner. I do not need master nor pilot. God alone is master and pilot to guide and deliver us. Commend yourselves to him and beg mercy. Let no one speak to me of putting back. Know for certain that if I find not what I have come to seek, to Portugal I do not return.' (Quotations in this account are from Correa through Stanley.)

All question of mutiny faded. Gama ran the S. Gabriel close to the other ships and called out to them what he had done: how he had master and pilot in irons; how he had destroyed their navigation instruments; how henceforth he would sail the ship himself. God would direct them. Let the other ships secure themselves as they pleased. Then he let his ship fall away without giving time for answer. And the other ships followed. Once again the wind began to blow strong, but from south of west, driving forward against the current, the seas lessening. Gama set course to make a landfall.

All accounts speak of the great storm; not all report a mutiny. Such sudden, fierce, violent storms are not uncommon at the back end of the year between Cape Alguhas and Cape S. Francis. Crew unrest was not uncommon in the fifteenth century, in Portuguese or in other nations' ships. As the story is told, Gama's handling of the unrest is in character. He was sharp, decisive, demonstrative, unyielding. He also showed guile: for, though he threw overboard the pilot's instruments, he had still his own; and, though he put the pilot in irons, he was himself able to navigate the ship at need. Against the mutiny, there is the fact that his was a picked, elite crew, which later suffered greater ills without revolt or murmur; and the pilot was Pero d'Alenquer, a man of great experience, highly valued. If a mutiny did occur, it may be that d'Alenquer, an older man, was ill and not able to act.

Within seventy-two hours the storm had run its course. During its last day the Berrio dropped out of sight; but at sunset she was seen from the top of the S. Raphael to be about sixteen miles astern. The other two vessels put out signal lights and lay to for her to come up to them, which she had done by the end of the first watch. Winds were slight; progress was slow. When, next day, the ships made their landfall by the 'Flat Islands' (probably the Bird Islands of Algoa Bay), they were fifteen miles east of the island of S. Croix, so named by Dias. They had made less than 200 miles in eight days (including those of the storm). Moving parallel with the coast, they advanced little—only twenty miles by the

next morning, when they passed Cape Padrone. There they could see the last
pillar put up by Dias, and, having sailed beyond, passed into waters probably
never before entered by mariners from Europe.

Sailing close enough to the shore to notice that there were many cattle and
that the country was well wooded, they found the landscape becoming more
attractive, more varied, with higher trees. During the night after they had passed
Cape Padrone, the fleet lay to; and, the next day, 17 December, a stern wind
took them forward till evening, when the wind reversed to blow from the east.
For two days they tacked into this wind, keeping off the shore. At last light on
19 December, the wind coming again from the west, Gama gave the signal to
lay to, so that they could have sight of the coast and judge where they were.
Making straight for land, next morning at ten o'clock they saw once more the
200-foot peak of S. Croix island, with its colonies of penguins and gulls.

The fleet was 200 miles west of its reckoned position, fifteen miles west of the
Flat Islands, which had been sighted five days earlier. With contrary winds, it had
been swept back by the great Alguhas current, 'an enormous body of warm
water', says the *Africa Pilot*, which from north-east of Natal runs south-west-
ward and westward, skirting the coast of Africa and extending from three to
about 120 miles off, 'sometimes running with a velocity of three to four and a
half knots'. It is at times checked by westerly gales, such as Gama's fleet had
met; but after them it runs with increasing strength.

That same day of amazed dejection, 20 December, their luck turned: a
strong stern wind came up to carry them forward against the current for
several days. But during Christmas Day, in honour of which they named the
coast along which they were sailing Natal, the crew of the *S. Raphael* found,
when setting a bonnet, that the mainmast had sprung about six feet below the
top, with a crack that opened and shut with the movement of the ship. They
made it secure with lashings, hoping that they would soon find a sheltered port
in which to carry out a thorough repair.

After another three days keeping course along the coast, the fleet anchored
some thousand yards off Durnford Point (Ponta da Pescaria on the old charts),
where they caught plenty of fish and the *S. Raphael* lost an anchor through a
cable snapping. Since they had left S. Croix island for the second time, eight
days earlier, they had made, in spite of the following wind, less than fifty miles
a day. When at sunset he gave the order to make sail, Gama led the fleet out to
sea, setting a course at first somewhat south of east. It would seem that he was
looking for ocean winds and some relief from the drag of current against him.
After three or four days, at about the turn of the year, he changed course north,
and later north-west. But, from the point from which he had put to sea, the
coast had drawn back on itself, and he found himself far from land. Drinking
water ran short. Probably some of the casks had broached during the great
storm. The ration was reduced to about half a litre a day; they had to cook with

sea-water. Fourteen days after leaving Durnford Point, thirty-six days since they were last on land, they eventually found a small river and anchored near the coast. In their wide sweep they had gone past the mouth of the Limpopo and reached the Zavora. In direct course they had advanced a little more than 300 miles in two weeks.

When the ship's boats went close in shore the next morning, 11 January 1498, a crowd of Africans, women as well as men, was on the beach. They were tall people and among them was a man who seemed to be a chief. His friendly welcome to Martin Affonso and another man ordered ashore to speak with him encouraged Gama to send him a jacket, pantaloon breeches and a Moorish cap— all of red—and a copper bracelet. Affonso, not certain of the language, thought the chief said that the visitors were welcome to anything of his country that they might need.

In the afternoon Gama gave permission for the two men to accept an invitation to go with the chief to his village, the rest of the Portuguese returning to their ships for the night. On the road the chief put on the finery he had been given and showed himself off all through the village, to delight and applause from his people. Affonso and his fellow were quartered in a compound, given for their supper a porridge of millet and chicken, and all through the night were subjected to the gaze of inquisitive men and women come to see them. But none interfered with them or tried to harm them in any way. Soon after daybreak the chief sent them back to the ships with a present of fowls for their commander, and message that he would show their presents to him to a greater chief, who ruled the country.

It seemed to be a densely peopled region, with about twice as many women as men and many chiefs. The people lived in houses made of straw, and carried spears with iron heads, long bows and arrows. From the number of copper ornaments on their legs and arms and 'in their twisted hair' it seemed that the metal was plentiful, and also tin, which they used for the hilts of ivory-sheathed daggers. Linen they valued highly, exchanging large amounts of copper goods for seamen's shirts. They collected salt by carrying seawater inland in large calabashes and pouring it into pits. This place the Portuguese named Terra da Boa Gente, the 'land of the Good People', and the river they named Rio do Cobre, 'River of Copper'. The whole of their stay there passed off in good humour and without strife, as the captain-major desired.

For five days the ships rode at anchor, exposed to the swell of the sea outside the river. All daylight hours were spent with the boats, ferrying water, which the Africans brought out to them from the waterholes. But at the end of five days came a favourable wind. Gama broke off the watering, ordered the fleet to sail, and set course due north. They crossed the great bay of Beira, leaving Sofala out of sight to the west, and met the coast again—low-lying and thickly wooded, with tall trees—after six days. Two days later, having travelled 480 miles in eight days, they came to the mouth of the Kiliman river, about two miles wide; the land thereabouts is low, sandy and covered with trees, and lies either side of a gap clearly seen when approaching on a line north-north-east, but through which no land is visible until one is close upon the entrance. There the fleet anchored. Next morning Gama sent Coelho with the *Berrio* to find a way across the bar and sound for anchorages inside. The *S. Gabriel* and *S. Raphael* spent two uncomfortable days turned by the coastal current to lie rolling broadside to the swell. On the night of 25 January, with the tide turned in their favour, the two ships entered. Either side of the channel were swampy islands formed by mangroves. They and the riverbanks carried many tall trees 'yielding an abundance of fruit, which the inhabitants eat'.

For thirty-two days the expedition rested and worked there, among a friendly people, who used dugout canoes to ferry out to the ships wood, food and water. These people were for the most part black, well proportioned, naked but for a cloth hanging at the loins, their young women handsome, decorated with pieces of twisted tin in their thrice-pierced lips. A few, who were less dark than the others, seemed to be of mixed blood; with these Fernan Martins, one of Gama's servants, was able to speak some Arabic. On the bank of the river the Portuguese beached and careened their ships one by one to clean their bottoms from the accumulated growth of seventy days at sea. Water casks were mended and this time the whole complement was filled. Yards, sails, rigging, masts and rudders were overhauled and repaired.

When they had been a few days in this place two men from up country visited the village, whether of the same nation or another is not clear. Their clothing was different: they wore caps, one with a fringe embroidered with silk, the other of green satin. They 'were very haughty and valued nothing which we gave them'. Apparently they were traders; for they had some huts built for them beside the river near to the ships. They stayed for a week, every day sending to the Portuguese cloth marked with red ochre, which they offered for barter. These men had with them a young attendant who, so their signs seemed to indicate, had come from a distant country and 'had already seen big ships like ours'. The Portuguese named the river Rio dos Bons Signaes ('River of Good Tokens'), for 'these tokens gladdened our hearts, for it appeared as if we were really approaching the bourne of our desires'. The two traders soon tired of being there and 'left in their *almadias* [dug-out canoes] for the upper river'.

The signs may have seemed good for the future, but for the present they were bad. In this place, for the first time, many men fell to scurvy, the killer sickness of those who ventured in the oceans and on far shores, the deadly fate of those whose daily food was salt-meat and grub-infested biscuit. It rots the gums, which give out black and putrid blood. The gums grow over the teeth so that a man cannot eat. Jean Mocquet, a French physician who sailed in these waters during the next century, described how his knees were so contracted that he could not bend his limbs; 'my legs and thighs were as black as members gangrened and I was constrained to be continually lancing to get out this black and putrid blood.

'I lanced also my gums, which were black and blue and surmounting my teeth, going every day out upon the side of the ship, holding by the cordage, with a little looking glass in my hand to see where to cut: when I had cut away this dead flesh, and drawn away abundance of black blood, I washed my mouth and teeth with my urine, but next morning there was as much; and my ill fortune was that I could not eat, having more mind to swallow than to chew, upon account of the great pains which the disease causes.'

This first onslaught of the scurvy, later in the voyage to strike so hard, seems to have been relatively mild, for no deaths are recorded of this outbreak. Moreover, so Castanheda writes, the effects of the sickness would have been far greater but for Paulo da Gama, 'who visited the sick night and day, and comforted and tended them, and divided liberally among them those things for the use of the sick which he had brought for his own use'. What sort of 'things for the use of the sick' there might have been has been discussed by Peter Cooper in his note on 'Buccaneering Medicine'. The anaesthetic was rum, the haemostatic and antiseptic were pitch from the carpenter's caulking store. Eye-sockets were plugged with carpenter's oakum. For purges there would be brimstone or mercury; vinegar and treacle were used to get the more virulent doses down. Bezoar stones, concretions of hair and other things found in the stomach of the llama, were highly prized. Garcia da Orta, who practised medicine in India from 1534 to 1570, serving as physician to several viceroys, recommended conessi bark for dysentery, and betel-nut as 'very good food for the sea' and useful against fevers and other illnesses.

Van Linschoten says (1597), 'onyons and garlicke are eaten in the beginning of the voyage, as being of small value, other provisions, as sugar, honey, reasons, prunes, ryce and such like are kept for those which are sick'. Dr Mocquet wrote that he 'found no better remedy [for scurvy] than the syrop of gilly-flower and good red wine'.

Whether the sick had recovered before the fleet sailed again is not reported; but the Roteiro records that, before sailing, the Portuguese had the help of the local people in raising on the shore a pillar dedicated to S. Raphael. On 24 February they left that place and gained the open sea. To keep away from the land, which, however, 'was very pleasing to look upon', they stood out northeast that night and took the same course the following day, till, at vesper, they passed the Primeira islands, which lie on a coral bank some miles off shore.

For five more days they kept this course, sailing by day, lying to at night. Late in the evening of 1 March they sighted some islands and also what appeared to be mainland; but as it was late they stood out to sea again until morning. Then again they moved in towards the land.

Four

Pilot for Calicut

'They sought for information about the Indian Sea'

Moorish Africa

All the fleet sailed steadily forward and dropped anchor at some islands off what appeared to be mainland. As had become the usual practice, Coelho, accomplished young navigator, whose caravel was the smallest vessel and the easiest to handle, was sent ahead to sound a way into harbour. While he was making for what seemed to be a channel between one of the islands and the mainland, and the other ships were manoeuvring to anchor in the roadstead off the islands, several boats put out from a village. They paddled towards the flagship with horns playing and with cheers and cries, apparently of welcome. They called out and signalled to the Portuguese to follow them further into the bay.

Nicholas Coelho meanwhile, looking for an entrance, mistook the channel and ran against a bank by the nearest island. Though his helm was damaged he got off into deep water, made his way between two islands, and dropped anchor 'two bowshots' from the white sandy beach of a larger island near a small town. There he received a visit from the local commander with several followers. Coelho greeted him with such ceremony as he could muster at short notice, gave him a red hood, received from him 'a black rosary, which he made use of when saying his prayers, as a pledge', and sent him ashore with some men of the *Berrio*, who attended him to his house. He in turn fed the men and sent them back to Coelho with a present of a jar of bruised dates made into a preserve with cloves and cumin.

Later the same day Gama brought the other ships in to the anchorage. After eight months' voyaging, the expedition had made its first real contact with Moorish east Africa. They had reached Mozambique, an island within a great bay, 'a verie great and safe haven, fit to receive and harbour all ships' (Linschoten). It is described as 'a little island, distant about half a mile from the firme land, in a corner of the said firme land, for that the firme land on the north side stretcheth further into the sea then it doth, and before it there lie two small Ilands named St George and St Jacob, which are even with the corner of the firme lande' (Astley).

The 'people of this country', described by the eye-witness as 'of a ruddy complexion and well made', were identified as Moors—a strange word for people who were surely Swahili. Their clothes were of fine linen or cotton stuffs, with variously coloured stripes, 'of rich and elaborate workmanship'; 'all' wore caps with borders of silk embroidered in gold. The 'all' were the merchants of the place. These traded with 'white Moors, four of whose vessels were at that time in port, laden with gold, silver, cloves, pepper, ginger and silver rings, as also with quantities of pearls, seed pearls and rubies'. Thus here, the Portuguese met for the first time the trade which in a few years they were to destroy, taking it for themselves alone, and saw for the first time the Moorish trading ships of the Arabian sea which were 'of good size and decked', made without nails (the planks being held together by cords), and with sails made of palm-matting. Such 'sewn boats' had been used for trade from Egypt to western India since Roman times and before, guided by such pilot-books as the *Periplus of the Erythrean Sea* (first century AD). Strabo the Greek had written some ten years before Christ that in those days about seventy ships engaged in the India trade.

Gama and his men received a warm welcome from the Moors of Mozambique, who apparently thought them 'Turks or Moors from some foreign land'— though the great crosses on their sails made bold denial of this. On the second day the sheikh, attended by a number of armed men, made a visit to the ship. He came 'with drums and trumpets playing before him', and wore 'rich embroidered cloaths' and a fine sword with diamonds. Warned of his coming, Gama had sent all sick men below and had gathered in the *S. Gabriel* all the whole men of the fleet. 'Armed in the Portuguese manner', they formed both a guard of honour for the visitors and a precaution. For Gama thought it foolish to trust the Saracens, and resolved to be upon his guard continually.

There seemed little basis for such doubts. The visitor dined with the captain-major and his officers, conversed through the interpreter Fernan Martins, who had 'formerly been a prisoner among the Moors', asked to be shown the bows of their country (apparently thinking them Turks) and to see their books of the law—which request Gama evaded. He did indeed show contempt for the presents that Gama offered him—hats, silk surcoats, corals and other trinkets— asking to be given scarlet cloth. But later he sent many things to the captain-major, not least good fresh food and fruits for his table; and he or his servants made several visits aboard in the days that followed. Among the fruits of the country brought to the ships for barter were many melons and cucumbers and the fruit of palms 'as long as a melon, of which the kernel is eaten', having a nutty flavour. Many people of the country came daily to offer these and other foods. They told the Portuguese that all the riches in the trading vessels in port, except the gold, were brought by Moors, and that further on, on the places that the Portuguese sought, these goods were very plentiful. Along the route they were to follow they would meet many shoals; the cities were numerous; and they would find an island one half of whose people were Moors, the other half christians, an island very wealthy. They were told, too, that Prester John's country was not far off, and that it included many large ports frequented by great merchants with big ships. Prester John himself, however, was said to reside far inland, in a place to which it was necessary to travel by camel.

Such tales of the lands that lay ahead were deeply moving to the Portuguese, thirsty for knowledge and for reassurance that theirs was no unending, no fruitless, quest; and eager, too, to find the christian kingdom which they believed lay in the east. 'We cried with joy, and prayed God to grant us health, so that we might behold what we so much desired.' One day among those who were bringing provisions aboard were two 'christian captives from India', who, to the delight of the Portuguese, knelt down and worshipped the gilt image of the archangel Gabriel which stood at the forward end of the ship; but, when Gama showed interest in speaking with them through his interpreter, the Moors took them away and they were not seen again.

Feeling the need for local knowledge, Gama bargained for the help of two pilots, with whom he agreed a payment for each of them of thirty crowns of gold (rather more than 130 grams) and two scarlet jackets, a condition being that there should always be one of them aboard. It was a condition wisely made; for one had gone off visiting his kin when Gama, preparatory to continuing the voyage, moved the fleet out from the harbour into the roads by S. George island. By chance the missing pilot lived on that island, and learning this Gama sent two boats armed with bombards at the bows, and commanded by himself and Coelho, to search for the man. At once the first clash came, the first sign of a change from ten days' amity. As the two boats neared the shore, five or six small sailing craft put out towards them—crowded with people carrying bows and long arrows. They signalled to the Portuguese to go back to Mozambique, and loosed off a few shots. Gama's instant answer was to bind the pilot he had with him and order the bombards to fire. This gunfire served as a signal to Paulo da Gama; on standby in case of need, he started to move the *Berrio* in to give support. This served only to make the Moors fly the faster; by the time she was able to come up, all had escaped.

In the early morning next day, mass was said under a tall tree on the island of S. George, a spiritual preparation for the next—as they thought the last—stage in the voyage to India. The wind blowing fair and strong, they returned on board without delay, raised anchors and set sail, the ships being well stocked with water and with fresh food, fowls, goats and pigeons, which they had bought in exchange for small glass beads. The next morning they saw ahead of them a low coast with a sparse cover of trees 'resembling elms', and beyond it a cape and high mountains. In twenty-four hours they had made over eighty miles; but the wind died away, leaving the fleet becalmed for the rest of that day and the day following. On the night of Wednesday 14 March, with a light breeze from the east, they stood out from the coast.

At first light next morning, they saw themselves back a dozen miles south of Mozambique. All through the year the Mozambique Channel current runs south down the coast; its speed varies from thirty-five to seventy, even 100 miles in twenty-four hours during the northern monsoon, which was nearing its end as Gama's fleet struggled northwards. With a small wind behind them they made progress north again, enough to anchor once more off the island of S. George.

There followed eight days in the roads, waiting for a favourable wind. During these dragging days a Moor with his little son visited one of the ships asking passage north, saying he was a pilot of Mecca who had brought a ship to Mozambique. There was, too, a peace-making message from the sheikh, brought by 'a white Moor and a sharif, that is a priest, and at the same time a great drunkard'. Things turned out far from peaceful. After eight days, the wind still being contrary, Gama moved the fleet into harbour to top up the water-casks. Boats were lowered in the dark (why then is not explained) and, with Gama and Coelho in command, were rowed to the watering-place. They took with them the Moorish pilot, but he either would not or could not find the right spot, though they searched till morning. Back again the next evening, they came upon some twenty men with javelins who warned them off the beach. These were answered by fire from three bombards and ran off into the bush, leaving the Portuguese free to land and fill their casks. Somehow, though, they lost a slave of Joan de Coimbra, Paulo da Gama's pilot.

It was by this time two weeks since they had said mass on S. George island and set out on the journey north. There was no longer any exchange with those ashore: no visits, no barter, isolation. During Sunday, the eve of Lady Day, they received a shouted message from a small boat sailing by that if they wanted water they could go to look for it and perhaps find something less pleasant. This taunt the captain-major answered at once by arming the boats, with bombards in the poop, and making for the town. There the Portuguese found palisades of lashed planks lining the shore, and many men walking the beach—armed with assegais, swords, bows and slings—who incontinently greeted them with showers of stones. But when the bombards spoke they dodged behind their fences and some were killed.

For three hours the Portuguese bombarded the town. When 'weary of this work we retired to our ships to dine', the people of Mozambique piled household goods into canoes, skiffs and dinghies to make for safety on the mainland. During dinner the Moorish pilot who had not escaped was tied up in the sun, flogged, left to roast, and flogged again; which so far improved his frame of mind that he let out how the sheikh had discovered his visitors to be not Turks but christians and had planned to trick, seize and kill them. Dinner and torture done, the Portuguese manned their boats again to search for hostages, their hope being to exchange them for the 'Indian christians' and the absconded slave. From three ferry-boats which they chased they secured four Africans and a quantity of fine stuffs, palm-frond baskets, butter, glass phials of scented water, books of the law, skeins of cotton, cotton net and many small baskets filled with millet. Gama distributed all these goods among the sailors of the fleet, except the books of the law, which he kept for King Emanuel. More water was loaded during that day and the following day, when they again 'discharged a few bombards' on the town. The next day, 27 March, they moved out to anchor near S. George island; and there for another three days they waited for a fair wind.

It came at last on 29 March—light, but enough to get them moving and to carry them in three days once more to the coast by which they had earlier been becalmed. They were off the Kerimba islands, an archipelago running close to the coast for 100 miles, up to Cape Delgado. Though there is an inner channel, Gama kept his fleet outside, having little trust in his pilot, after whom one of the islets was named Ilha do Acoutado—the 'Island of the Flogged One—he having been punished there for lying to the captain-major. A week's slow sailing off and on these islands brought them to a group that the pilot recognised. They had gone beyond one of their objectives, Kilwa, seat of east Africa's most powerful king, overlord of Mozambique, the Zambesi and Sofala. The Portuguese believed the people of Kilwa to be christians and wished to visit the place. All day they worked to and fro, but they could not get back. They had to contend not only with the wind but with the set of the water also. Being above the tip of Madagascar they had entered the region of north-flowing currents. The flow of the sea and the general trend of the winds were at last with them. It is the land-mass of Madagascar, which they had not seen, that causes the great westward drift of the south Indian ocean to divide near Mauritius, forming two powerful streams north and south, the southward being the Agulhas current, which had caused them so much trouble. At night they gave up; with the wind high they stood out to sea to make for Mombasa. The next morning they were out of sight of land; steering north-west they made the coast again in the evening; and at night they turned seaward again.

During the morning watch of 6 April they again set course for land, north-north-west, till, two hours before daybreak, S. *Raphael* ran aground on a shoal. Immediately she touched the crew shouted warnings to the other ships, which dropped anchor and lowered boats to help. By daylight the tide had left her standing dry on the bank. They were off the Tanga coast beyond Zanzibar, in a roadstead that Burton says 'the long roll of the Indian Ocean renders a place of trembling to the coast trader'. Inland they could see 'a lofty range of mountains, beautiful of aspect'—the Usambara mountains. They named these the Serras de S. Raphael and the shoals the Baizas de S. Raphael. While the S. *Raphael* sat on her sand bank two canoes paid a visit, bringing fine oranges, 'better than those of Portugal', and left with the fleet two of their number who wanted a lift to Mombasa.

To the sound of cheers and trumpet calls, the S. *Raphael* was refloated in the afternoon. Next morning the fleet, following the coast, passed between the mainland and Pemba island (some twenty-odd miles off shore), an island of luxuriant vegetation. Its tall trees, the fleet's African passengers said, were used to make ships' masts. By early evening the fleet was making for a gap between the Shimba range (rising to about 1,400 feet) and, to the north of them, a lower range of flat-topped hills. Closer in, three distinct hillocks could be seen on the starboard bow, the northern guardians of the entrance to the firth in which Mombasa island lies.

As they cast anchor off the island a small dhow put out to them. Before them stood a sizable town on a shelf washed by the sea; it seemed to Gama's men a city of many beautiful houses built of stone and mortar, with windows and terraces as they knew them at home. A pillar stood at the entrance to the port, and a large, low-lying fortress could be seen at the sea's edge.

Many vessels dressed in flags lay in front of the harbour. To show respect for them, the Portuguese too dressed their ships 'and we actually surpassed their show, for we wanted in nothing but men, even the few we had being very ill'. Their hearts were full of anticipation, of hope that next day they might go ashore to hear mass jointly with those christians who they had been told lived there with their own mayor in a quarter separate from the Moors. Their Moorish pilot and passengers had told them this, leading them to believe they would be received with honour, welcomed in the houses of men of their own faith.

In the dark, towards the end of the first watch, a larger dhow closed up to the flagship, carrying about a hundred armed men with cutlasses and bucklers. They tried to board but were stopped. Four or five of their leaders, invited in and entertained, stayed about two hours and left after a good look-see, as it seemed to Gama and his men. They were followed next day by two pale-skinned emissaries from the Sultan of Mombasa, who sent the captain-major a sheep, many oranges, lemons, sugar-cane, a ring as a pledge of safety, and an offer to supply his necessities if he would enter port. The Sultan's messengers professed to be christians, which seemed to the Portuguese true. Gama sent back in return a string of coral beads; later in the day four Moors of standing came visiting. In response two men were sent ashore, with further messages of peace to the Sultan. At his palace they were passed through four doors, each guarded by a doorkeeper with drawn cutlass, to be well received in the presence. They were given a tour of the city. On the way they were taken to the house of two

Navigation Section

The caravel (fig a) with which the Portuguese explored the Atlantic coasts of Africa was valued for its speed and handiness; but it was not powerful or roomy enough for the deep ocean, at sea for many months. For Gama's purposes the Portuguese designed a new type of vessel – they called it simply *nau* – 'ship'. Just as they had created a new science of navigation (figs m to q), for Gama they established a new style of vessel whose rigging set the basic pattern for ocean-going craft for more than two hundred years. The caravel could sail closer to the wind; but in a 30-tonner all fifteen men of the crew might be needed to move the towering yards from one side to the other when tacking; and the shrouds, fastened by tackles inboard on the deck, had to be reset each time. The new ship (fig b, c, j, k, l) could not get so close to the wind but it stood higher, was stauncher in high seas and less onerous. Its ratlined shrouds for fore and main masts, fastened outboard, needed only occasional adjustment; and perhaps a fifth of its crew of 50 could handle its running rigging (fig f, k). Two heavy jobs still called for a lot of men – hoisting the mainsail (which needed all hands according to Morison (1942) and weighing and letting go anchors (Gama's ships probably had no windlasses).

Reefing was not used. To increase power a 'bonnet', even two or three, would be fastened to the foot of the main and sometimes the fore sail (fig e, f) To shorten sail in a strong wind, the yard carrying the sail had to be partly lowered for the bonnet to be unlaced. To meet bad weather sails would be furled by lowering them to the deck, bunching them and lashing them to the yard. Furling in fair weather could be done by men aloft sitting astride the yard, a precarious task without foot ropes (fig g). In the sudden storms of the Equator or the Guinea Coast, survival could depend on the speed with which sails were let go to fly loose, or the yards dropped to the deck. It might also be necessary to rely on anchors. Two bowers (bow anchors) and one stream (stern) anchor were normally used for mooring, the bowers being lashed outside the bulwarks below the 'catheads' (fig b) when sailing. In dangerous weather more anchors would be let go, up to eleven being carried in a ship of those times.

V. J.

a

a This nineteenth-century reconstruction of a caravel shows the massive yards which had to be manhandled from one side of the mast to the other when changing direction into the wind. Osorio (1576) praised the ability of the caravel to sail 'from whatever quarter the wind blows'. (The picture is wrong in showing ratlines on the shrouds and hull gunports.)

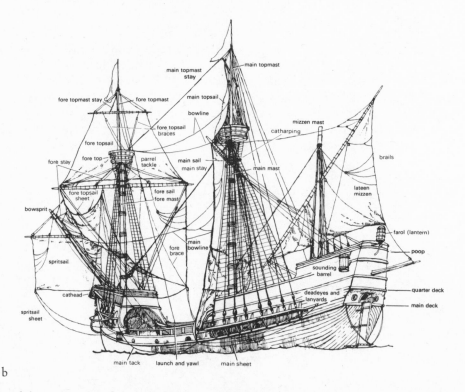

b

b A *nau* of about 1520, drawn to show details of sails, rigging and parts of the ship: the ratlined shrouds of main and foremasts are fastened to wood blocks on ledges ('chain-wales' or 'channels') outside the bulwarks; a bower anchor can be seen lashed below the cathead. Morison (1942) says that the main mast was made in one piece, higher from the keel than the ship was long, and the main yard as long as the keel. Gama's ship almost certainly had a round stern. *See* chapter 2/page 27 et seq detail of caravel and *nau*.

c

c A Portuguese reconstruction of the possible appearance of Gama's flagship *S Gabriel* – probable length 22 metres.

d   e

d A pen wash and ink drawing (*c* 1535) of a *nau* sailing in Lisbon harbour with wind on the port quarter, the spritsail seems to be furled and lashed to the bowsprit; the main sheet can be seen passing outside the hull aft to a porthole and

e (from the same drawing as *d*) a *nau* sailing before the wind, both fore and main sails having 'bonnets' fixed: these additions to the sails were fastened by looping a continuous lace, which was stitched to the bonnet, through grommets (rope rings) in the foot of the sail above.

f

f In Peter Bruegal the Elder's engraving (*c* 1560) of a warship before the wind with bonnets set, the running rigging (fig k) looks complicated but it could be handled by fewer men than were needed for the lateen rig rig of the caravel: although the ship dates from 60 years later it is essentially the same as the rigging of Gama's vessels – which established a basic pattern that changed little in two hundred years.

g

h

g This detail from the painting 'Portuguese Carracks' (*c* 1520) shows men carrying out their hazardous tasks aloft without footropes.

h Though mizzen, top and sprit sails have been furled and fore and main sails half-dropped, this ship from the picture 'Jonah and the whale' by Cornelis Verbeeck (*c* 1620) seems to be heading for trouble: the 'catted' bower and the forestays of the fore and main masts are clearly shown: again though a hundred years later, it differs little in principle from Gama's original ships.

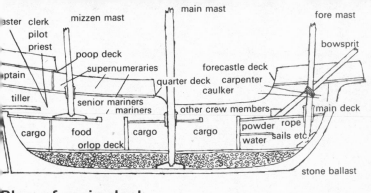

master clerk
pilot
priest
mizzen mast
main mast
fore mast
poop deck
bowsprit
captain
supernumeraries
forecastle deck
carpenter
quarter deck
caulker
tiller
senior mariners
mariners
other crew members
main deck
cargo
food
cargo
cargo
powder rope
sails etc
water
orlop deck
stone ballast

j Section and plan showing the probable arrangement of a *nau* of Gama's time.

Plan of main deck

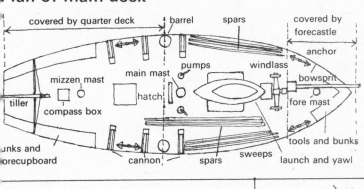

covered by quarter deck
barrel
spars
covered by forecastle
anchor
pumps
windlass
mizzen mast
main mast
bowsprit
tiller
hatch
compass box
fore mast
bunks and
storecupboard
cannon
spars
sweeps
tools and bunks
launch and yawl

k Running rigging of a square sail: 1 yard lifts, 2 braces for swinging the yard round, 3 sheets for controlling the corners of the sail, 4 tacks to pull sail corners forward as needed, 5 bowlines to pull forward sail edges, 6 clews to haul corners upwards, *eg* for furling – all of these were controlled from the main deck, the two mainsail sheets being taken aft outboard and returned through a porthole near the steersman.

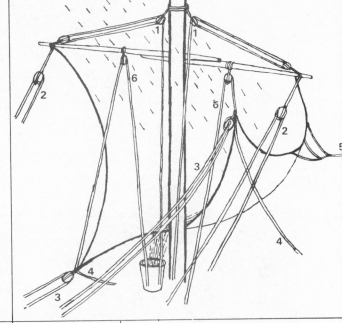

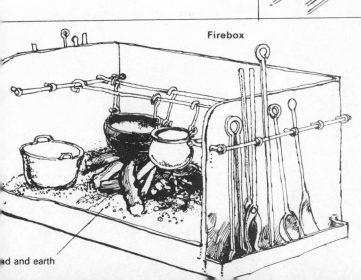

Firebox

wood and earth

l Sketch showing possible appearance of the cooking box on one of Gama's ships.

m

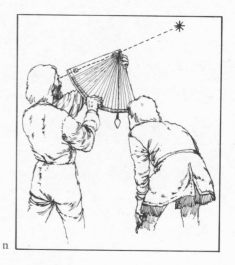

n

o

ORIZONTE

p

m Sea compass of about 1500.
n Using a quadrant such as Gama probably had aboard though he will have relied mainly on an astrolabe.
o Using a mariner's astrolabe to observe the meridian altitude of the sun, reproduced from a Spanish navigational guide based on Portuguese information, Pero de Medina's *Regimiento de Navegacion* published in Seville 1563.
p Traverse board, used to keep a record of changes of course during one watch. For details of navigation instruments and their use see Chapters 2/page 34 and 3/page 40.

q Possibly the oldest surviving mariner's astrolabe, dated 1555.

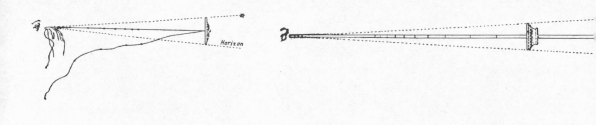

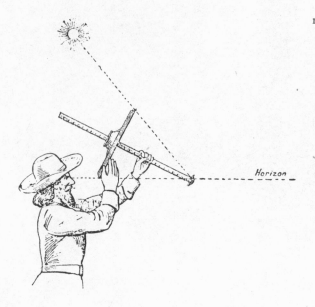

r This group of drawings shows Moorish navigation instruments such as will have been carried aboard the *S Gabriel* on 24 April 149[?] by Anmed Ibn Majid (he will also have had [at] least one astrolabe) see Chapter 4: The *Kam[al]* (i), simplest of the Moorish instruments, a[nd] the slightly more sophisticated *Bilisti* (ii) we[re] both used for finding the altitude of a star; t[he] cross-staff (iii) – later taken up also by Euro[o]peans – could be used for taking the altitude [of] the sun as shown here or, the other way roun[d] focused on a star; (iv) shows a variant of t[he] *Kamal* as still used in the Indian Ocean in t[he] nineteenth century and perhaps today. (i) an[d] (ii) from Prinsep (1836), (iii) from Bigourd[a] (1911), (iv) from Congreve (1850).

supposed christian merchants, who showed them a 'picture of the Holy Ghost', an object of adoration; in fact these were Hindus, the picture probably of an incarnation of Shiva and his wife. The men arrived back at the ships carying samples of cloves, pepper and sorghum, with an offer to allow loading of these goods in the Portuguese ships. With such encouragement Gama prepared to enter harbour the next morning.

Soon after it was light, more messengers from the Sultan visited the fleet; sails were shaken out ready for the move, with the flagship leading. As luck had it, when weighing anchor the *S. Gabriel* would not pay off, started drifting towards a shoal and was jostled by the ship following astern. Gama bellowed to let go the anchor, whistles shrilled from master and bosun—there was a rush of action and a hubbub. Incontinently all the Moors aboard scrambled into a dhow which was hitched to the *Gabriel*'s stern, cast hastily off, and picked up from the water the two Moorish pilots (one commissioned, the other a passenger) who had jumped over the side.

In the dark of the first watch that night, lit by the flames of torches, two men taken from Mozambique were questioned. It was a standard method: olive-oil let fall boiling drop by drop on the bare skin of back, shoulder or chest, or inside the thigh, with suitable pauses between the drops so that each separate place could burn and blister and have its proper effect. Which it did; for the two let out that the Sultan, alerted by news from Mozambique, had planned to attack and capture the Portuguese once they were safely in port. During a second questioning, one of these men, though his wrists were bound, threw himself into the sea; came the morning watch, the other followed him. Cool death was to be preferred.

Soon after midnight lookouts on the *Berrio* heard splashing. At first they thought it was made by tunny fish; but then came a tremor on the ship. In a moment they were calling out warnings to the others. A number of Moors, having swum to the caravel from two ferry-boats, were starting to cut her cable; some had already reached the rigging of the mizzenmast; other were swimming towards the *S. Raphael*. With the shouts of discovery they slid back into the water and made off. 'These and other wicked tricks were practised upon us by these dogs', says the narrative, 'but our Lord did not allow them to succeed, because they were unbelievers.'

Despite the wicked tricks, Gama hung on for two more days—perhaps partly in hope of finding or seizing another pilot, probably also for the health of his men. For on arriving at Mombasa all his sick had recovered. This, it was said, was because the air of the place was very good; but the true reason was that they had reached a region of citrus fruit. When the *S. Raphael* was aground, they had come by their first oranges for many months; and at Mombasa, before the attempt on them—perhaps afterwards, too, since profit is always good—the Moors had sold them many oranges and lemons.

On the seventh day from their arrival at Mombasa, 13 April, they moved on; but, the wind being light, they made little more than thirty miles and then again anchored. The next day, Good Friday, two small sailing vessels were sighted at daybreak about ten miles out to sea. Mainly to lay hands on another pilot, Gama went after them, and in the late afternoon one of them was caught, the other scudding off among reefs into the haven of a small river-mouth. All those in the one taken leapt into the water, but seventeen were picked up by the boats, among them an elderly Moorish noble and his young wife. In the boat were found gold, silver and much maize and other food. All the captives were taken aboard the flagship, and though there was no pilot among them, with them were men with good knowledge of Melinde, which lay on Gama's course. Melinde road, they could report, was surrounded and sheltered by reefs, and there was anchorage with a bottom of sand and coral. Melinde's ruler, they said, was a man of humanity. That evening at sunset, the fleet dropped anchor off the town.

On Easter Sunday Gama spoke to his captive guests of his desire to find local pilots for the passage to India. They told him that at Melinde there were several ships belonging to 'christians' from Cambay; that he should be able to secure pilots from them in exchange for themselves; and that in the town he could get water, wood and other supplies. The fleet had anchored about two miles off shore and there Gama waited. For a time nothing happened. The Portuguese were doubting and watchful; the people of Melinde were cautious, knowing that one of their vessels had been taken. More talk with his guests decided Gama to set the elderly Moor ashore on a sandbank in front of the town and withdraw. A canoe soon picked him up. He was a man with access to the Sultan, to whom he spoke of the desire of the Portuguese for relations of peace and of their wish for a reliable pilot for passage through the Arabian Sea to India. Soon after noon he was sent back in a dhow with a sharif of the Sultan's body-guard, who brought a present of three sheep. The Sultan, he reported, would gladly welcome peace and friendly relations and was ready to give help with all his country could offer, pilots or whatever else were needed. Gama answered that he would enter harbour next day, and sent presents of a surtout, strings of coral, three hand-basins, a hat, little bells, and pieces of striped cotton cloth. A further embassy came back with an offer from the Sultan to go out in his dhow and meet Gama on the water; with this message he also sent six sheep, together with cloves, cumin, ginger, nutmeg and pepper.

So it happened next day: in the early afternoon the Sultan moved up close to the ships in his barge, seated on two cushioned chairs of bronze under a round sunshade of crimson satin, his royal cloak of damask trimmed with green satin, a richly decorated cap on his head. His chief attendant was an old man, who carried a short sword in a silver sheath. With him were many musicians playing on tubas, and two men blowing the *siwa*, a double trumpet of carved

ivory (an instrument originating with the Persians of Shiraz). Clarions sounded
from the flagship as the captain-major with his gentlemen-at-arms climbed
down into the ship's boat, furbished and equipped in some luxury with cloths
and cushions; and through their interpreters, the Africans and Portuguese,
conversed in friendship from their two vessels as these lay side by side. Gama was
invited by the Sultan to rest in his house ashore, but he averred that this was
forbidden by his master, the King of Portugal. To the Sultan's question, 'But
what will my people say of me if I visit your ships?' he replied with evasion.
The Sultan asked the name of the King of Portugal, which was written down
for him; and he said that when the Portuguese returned he would send an
ambassador or a letter with them. Before they parted Gama handed over to the
Sultan all the prisoners he had in his ships, which gained him gratitude. In the
flow of goodwill the Sultan and his train of boats, with flags and banners, flutes,
tubas and kettle-drums making great noise, sailed round the Portuguese fleet
while the bombards fired a salute and the trumpets sounded. After some three
hours of these exchanges, the Sultan turned ashore, leaving with Gama one of
his sons and a sharif, and taking with him to visit his palace two men from
Gama's staff. For the next day he promised a display on the beach by his
horsemen.

With bombards on the poops of the longboats, Gama and Coelho next
morning paid their visit. They rowed down the front of the town, and remarked
how much like Alcochete, on the left bank of the Tagus estuary above Lisbon,
the inner shore of the way was. The houses were lofty, well-whitewashed, with
many windows; palm groves grew on the landward side and all around were
fields of maize and market gardens. As the Portuguese neared the front many
people gathered. Two horsemen gave a sham fight. The Sultan was carried in
his palanquin from the stone steps of his palace to the quay beside the longboats,
where he conversed again with the captain-major, urging him to step ashore to
meet his father, who was too old and sick to move, and offering himself and his
sons to stay meanwhile as hostage on board the ships. Thus is became clear that
this man, whose name was Sheikh Wajeray, was regent rather than Sultan.
Gama, however, always excused himself, fortified in his resolve by the words of
the 'christian' merchants from the Indian ships in port, who warned him not to
go ashore and not to trust the 'fanfares' of the Moors, which came neither from
the heart nor from goodwill—a slander, as the behaviour of the Sheikh Wajeray
towards the Portuguese then and later proved.

The Indians had their first meeting with Gama on his second day in port,
when he happened to be in his brother's ship, the *S. Raphael*. These men the
narrator describes as tawny, wearing little clothing, long beards and long hair,
which they braided. Paulo showed them an altarpiece representing the Mother
of God at the Foot of the cross, with Jesus Christ in her arms and apostles
round about her. Before this they threw themselves worshipping on the deck

and on the following days repeatedly came to pray before it, bringing with them offerings of cloves, peppers and other things. For a second time the Portuguese were convinced that they were indeed to meet with christian people when they reached India. This illusion was further fostered on the day when Gama went to the town in the longboats. As he passed, the traders from Cambay saluted with many bombards, raised their hands and, as it appeared to the Portuguese, called out, 'Christ! Christ!' Further, they asked leave of the captain-major to honour his fleet with a night fête, for which they fired off their bombards lavishly, sent up rockets and made a great din of shouting.

By the following Sunday, when two days had passed without further message from the palace, Gama became impatient; he held on board a servant of the Sheikh Wajeray's who had come out to him in a dhow, and sent word to the sheikh that he was waiting for the promised pilot. The sheikh responded. Later that day, at his request, an elderly man and his attendants went out by barge to the S. Gabriel.

As this rather venerable man climbed over the side of the ship, Vasco da Gama and his band of adventurers, new men from the west, stood in the presence of a thousand years' experience, of the sort of expertise that had made possible the fructifying civilisation to destroy whose trade they had come to sail those seas.

Lion of the angry seas

Some said he was a christian from India. Travellers gleaning their stories later called him a Gujerati, naming him Canaqua or Malemo Cana—Portuguese versions of his title, mu'allim kanaka, 'master of navigation and astronomy'. His real name was Ahmed Ibn Majid (more formally, Sihab ad-Din Ahmad ibn Majid bin Muhammad bin 'Amr bin Fadh bin Duwik bin Yusuf bin Hasan bin Husain bin Abu Ma'lak as-Sa'di bin 'Ali ar-Rakaib an-Najdi). Men such as he were already guiding ships through the Indian seas and out to the waters of Cathay when Constantine ruled in Byzantium, and no doubt earlier.

At about that time it was written in Sanskrit how a master pilot 'knows the course of the stars, with never a difficulty to orient himself; knows to perfection the worth of portents, regular, accidental or abnormal; knows favourable and unfavourable weather; can tell the different regions of the ocean from their fish, the colour of the water, the nature of the bed, the birds, the mountains and other signs; has a good memory, in full control of himself; can stand heat, cold, rain, weariness; is ever alert, without weakness of character; is sought after by traders for his ability to guide a ship and bring it safe to port' (translated from Ferrand).

At the end of the thirteenth century, Mahmud Sah, in setting down in his Sea Code of the Kingdom of Malacca the laws to be observed on junks, ships and all other vessels at sea or in harbour, gave the duties of the Malim (mu'allim) as follows: 'to be attentive for the good guidance of the ship, keeping watch whether at sea or on land for the winds, broken waters, currents, the path of the moon and stars, the seasons of the year, the monsoons, the bays and beaches, capes, islands and coral reefs, channels, uninhabited shores, mountains and hills. He must know these all so well that the crew be safe and sure at sea or on land, and so that he may be wholly free from fault; but let him above all pray to Allah and his Prophet to keep all safe from danger. The Malim is like the Imam; so says the law. Should he want to leave the ship, in what place soever, he cannot be allowed. Such is the custom.' (Translated from the Sanskrit of Arga Sura by Sylvain Levi in *Journal Asiatique*, Jan.–Feb. 1918, pp. 86–7, and cited by Ferrand.)

In that tradition was Ahmad Ibn Majid, whom the Turkish admiral Sidi 'Ali half a century later praised as 'the enquirer after truth, the most worthy of trust among all pilots and mariners of the west Indian coast in the fifteenth and sixteenth centuries'. He was the latest in a line of preceptors of seamanship going back to the Abbasids. Twenty years before he met Gama, in 1475, he had already produced his first classic, *Sailing Directions*, setting out for the coast of Araby and the Indian, Andaman and China Seas the principles and foundations of nautical science, observations on the nature of monsoons, and instructions on pilotage. Other works followed, thirty-three in all, of which the latest was finished in about 1495. He was the first modern author on pilotage. 400 years later mariners of India and the Maldives were using a pilot's guide known as *The Book of Majid*. In the Gulf of Aden, so Richard Burton reported in 1856, 'before venturing into the open sea we repeated the Fatiha-prayer in honour of Shaykh Majid, inventor of the mariner's compass and evening saw us dancing on the bright clear tide, whose "magic waves", however, murmured after another fashion the siren song which charmed the senses of the old Arabian voyagers'. Ibn Majid had passed into the communion of saints of Islam though by the beginning of the present century his name as a navigator was no longer known to the seamen of his native coasts. He was probably a Shiah, as were the heterodox militants whose insurrections in twelfth-century Portugal weakened moslem power in face of christian attack.

Ahmad Ibn Majid, son and grandson of pilots 'of the two coasts', spoke of himself as 'poet of the two Kibla, Mecca and Jerusalem,' who had made the pilgrimages to the 'two illustrious holy places, descendant of lions, lion of the angry seas. I, Ahmad Ibn Majid, am the Arab master of navigation.' His grandfather and his father, both authors of pilots' guides, knew the pilgrim routes precisely and in detail. 'When our own hour came and in the course of forty years we followed their experience, corrected the learned work of these two exceptional men, and wrote down the results of our experience and recorded observations, we brought to light facts and principles which no one had

collected in our times—only to be found dispersed among individual people.'
(Ferrand).

Such was the tradition, such the man who was received by the captain-
major. Once again Moor and Portuguese were face to face; but in commerce.
Ibn Majid (who had not been made drunk, as Kuth ad-din's pious lie would
have it) agreed to pilot Gama for a fee. (During the next sixty years Portuguese
commanders often hired Moorish pilots.) For Gama his first discussion with the
great navigator brought a tangible aid of great value: a map of all the coast of
India. The appearance was new to him: it was set out 'in the Moorish fashion',
without the points of the winds but with close-set meridians and parallels; these
formed squares so small that the direction of the coast through the two rhumbs,
north–south and east–west could be laid down with great accuracy without the
clutter of wind-direction signs and compass points that were used on European
charts. Here was a source of pleasure and satisfaction to the Portuguese commander, who had travelled so many thousand miles with little or no guidance.
In return he showed the Moor his astrolabes, the big one of wood and the
others of metal. But he met no surprise. Red Sea pilots, he was told, were
accustomed to using brass instruments, both triangles and quadrants, for taking
the height of the sun and, especially, the stars. Ibn Majid, in common with the
navigators of Cambay and of all India, steered by certain northern and southern
stars, and also by a number of stars that traverse the middle of the sky from east
to west. For this they used a device made from three strips of wood, the *bilisti*.

Possibly learning from the Chinese, Arab navigators had long (probably
since the eleventh century) known how to use magnetised metal for finding
south. But the magnetising was weak and ephemeral, needing renewal each
reading. By Ibn Majid's time, for practical purposes, when sailing the Indian
seas, the simple *bilisti* was good enough. It was based on finger measurements,
and had been developed from a method of gauging altitudes by holding out a
hand at arm's length and perpendicular to the horizon. James Prinsep, an English
pilot, found different forms of this device still in use in the Maldives and described them in the *Journal of the Asiatic Society of Bengal* in 1836. The simplest
was the *kamal* (see illustration), a piece of horn about two inches by one,
through the centre of which ran a string carrying nine knots. The intervals
between the knots were multiples of an *isba*, or finger width (about 1°36'). With
one end of the string held between his teeth, the pilot held the horn cursor
vertically and stretched his arm so that the bottom edge was aligned with the
horizon and the upper end with his chosen star: the nearest knot in the string
gave him the altitude. (This *kamal* was described in the *Muhit* by Sidi 'Ali in 1554.
A similar device used by pilots on the Coromandel coast was reported by
Captain H. Congreve of the Madras Artillery in the *Madras Journal of Literature
and Science* in 1850—quoted by Ferrand.)

The more sophisticated form of this device described by Prinsep—the *bilist*

proper—corresponds exactly with the one which Ibn Majid showed to Gama: a
square rod of ebony, the cursor sliding upon it at right angles (see illustration).
Each side of the rod carried a different scale, to correspond with one of four
cursors of different size, so giving a greater range of use without lengthening
the rod. Both the *kamal* and the *bilisti* were designed for navigating by star. A
third instrument probably used by Ibn Majid and described by Prinsep (here
illustrated by drawings from M. G. Bigourdan's *L'Astronomie*, Paris 1911)
could be adapted for taking the sun's altitude. Standing with his back to the sun,
the pilot made his reading from the point at which the solar shadow fell. This
'crossbow' could also be turned the other way round, for taking observations
at night. For all three instruments the basic observations of star heights from
which the divisions were calculated were made with the astrolabe, the origi-
nation of which Ibn Majid attributed to the prophet Idris.

With such instruments, refined through many generations, the Moorish
pilots sailed with confidence through the Asian seas. They were the product of
intra-tropical latitudes where the heat of day oppresses, where night skies are
usually clear, and where the azimuths of prominent stars vary only by small
amounts. Portuguese mariners who took them home found them less suitable
to the overcast skies and higher latitudes of the north Atlantic.

As he talked with Ibn Majid, Gama formed the impression that he had
'gained in him a great treasure'. He lost no time in acting on it; for, forty-eight
hours after the navigator had come aboard, they set sail for India.

Monsoon

Some feeling of regret hung about the fleet when the order came to prepare to
move, for 'we remained in front of this town during nine days and all this time
we had fêtes, sham fights and fanfares'. Furthermore, during all this time they
were free from strife, in friendly trade with both ruler and people. With the
goodwill of the Sultan they had been able to load fresh food, rice, butter, coconuts, live sheep, chicken, vegetables, fruit, sugar, as well as salted mutton. It is
said that here Gama was shown how to replace his water-casks by fitting below
decks large tanks formed of planks sewn together and caulked with pitch, four
tanks for each ship. By this means more water could be carried in less space. Also
in these last days the Sultan gave leave for Gama to raise a pillar on his shore in
the name of the Holy Spirit. It was said to attest 'peace and friendship estab-
estalished', but was in truth a symbol of subjection.

On the eve of their leave-taking the Portuguese dressed their ships. They put
on their best clothes, served out wine and fruit and danced to the sound of
trumpets and pipes. A parade of boats sent out by Sheikh Wajeray circled the
fleet with flags, music and shouting. They carried to Gama and his captain's the

Sultan's parting gifts of fresh poultry, figs, thin cakes of wheat and rice flour, and brought a message urging that without fail the Portuguese should visit Melinde again on the way back from India. These messengers were entertained in the ships, with food, drink and music. As they went over the side into their boats, the fanfares played, 'and then all the crews gave a shout of "Lord God have mercy, farewell!", after which night fell.'

Daybreak the next morning, 24 April, brought a clear sky and a fair wind from the south, not strong but steady. *Jam lucis orto sidere*, the morning's first hymn, was apt to the mood as the sails were loosed for Calicut; and as they moved north to cross 'the great gulf of seven hundred leagues' those who listened or muttered with the chaplain could gain strength from the psalm of Prime: 'Judge me, O Lord; for I have walked in my integrity; I have trusted also in the Lord; therefore I shall not slide.'

After two days of sailing north-east, in sight of the coast, Ibn Majid altered course to east-north-east, leading the fleet out, into the first, soft days of the south-west monsoon, to the path found by Hippalos the Greek in AD 45 and subsequently used by Greek, Roman, Jew, and Arab for trade with India. During its greatness and its decline Imperial Rome took in large, rich cargos of spices, and in AD 405 Alaric secured as part of the ransom that he demanded from the city 3,000 pounds of pepper, imported from that coast towards which, for the first time three small ships out of Europe were reaching, the coast of Malabar.

No incident of the twenty-three days it took to cross to India is anywhere recorded, except that on the fifth the adventurers saw once more the Pole Star, which they had not seen for more than 200 nights. After many months of baffling winds and currents it was new to move on day after day with a steady breeze, probably gathering force as the days went by. They were travelling with the front of the young monsoon carrying the rains to the rich, diverse country that lies between the sea and the great range of the Western Ghats. The chief port and principal city of that coast was Calicut.

From the Ghats (with peaks reaching 7,000 feet) the land of Malabar breaks up into a densely forested country of long spurs and ravines, which to the westward softens into rolling hills and wide valleys, and then rice plains, separated from the coast by backwaters fringed with coconut palms. As the monsoon draws near, the air grows heavy and the heat oppressive. During the day clouds build up over the mountains, and sheets of lightning flare ever more often through the sky, turning into brilliant darting forks at evening; but at first no rain falls and the nights are clear. So it is for a few days; then suddenly after sunset, comes a rush of wind from the east, heavy rain, thunder and lightning, for perhaps a hundred minutes. The rain breaks off. Growing weaker, the wind steadies, veering to south-west; and thunder grumbles far away among the hills. By such signs as these the people of Malabar know the monsoon is on its way. Travelling with it Gama's flotilla passed south of the Manigal Par coral reef, named by the Portuguese the 'flats of Padua'; they were sailing due east.

By this time they were sounding right through the dark hours. By day a far haze made uncertain the interface of sky and sea. On Friday 18 May 1498, as the lead struck bottom at forty-five fathoms, land, apparently the top of Mount Dilli—at about 900 feet the most striking headland of that coast—was seen about twenty miles off.

But Ibn Majid turned away. During the night he set the ships on a course south-south-west to stand off from the coast. Next day he turned in again, but suddenly rain beat down, with a crash of thunder. They had arrived at the coast just as the monsoon burst. As they sailed down the shore of sandy bays, the storm was too thick for Ibn Majid to see just where they were; but on the next day, Sunday 20 May, with the thunderstorm past, some hills could be seen. 'And when we were near enough for the pilot to recognise them he told us were were above Calicut, and that this was the country we desired to go to'. Another account says, 'The twentieth, he discovered the high hills, which are over Calicut, then going cheerfully to the general, demanded *Albrisias* [fee], saying, that was the land which he and his people so greatly desired to see. Da Gama, overjoyed, gave Kanaca his demand; and making a feast on shipboard, came to anchor two leagues below Calicut, in an open road; the city having no harbour or shelter for ships.'

In the *Lusiad* Camões writes,

> Aloud the pilot of Melinde cries,
> Behold, O chief, the shores of India rise!
> Elate the joyful crew on tip-toe trod,
> And every breast with swelling raptures glow'd;
> Gama's great soul confest the rushing swell,
> Prone on his knees the hero fell,
> Oh bounteous heaven, he cries, and spread his hands
> To bounteous heaven, while boundless joy commands
> No further word to flow. (Translated by W. J. Mickle.)

314 days since they left Restello, Ibn Majid had placed Gama and his men at the mouth of the Elatur river, seven miles north-north-west of Calicut, where they anchored about six miles off shore. Four fishing boats sailed near them during the day, their leading man calling out to know who they were. In the exchange of hails, the fishermen, 'brown, and all naked, excepting a little piece of linen before', pointed out to them Calicut, just down the coast. Next day, when they came back selling fish to the crews, Gama sent among them one of his convicts, Joan Nunez, a 'new christian' (which means a converted Jew) who could speak some Arabic and Hebrew; he was to go ashore to test the feeling. Many

crowded about him on the beach, in a clamour to know what sort of man it was, so clearly was his dress not that of the Moor he claimed to be. As he moved up the beach through the confused noise, bustle, and chatter of an unknown tongue he heard a shout in clear Castilian and in Genoese: 'May the devil take thee! What brought thee hither?'

Two men in Moorish dress drew Nunez from the crowd. What was he seeking so far from home? Christians and spices. Why had not the King of Castile, he of France or the Signoria of Venice sent such messengers? The King of Portugal would not allow it. Wise was the King of Portugal. As they put their questions the two Moṵrs, traders from Tunis, they said, led Nunez to their house and there fed him on wheaten bread and honey. He in turn, questioning them about Calicut and its ways, persuaded one of them to go back with him to the ships to speak with the captain-major. As he crossed the ship's rail and stepped on deck, this man from Tunis called out loudly to Gama, 'A lucky venture, a lucky venture! Plenty of rubies, plenty of emeralds! You owe great thanks to God, for having brought you to a country holding such riches!'

The long search was over; here the discovery began: began with Gama eagerly questioning Monçaide, the Spanish-speaking Moor, whom good fortune, or destiny, had brought to him.

Yet there was a sour note to the arrival of the Portuguese, as is plain from the first words of description that the anonymous eye-witness in Gama's ship gives about the land to which they had come. Immediately he becomes the self-satisfied, patronising European loftily disdainful of the appearance and customs (but not the wealth) of a people other than his own: 'They also wear moustaches. They pierce the ears and wear much gold in them. They go naked down to the waist, covering their lower extremities with very fine cotton stuffs. But it is only the most respectable who do this, for the others manage as best they are able. The women of this country, as a rule, are ugly and of small stature. They wear many jewels of gold round the neck, numerous bracelets on their arms, and rings set with precious stones on their toes. All these people are well disposed and apparently of mild temper. At first sight they seem covetous and ignorant.'

The next day Gama moved his ships seven miles down coast, to drop anchor 'in front of the most noble and rich city of Calicut'—a noble city, but on an unprotected shore.

'Outside the law of Jesus Christ'

'Although by common right the seas are common, and open to all navigators, and also by the same right we are obliged to give conservation to the property which each one may bring into our presence, because it suits him to go that way, not having any other public way, yet this law has force only in Europe, among the christian flock; which, as by faith and baptism, it is contained in the bosom of the Roman church, so in the government of its policy it is ruled by Roman law. Not that the christian kings and princes are subject to this imperial law, especially this kingdom of ours of Portugal, and others which are drawn close to the Pope by obedience, and not on account of being his feudatories; but they accept these laws inasmuch as they are just and conformable to reason, which is the mother of law. But with respect to these Moors and gentiles, who are outside the law of Jesus Christ, which is the true law, which every man is obliged to hold and keep, under pain of being condemned to eternal fire: since they are condemned in the principal part, which is the soul, that part of them which it animates cannot be privileged with the benefits of our laws, because they are not members of the evangelical congregation, although they are near to it as rational beings, and are, as long as they live, in the possibility and way of being able to enter into it. And even conforming with ourselves with the common right itself, not speaking of these Moors and gentiles, who have lost this faculty from not receiving our holy faith, yet any member of it [our faith] cannot claim preservation in those eastern parts; because before our entrance into India by which we took possession of it, there was no one there who had any property inherited or conquered; and where there is no preceding right of action, there is no present or future right of safeguard. Because as every act, to continue itself for a long time, requires a natural origin, so legal action to be just depends upon an origin of preceding justice, which in common right is a universal centre, with which all acts of men must concur, who live according to the law of God.' (Barros, liv. vi, cap. i, trans. Stanley.)

Five

Ambassador

'They did reach and discover India'

Bruges of India

From the hour of their arrival the Portuguese persisted in an illusion. 'The city of Calicut is inhabited by christians', says the report. 'They are of tawny complexion. Some of them have big beards and long hair, whilst other clip their hair short or shave their head, allowing only a tuft to remain on the crown as a sign they are christians.' Not till later voyages did they begin to unravel the stratified complexities of this society on which they had burst, a society already centuries in being when the Portuguese-to-be descended from the Galician hills to war against the Moors. There had been christians in Malabar since the fourth or fifth century; but none in Calicut.

When the armies of the Prophet first carried their faith among the infidel, on the blades of their crescent swords, Malabar had long been a staging post on the trade route between China and the Persian Gulf. From the start of the eighth century AD, the second of the Hegira, the western part of this trade passed into moslem hands. As the Arab empires grew out from Morocco to Sind, the ports of Malabar, of which by the fourteenth century Calicut was foremost, developed close trading links with Cairo, Tunis and Bussorah. 'Calicut', wrote the ambassador of Shah Rokh, Abdur Rezzak, in 1443, 'brings together merchants from every city and from every country; in it is found abundance of precious articles brought thither from maritime countries, and especially from Abyssinia, Zirbad and Zanguebar.

'From time to time ships arrive there from the shores of the House of God and other parts of the Hedjaz, and abide at will, for a greater or longer space, in this harbour; the town is inhabited by infidels, and situated on a hostile shore. It contains a considerable number of musulmans, who are constant residents, and have built two mosques. . . .

'Security and justice are so firmly established in this city, that the most wealthy merchants bring thither from maritime countries considerable cargoes, which they unload, and unhesitatingly send into the markets and the bazaars, without thinking in the mean time of any necessity of checking the account or of keeping watch over the goods. The officers of the custom-house take upon themselves the charge of looking after the merchandise, over which they keep watch day and night. When a sale is made, they lay a duty on the goods of one fortieth part; if they are not sold, they make no charge on them whatsoever. . . .

'From Calicut are vessels continually sailing for Mecca, which are for the most part laden with pepper. The inhabitants of Calicut are adventurous sailors: they are known by the name of Tchini-betchegan (sons of the Chinese), and pirates do not dare attack the vessels of Calicut. In this harbour one may find everything that can be desired.' (Major's translation.)

So far Abdur Rezzak; though, at least when Gama arrived, the city's only adventurous sailors were the moslems.

This Calicut off which Gama's ships were anchored was a city some eight miles round, without walls or formal defences; its buildings were of wattle, excepting the palace and the temples, which were 'of lime and stone'. It was the great centre of the western trade of India, later described by King Emanuel as 'the Bruges of India', and its ruler, the Zamorin, was the wealthiest and most powerful on the coast. The whole seaborne trade was in the hands of the Moors, who brought wealth, arms and horses, giving power to the state and were organisers and commanders of the Zamorin's naval forces. They were, said Ibn Battuta, the Marco Polo of the moslems, extremely rich—so rich that one of their leading merchants could buy up the whole freightage of such vessels as put in there and fit out others like them. But, as Zain Al-Din insists, the Moors did not encroach on the civil power or on the rights of the people: 'I would have it understood that the mohammedans of Malabar lived in great comfort and tranquillity in consequence of their abstaining from exercising any oppression towards the people of the country as well as from the consideration which they always evinced for the ancient usages of the country and from the unrestricted intercourse which they preserved with them.'

It came as no surprise to the Portuguese to find themselves faced with the Moors at this centre of the spice trade, but it seemed to them truly astounding that they should find there someone who spoke the language of Castile. 'The general and the rest were so surprised to meet with one who could speak their language so far from home that they wept for joy.' Gama, sitting him down at once, asked Monçaide whether he was a christian and how he came to be in Calicut. 'The Moor told him what religion he was of and that he arrived at India by way of Cairo.' This man was later said to have done business with the Portuguese at Oran in the days of the Perfect Prince. By one account he was born a christian in Seville, was taken prisoner by the Moors when he was five, was long a slave, and, though remaining at heart a christian, had, to save his life, taken the name and ceremonies of the Moor'. To all others he was the 'Moor of Tunis', as King Emanuel later called him. That day on the deck of the *S. Gabriel* he 'concluded by speaking in favour of the Portuguese and saying that as he had on all occasions before been their friend, so he would continue to further them in their designs to the utmost of his power'.

Gratified but cautious Gama promised Monçaide bountiful rewards if he should do service to the Portuguese in their mission of discovery; for doubtless God had sent him thither before them to give them success. In the meantime there was the immediate question: where was the ruler of Calicut—and what sort of man was he? He was, said Monçaide, a prince of very good disposition, and, as most of his revenues came from duties on goods, would no doubt gladly receive Gama as the ambassador of a foreign king interested in trade. He was then at Panane, a coastal village fifteen leagues south, to which Gama should send messengers with notice of his arrival.

It was done that day. With Monçaide as guide Fernan Martins and another set off with the message from Gama that he bore letters from the King of Portugal, a christian prince. They were to say that the captain-major was ready to attend on the Zamorin where he then was. Three days passed, uncomfortably spent at anchor on a stony bottom, in mist and rain off a coast that was open, low, sandy and fringed with coconut trees. For the men who were not let ashore or even allowed contact with the people who came hawking their fish and fowls (the pilot bought what was needed, on behalf of all), they were days of frustration.

For Gama and his captains they were days of conference and of controversy. The captain-major was firm in his intention to go himself to see the Zamorin, to conclude with him 'a pact of commerce and perpetual amity'. In this, Castanheda says, Paulo stoutly opposed him. Though he believed the ruler and his own people to be christian, he saw that the many Moors amongst them were influential and powerful, and argued that they would always be mortal enemies to the Portuguese, whose arrival would make them fear for their trade. This being so, they would be ready for who knew what treachery: 'they would attempt with all their force possible to destroy him [Gama]'. The others reinforced Paulo's arguments, saying it was not prudent to risk the life of the commander, on whose safety they all depended. Someone else should be sent first. The arguments went on for many hours, at more than one meeting. But Gama would not be persuaded. He made his position uncompromisingly clear. He carried his king's commission. He had undertaken a charge. He would rather die than go back to Portugal without sure proof of his mission from the ruler of Calicut. What cause for anxiety was there, he argued, when he was going to treat with a christian king and one who wanted trade? However, if the worst happened, if he were imprisoned or murdered, he said, there was on no account to be any attempt at rescue or reprisal. The mission came first; and the others must at once go back to Portugal with the news that the sea-way to India was open.

Martins and his companion came back bringing presents and goodwill—presents of fine cloth for themselves, messages of goodwill and welcome for the captain-major. The Zamorin would see him, they reported, but at Calicut; and for his visitors' greater safety he sent a pilot to guide them to Pandarini, a better anchorage a dozen miles to the north. There they would be protected by a mudbank, the shore was free from surf, and the ships' boats could land with ease. Gama lost no time in giving orders for the move, which was completed before evening, but caution still prevailed—'we did not anchor so near the shore as the king's pilot desired'.

Within a short time a message came to say that the Zamorin was already in the city: he had set out from Panane 'with great retinue' as soon as the strangers had left. The Zamorin in progress was no mean show. 'The King comes forth borne by two men in his litter which is lined with silk cushions', wrote accurate Duarte Barbosa of the enquiring mind. 'The litter is of silk, and is slung on a bamboo pole covered with precious stones; it is as thick as the arm of a man and they carry him with certain turns and steps to which they are trained from their birth.'

Many instruments of metal were played before the Zamorin; many archers preceded him, with bows and arrows 'like those of the English'. Others carried long spears with heads an ell in length, 'brandishing them as they go'. Others, again, had drawn swords in their hands, with rings on the hilts 'with which they make great disturbances', and 'they shout one to the other in a loud voice "Go on!" "Go on!" ' Some fenced with one another as they passed in front of the Zamorin and cleared a space so that he might see them.

One page carried before the Zamorin his sword and shield, another bore a golden sword of state, another a sword 'which belonged to that King who ruled over the whole of Malabar and became a Moor', within his left hand 'a weapon which is like unto a flower of luce'. On each side walked a man with a fan, the one carrying a large round fan, the other a fan made from the white tail of an animal like a horse. At the Zamorin's right hand walked a page with a golden ewer of water, at his left two pages, one with a ewer of silver and one with a towel. Right and left also were a page with a cup of betel covered with gold and one with a silver spittoon. Four parasols were borne in front of the Zamorin two of very fine white cloth, and two of worked and embroidered silk. Near him also was carried an umbrella on a high support, which kept off the sun.

With such ceremony the Lord of the Hills and the Sea made his way to Calicut, from which, that evening, he sent to Gama the 'Catual', his civil minister and police chief, with a guard of 200 men armed with sword and buckler. Their instructions were to conduct the visitor to the palace, but Gama deferred leaving till the next day, since it was already late and he was not prepared. Next morning the ships' boats gathered alongside the S. *Gabriel*, bright with bunting and with standards. Bombards were mounted in them. With them were all the fleet's trumpets. Captains and men were in gala order. They made a sparkling sight, a gay and glorious sound came from the salute of bombards and the peal of trumpets carrying over the water as the oars dipped and sparkled spray and the line of boats made steadily for the shore. Paula da Gama stayed with the ships. Coelho commanded the boat party, his orders being to stand by for the commander's return. In the landing party or embassy, Gama took with him thirteen men, among them the three pursers—Diogo Dias, Joan de Sá and Alvaro de Braga—and Alvaro Velho (a soldier), Joan de Setubal, Gonçalo Pirez (a master mariner and a retainer of Gama's); and the unknown officer who wrote the one surviving record of the voyage. To greet them on the beach were the Catual, his guards with swords drawn, many other followers and a great crowd of people.

Cries that seemed welcoming and friendly greeted them. For Gama there was a palanquin—a mark of distinction for the eminent, but for merchants a privilege for which they had to pay a handsome fee to the Zamorin. Six men carried him in relays; his company followed on foot along the road to Calicut, so closely brushed by the loud, nudging throng from the beach that they sometimes were nearly lost among them. On the way, at Capua, or Capocate, where the Elatur river opens into the sea, a stop was made at some notable's house. The food offered there was refused by Gama, but his companions ate with pleasure a dish of 'rice with much butter and excellent boiled fish'. When they left again for Calicut it was by ferry across the river mouth—two boats lashed together with planks above and railed round. Their throng of sightseers went with them in a swarm of crowded boats for about four miles, passing many large ships drawn up high on the banks. New thousands were attracted when the party reached the other side, where the captain-major was once more taken up in his palanquin, with the others following on foot as best they could. There was 'a countless multitude anxious to see us', and 'even the women came out of their houses with children in their arms and followed us'.

So they came at last to Calicut; but before entering the city they were led to 'a large church'—large as a monastery, all built of hewn stone and covered with tiles. Along the walls by the main gate hung seven small bells. Before the gate rose 'a pillar of bronze has high as a mast', on top of which was perched a bird, apparently a cock. Nearby was 'another pillar as high as a man, and very stout'. At this pagoda or temple, with its high metal-cased flagpole crowned by the image of Subraumainar, the god of war, and its lamp standard, the Portuguese found some assurance for the moment that these were indeed christians among whom they had come.

In the centre of the body of the church was a chapel of hewn stone, with stone steps leading up to a door of bronze, and through this door as it stood open they could see a small image; this they were told, or thought they were told, 'represented Our Lady'. Infinite possibilities of self-delusion flow from a wish to believe, allied to ignorance of the language being spoken. For the Portuguese saw four priests go into the chapel; they heard, or thought they heard, these men call out, as they pointed to the image, 'Maria, Maria'. At this cry, all the Indians threw themselves prone upon the ground; the Portuguese knelt to adore the Virgin Mother of God. But who really was it that the priests were calling upon? Was it Gauri the 'white goddess', as Burton suggests? Was it Maha Maja? Or perhaps a local diety, Mari or Mariamma, goddess of smallpox?

At this church, but not within the sanctuary, where only the priests might go, the captain-major said his prayers, joined by his companions. The priests 'wore some threads passing over the left shoulder and under the right arm, in the same manner as our deacons wear the stole'. Clearly these were Brahmins, who then 'threw holy water over us and gave us some white earth which the christians of this country are in the habit of putting on their foreheads, breasts, around the neck and on the forearms'. When they threw holy water upon the captain-major and gave him some of this mixture of dust, cow-dung, sacrificial ashes, sandal wood and other delicate ingredients bound with rice water, he passed it to his servant, saying gravely that he would put it on later.

Some doubt about the orthodoxy of these christians was caused by wall pictures of crowned saints with teeth protruding an inch from the mouth and with four or five arms. As Joan de Sá knelt beside da Gama he murmured, 'If these be devils, I worship the true God'—at which his captain smiled. It was no doubt because of such aberrations Emanuel the Fortunate found it necessary to say to the King and Queen of Castile that he expected 'the christian people whom these explorers reached, notwithstanding that they are not as yet strong in the faith . . . to do much in the service of God and the exaltation of the Holy Faith, once they should have been . . . fully fortified in it'.

At that moment in Calicut, however, it was the Portuguese whose faith was fortified, by what they imagined to be proof that they were among christians, though untutored; and so fortified they were led into the city itself, past another such church. The crowd about them became a multitude. Passage through the street was stopped by the excited mass. Gama and his company were led aside into a house to rest. Thither the Zamorin sent a brother of the governor and with him 2,000 armed men to escort the party to the palace. Drums were beaten, tuba-trumpets and screaming bagpipes were blown, and matchlocks were fired. Unnumbered people surrounded the procession and clambered on to rooftops to watch it pass as the captain-major was conducted forward with 'much respect, more than is shown in Spain to a king'.

An hour before sunset they reached the palace, which stood among trees of many kinds and gardens graced with fountains. Noble lords and men of much distinction, as it seemed, came out to greet the strangers. They passed through a gate into a courtyard of great size; then, to reach the Zamorin's audience chamber, they were led to four doors each guarded by ten porters, 'through which we had to force our way, giving many blows to people'. It seemed that in the crowd Gama's followers were being cut off from him as he was carried along in the palanquin of state; and knives were drawn.

'At last we reached the door where the king was. There came forth from it a little old man, who holds a position resembling that of a bishop, and whose advice the king acts upon in all affairs of the church. This man embraced the captain when he entered the door. Several men were wounded at this door. We only got in by the use of much force.'

This door led them into a small court and into the presence. They saw reclining on a couch a small elderly man—'tawny, almost white' says one account, 'very dark' says another. He was naked to the waist, clad in cloths of white silk below, one of them threaded at its point with gold rings and rubies; his hair was tied up on the top, with a string of pearls round the knot; he was beardless but with 'short moustaches after the manner of the Turks'. In his ears were rich jewels of precious stones filled with great pearls. A bracelet that seemed like three rings together adorned his left arm above the elbow; it was 'studded with rich jewels' and from it hung a diamond 'the thickness of a thumb': it seemed a priceless thing. Pearls the size of hazelnuts hung in two rings round his neck, reaching to his navel, above which was a thin round gold chain bearing a heart-shaped jewel all full of rubies and surrounded with pearls; and in the middle of this jewel was 'a green stone of the size of a large bean which was called an emerald'. On the Zamorin's toes and fingers were many diamond rings. On his chest, shoulder and forehead were streaks of ashes in groups of three.

His couch was covered with a cloth of green velvet, above it 'a good mattress', and on the mattress was 'a sheet of cotton stuff, very white and fine, more so than any linen', wrought with gold, with round cotton cushions after the same fashion. Overhead was a rich gilt canopy of subtle workmanship, which covered the whole room. Near the Zamorin a page, a silk cloth round him, held a red shield bordered with gold and jewels, and having a similarly precious boss, about a span in breadth and a sword (round at the point, and an ell in length, with a hilt of gold and jewels with pendent pearls). At the Zamorin's right side stood a gold basin so large that a man might just encircle it with his arms. It held a mixture of betel-nut (*Areca catechu*) and lime of oyster-shell bound with cutch. A page at his side constantly handed to him pieces of this mixture to chew, wrapped in a leaf of betel-pepper. At his left a second page held a large cup of gold to receive the blood-red spittle which came as constantly from the red-stained lips and black-stained teeth. This preparation, wrote Garcia da Orta, was 'a good medicine to open the gums, fortify the teeth and compose the stomach, as well as an emetic and a cure for diarrhoea'; and

Correa wrote that it made the breath very pleasant. In the presence of the Zamorin all held the left hand before their mouths, that their breath might not reach him; before him none might spit or sneeze.

From the door of the Zamorin's chamber Gama stepped forward, bowed three times from the hips, saluted three times 'in the manner of the country, putting his hands together, then raising them towards heaven, as is done by christians when addressing God, and straight afterwards opening them and shutting the fist quickly'; then he stood silent, his eyes on the ruler. The Zamorin gazed back at him and his head just moved, a nod so slight it was almost a negation of motion, but from him it was considered acknowledgement enough. Still Gama stood. The Zamorin beckoned with his right hand that he should come nearer; but Gama did not move until a seat was placed for him, for it was thought discourteous to approach the body of the king. Gama's companions in turn were led to a stone bench near him. Servants brought silver ewers of water for their hands and offered jack-fruits and bananas, which some ate, the Zamorin looking on at them, smiling and talking with his betel-page.

At length the Zamorin called on Gama, who sat facing him, to speak to the court, and to tell those noble and distinguished men whatever he desired, so that they in turn could interpret his wishes to their king. Nothing could have been less desirable to Gama. Such a procedure was totally out of keeping with the status he intended to establish for himself; and the idea of opening his business in the presence of the leading Moors did not please him at all. He was the ambassador of the King of Portugal, he answered—bearer of a message to be handed directly and in private to the ruler of Calicut and Malabar himself. His answer seemed to please. The Zamorin directed that he be led to a room at one side with his interpreter Fernan Martins and joined him there without delay, bringing with him only the chief Brahmin, his betel-page and his factor, controller of his household. Once settled on a couch covered with gold-embroidered cloth he asked again from what country the strangers had come and the reason for their coming. Then at last Vasco da Gama spoke.

The King of Portugal, lord of many countries, possessed of great wealth of every kind—greater, indeed, than the wealth of any king of those parts—had sent him, he said, as his ambassador to India to discover that great christian king who was famed to live there. Year by year for sixty years the ancestors of the present King of Portugal had sent out vessels of discovery to search for the way to India. They did this not from desire for silver or for gold, of which they had such abundance that they had no need of the wealth of other countries, but because they sincerely wished to become acquainted and to contract friendship with those of their fellow christians who ruled in India—especially, as the greatest and most powerful of them, the ruler of Calicut.

During those years of search, Gama explained, the captains sent out would travel a year or two years, depending on how their provisions lasted, and then return to Portugal, without having met success in their endeavours. But Emanuel, the great and present King of Portugal, had laid on him, Vasco da Gama, the charge to build three ships, had appointed him his captain-major, and had sent him out with the command not to return to Portugal without having discovered the king of the christians in India, failing which he would lose his head.

He had brought two letters from King Emanuel to be presented if he succeeded in discovering the king he sought; these he would present in person the following day. He was commanded also to say by word of mouth that the King of Portugal desired to be Calicut's friend and brother. He was furthermore to ask that the King of Calicut send to Portugal with Gama his own ambassadors, to confirm his amity.

At this meeting nothing was said of trade or spices. To the formal offer of friendship and fraternal relations the Zamorin answered that the embassy was welcome. For his part he was glad to hold the King of Portugal as friend and brother and he would send ambassadors. He then questioned Gama about the power of the King of Portugal, the distance of Portugal from Calicut, and how long the voyage had taken. In this way they talked far into the night, till at length the Zamorin enquired with whom Gama would wish to be lodged, with christians or with Moors. With neither, but on his own, was Gama's characteristic answer. And so the Zamorin ordered it.

'Four hours of the night had already gone' when the captain-major left the presence of the Zamorin and found his company resting on a verandah lit up by a huge candlestick. Led once again by the Catual and his guard, accompanied by the Zamorin's factor, a Moor, and followed once again by a great crowd, they set out, the commander again in a palanquin, to find the lodging. Rain poured down heavily; the roads ran with water. The way seemed to be without end. At length the captain-major asked for a pause and for shelter. They were taken into the factor's own house, to a court with a tile-roofed verandah which kept off the sheeting rain. There carpets were spread for them. Two large standards, each carrying great iron lamps fed with oil or butter, were lit. After a time the factor offered a horse to Gama; but, as it had no saddle (as was customary there), he refused to mount it. All set out again on foot to find the lodging. Perhaps the rain had lessened or stopped—the records give no hint— but at least they soon reached their resting-place. The Catual, or more probably the factor, had organized well; for at the lodging they found some of their men, who had brought from the ships, the captain's bed and other necessary baggage and supplies, with many things provided as presents for the Zamorin. To judge by the actions of his officers, the Zamorin intended friendship; but there remained the doubtful question of how the Moors would act.

Realities of power

Through the centuries for which it had been at the centre of trade between eastern Asia and the Mediterranean, Calicut had become the leader among the states of Malabar. Gama's reporter wrote that the Zamorin 'can muster 100,000 fighting men, including auxiliaries, for the number under his proper jurisdiction is very small'. The ruler appeared an autocrat, but was in reality at the head of a form of feudal power. His strength lay in his wealth, in his Moorish immigrants and the naval power they brought him, and in the rivalries of his ever-warring feudatories. These minor rajahs and great landed nobles, owing allegiance sometimes to more than one overlord, kept in being large private armies. The principal expression of their allegiance was support in time of war; this apart, they ruled their domains much as they willed, with little meddling from the Zamorin.

His authority was further limited by priestly power. For the Zamorin and the subsidiary rajahs and nobles were members of the second caste. Above them in the god-ordained gradation of mankind were the Brahmins, who controlled the practice of religion. In relation to the ruler they were more allies than subjects, forming a small theocratic oligarchy managing its own communal affairs, ready at any time to interfere with others; and owning much land. In Malabar the warrior caste, to which the Zamorin belonged, were Nairs. Below them came the merchants and husbandmen, then the artisans and labourers, then division after division until at bottom was the pariah, to all the rest a pollution, more animal than human.

From the first, the Portuguese were bemused by the kinship rules of this alien society, which to them seemed totally depraved, its women harlots all. The Brahmins as the highest caste, operated a rigid primogenitive system. In each family, the firstborn male inherited the whole estate, and he was the only male of his generation who was allowed to marry within his caste, which in this way was preserved small and undilute. The rest could only take women of the Nairs —to whom it was an honour that a Brahmin should grace their bed.

Far different the Nairs: 'these kings do not marry, nor have they any marriage law', wrote Duarte Barbosa. 'They keep as a concubine a woman of good family of Nair descent. Their heirs are their brothers, or their nephews, sons of their sisters. The firstborn son to the king's eldest sister is heir to the throne.' Without understanding it, he is describing a form of group marriage and its resultant matriarchal system. It was not concubinage, not harlotry, but a form of family organisation dating back to ancient tribal society, in which the fact that the identity of the father was not certain meant that it was the mother who counted in reckoning relationships.

This system produced very large family groups. Social obligations related not to the individual but to the family as is common in clan society. With the Nairs, traditional warriors, the family had further an unusual characteristic: it was virtually organised as a unit for military service. In each village was an instructor in arms and the arts of war. Boys and young men in the village were compelled to take military training and join in exercises. They formed in essence a conscript militia. Typically they had a family sense of honour, and family resentment of dishonour. Their skill at arms, their virtual monopoly of that skill and their caste sensitivity gave them great influence in the state and made them harsh oppressors of the lower castes. But they had also a strong tradition of loyalty to the rulers whose authority they upheld. The 2,000 swordsmen who attended the Catual and cleared for Gama the road to the palace were a small troop of Nairs in the Zamorin's train.

But it was not a straightforward Hindu society that the Portuguese found. Things were, and had long been, changing in Calicut. The cause was the moslem presence. To many parts of India the moslems had come as conquerors; to Malabar they came as traders. Their wealth, maritime skill, and the horses they brought with them all benefited the Zamorin, who as a result gradually extended his influence and power. As traders over generations they also became settlers—and gradually unsettlers also, for the moslem faith had great attractions for those of low caste.

Duarte Barbosa describes how 'in this land of Malabar there are Moors in great numbers who speak the same tongue as the heathens of the land and go naked like Nairs but as a token of distinction wear little round caps on their heads and long beards. They are so rooted in the soil throughout Malabar that it seems to me they are a fifth part of its people spread over all its kingdoms and provinces. They are rich and live well; they hold all the sea trade and navigation in such sort that if the King of Portugal had not discovered India Malabar would already have been in the hands of the Moors and would have had a Moorish king. For the heathen if displeased at anything become Moors; and the Moors show them great respect and if it is a woman they take her in marriage. . . .

'They marry as many wives as they can support and keep as well many heathen concubines of low caste. If they have sons or daughters by these they make them Moors, and oft-times the mother as well; and thus this evil generation continues to increase in Malabar. The people of the country call them *Mapuleres* [Moplas]. There are many other foreign Moors as well in the town of Calicut, who are called *Pardisis*, natives of diverse lands, Arabs, Persians, Gujarates, Curasanes and Daquanis. They sail everywhere with goods of many kinds and have a Moorish governor of their own who rules and punishes them without interference from the king.'

On the same point Correa comments, with greater venom, that from their great trade 'the Moors were very powerful, and had so established and ingratiated themselves that they were more influential and respected than the natives themselves so that many of the heathen became Moors, in such manner that they were more people than the natives, by a diabolical method which the Moors found.'

This is how that 'diabolical method' worked: 'In this region of Malabar the race of gentlemen is called Nairs . . . people very refined in blood and customs, separated from all other low people; so much do they value themselves that no one of them ever turned Moor: only the low people turned Moors, who worked in the bush and in the fields. These people are so accursed that they cannot go by any road without shouting so that the Nairs may not come up suddenly and meet them because they kill them at once.' So the Moors had said to the rulers of Malabar that they had great difficulties with their merchandise for lack of labourers because the labourers, being low-caste, could not go among other people, as the Nairs would kill them whenever they met them; 'therefore they would esteem it a favour if those of the low people who might turn Moors should be able to go freely wherever they pleased, for as Moors they would be outside the Malabar religion and usages and might be able to touch all sorts of people'. Thus these 'accursed that lived in the bush and in the fields where they ate nothing but herbs and land crabs by becoming Moors could go where they liked and gain their livelihood and eat as they pleased. . . . So many of them became Moors and were converted to the religion of Mohammed and they increased so much in numbers that all the country became full of them, which caused these Moors to be very influential and powerful by their trade . . . above all in the city of Calicut where they had their principal port for shipping drugs.' Such devilish work.

Of the commodities in which the Moors traded, the reporter from Gama's fleet records that ginger, pepper, cinnamon and cloves were the principal spices they carried (Barbosa adds cardamom, mirobolans and musk, and of other goods singles out aubergines, rhubarb, precious stones, porcelain and cotton cloth) and says that they carried their goods to Jidda, where they discharged them, 'paying customs dues to the Grand Sultan. The merchandise is then trans-shipped to smaller vessels which carry it through the Red Sea to a place close to Santa Caterina of Mount Sinai called Tunz [El Tar], where customs are paid once more. From that place the merchants carry the spices on the backs of camels, which they hire at the rate of four cruzados each, to Quanyro [Cairo], a journey occupying ten days. At Quanyro, duties are paid again. On this road to Quanyro they are often robbed by thieves such as Bedouin and others. At Quanyro the spices are embarked on the river Nile, which rises in Prester John's country in Lower India, and descending that river for two days they reach a place called Roxette [? Rashid/Rosetta], where duties have to be paid once more. There they are placed on camels and are conveyed in one day to a city called Alexandria, which is a sea-port. This city is visited by the galleys of Venice and Genoa in search of these spices which yield the Grand Sultan a revenue of 600,000 cruzados in customs duties.' Such was the trade and such the revenues which the Portuguese had come to take for themselves.

In one respect the planners in Lisbon with all their care had gone badly wrong. For they had failed to foresee the riches and highly developed culture to be found in Calicut. K. M. Pannikar points out in *Malabar and the Portuguese*, 'the Mammalis and Khoja Musas whom the Portuguese encountered were merchant princes to whom Cairo and Damascus were as familiar as Calicut and Cannanore. Through them, the Zamorin was in close connection with the rulers of Egypt, Persia and the northern Indian sultanates.'

It was for such a court and such a ruler that Gama and his servants, on the morning of Tuesday 29 May, prepared a present.

Entanglements

The Zamorin's factor and the Catual laughed and jeered when they saw the intended gifts. Laid out for them to see at Gama's lodging were twelve pieces of a striped cotton known as lambel (it had been popular in the African trade), four scarlet hoods, six hats, four strings of coral, a case containing six hand-basins, a chest of sugar, two casks of oil and two casks of honey.

Their sneers were painful, humiliating. This was no present to offer a king, they said. The poorest merchant from Mecca or from any other part of India would give more. The Zamorin would not accept such things. A present for him, they said, must be in gold. But Gama was no easy man to humiliate. Though downcast and, as some accounts say, resentful, he answered that he was no merchant but an ambassador; he was on a mission of discovery, his task to seek out Calicut; he was not supplied with gold. What he had assembled was a token gathered from his own possessions, not sent by his king. For his king could not know whether the fleet would reach Calicut, whether they would find the Zamorin, whether he would ever see his servants again. He would send rich presents, silver, gold and goods of price, when next he sent his ships, in the sure knowledge that the way to Calicut had been found. That might be so, was the answer; whatever the future might be, it was the custom that every stranger seeking to speak with the Zamorin should make him a present worthy of his state. A custom fit to be observed, said Gama; they should therefore allow him to carry to their king the only present he could muster; otherwise he would take it back to his ships. But factor and Catual were unyielding: on no account would they allow it.

The dispute suited their purpose. For in fact the presents were unsuitable. Whether from ignorance, parsimony or doubts of Gama's success Emanuel had sent him on his mission without proper goods or gifts. What was sent had proved popular in the villages of Africa; but Covilhan's report should have prepared the planners' minds for something different in the cities of Malabar. It was a blunder with evil consequences, a lever for Gama's opponents who were already moving against him.

But Gama would not surrender the initiative. Protesting vigorously, he said that, leaving his presents, he would go to make his explanations to the Zamorin, deliver his letters and go back to his ship. The factor and Catual consented. They promised to come back for him soon, but they stayed away all day, leaving the captain-major in a fume. At one moment he decided to go to the palace on his own; then he thought better of it and made up his mind to wait and see what would happen the next day. Apparently he kept his worries to himself; for 'as to us others, we diverted ourselves, singing and dancing to the sound of trumpets, and enjoyed ourselves much'.

During this lost day, while Gama was kept fretting at his lodging, the Moors had been working on the ministers, principally the Catual, and through them on the Zamorin. They fed them stories (which they embroidered in the telling) from their factors in east Africa, stories of bombardments and treachery at Mozambique and Mombasa—and at Melinde too, for good measure. According to Portuguese historians they supported their stories with lavish bribes. Monçaide tried to counter the effect of these polemics, arguing that the coming of the Portuguese brought promise of valuable trade, with good profit for the Zamorin. Probably he was able to speak direct with the old man, since it is said that the Zamorin wavered from one view to the other. His policy of welcoming all trade from any country inclined him to do business with the Portuguese; but his longstanding profit from the presence of the Moors, and his fear of losing their goodwill, argued for Gama's destruction.

To back the Catual's influence a group of leading Moors went to the palace to press their argument that the Portuguese were a mortal danger to their trade and to Calicut itself. Osorio records at length the sense of what they said: These people, they suggested, were corsairs, not merchants; men banished from their own country, vagabonds: their claim to carry letters from the King of Portugal was a fiction to hide their villainy. Was it credible, they asked, that a king so far off as the west of the country of the Franks should send an embassy only to seek the friendship of the King of Calicut? The miserable presents which they offered showed that they represented no king. And, if they did, nothing could be more dangerous to the Zamorin than to deal with the Portuguese, a nation of perfidy, lustful for power, who by artifice had made themselves masters of the towns of Africa. If they did come from the King of Portugal they came as spies; their talk of trade was no more than pretext. For the welfare of the state they should be destroyed before they could come again with greater power to ruin the great city of Calicut and its trade. Timely extinction of these Portuguese would put an end to this dangerous navigation and prevent any more of them from coming. In this way the ancient harmony between the

Moors and Calicut would be preserved and the revenues from their trade would continue and multiply.

Perhaps the views pressed by the Moors were not striking for their consistency; but they were not very wide of the mark. The Zamorin certainly paid attention to them, for the following morning, when the Catual and the factor fetched Gama and his company, the palace was crowded with armed men, and Gama was kept standing beside a closed door for four hours before word at last came from the Zamorin to admit him—with not more than two men of his own choice. This separation from his men seemed to him and to them a sign of trouble ahead. He took with him his interpreter, Fernan Martins, and his secretary; and he stepped into an angry-seeming presence.

Harsh words greeted him: all the previous day the Zamorin had been expecting him to bring his letters, but he had not come. Unwilling to speak of the previous day's dispute or to mention anything about a present Gama made excuse that the long journey had tired him and therefore he had rested. But the Zamorin brought him to the point at once: he had come from a very rich kingdom, ambassador of a great king, so he said; but he brought no gifts. A strange affair—what was to be thought of an embassy which came so ill supplied?

He had brought nothing with him because he had been sent on a discovery uncertain of what would be his fate, was Gama's answer. It was certain that, if he survived to return to Portugal, his king would send noble presents of great worth.

'What did your king send you to discover: stones or men? If men why did he send me no presents by you? But I have been told that on your ship you have a gold image of a saint: let me have that.' The Zamorin had been well prompted.

It was no gold image but painted wood, said Gama. But were it indeed gold, still he could not give it: it was the guardian of his ship and had guided him across the ocean and would guide him home again.

Watching Gama closely the Zamorin threw at him the accusations made by the Moors. Was he in truth a banished man? If he were, the Zamorin would aid him. Was it true he had no king, that he was more privateer than merchant, that he . . . ?

As the Zamorin spoke, Gama broke in. He could understand, he said, that the vassals of the King of Calicut should form fanciful ideas about people whose religion and customs were new to them; who had come, by seas never before navigated, as ambassadors from a powerful king. He could see, too, that they would have their doubts that this far-distant king had no other aim than to offer friendship and a new outlet for their spices. Portugal was in truth so rich in men, arms, horses, gold, silver, silk and other things necessary to human life that they had no need to seek out those of other men, especially of those so far removed as India. But the King of Portugal had heard the fame of the Zamorin and so had sent his ambassador to find him.

The captain-major's words poured out.

The King of Portugal had discovered 1,600 leagues of coast. He had required nothing from the many gentile kings and princes there found beyond instructing them in the faith of Jesus Christ, in whose service he had undertaken this enterprise. Besides this great benefit of the salvation of souls, the King had sent to these peoples ships laden with things they lacked and in return his captains brought him what was in those countries. By such trade those kingdoms which took his friendship flourished, became powerful and wealthy—all at the cost of the labour of the Portuguese and all done for the glory of serving God and for the fame of Portugal.

As for the Moors, they were the bitter enemies of Portugal, which had taken from them by force of arms four of the principal fortresses in the kingdom of Fez. Everywhere the Moors blackened the Portuguese and maliciously sought their death. Such treachery the Portuguese had never met with from the heathen, natural friends of the christians, similar in many customs and fashions. So long had the King of Portugal wished for the discovery of the way to India that even should he, Gama, not return, the King would certainly pursue his search until he got word of the Zamorin of Calicut. Therefore, he urged, the Zamorin should use his power to protect the Portuguese ambassador against the hatred of the Moors, not allowing them to be the cause of lighting up war in those parts.

Gama's great speech is only indirectly reported; but his words and his bearing clearly impressed. His eye-witness says that the Zamorin 'kept his eyes intently on him', searching his face and his expression, listening with concentration as Gama spoke with much temperance, fervour and constancy; 'it seemed to the Zamorin that he was sincere and steadfast'. At the end Gama was given leave to go back to his ships and to land his merchandise; but first he was to hand over the letters from his king.

Gama requested that 'a christian able to speak Arabic' be sent for, 'as the Moors wished him ill and might misinterpret him'. This seemed well to the Zamorin, who sent for a young man to do this. Gama explained that he had two letters—one in his own language, the other in that of the Moors: of the former, which he could read, he knew that it held nothing that would prove unacceptable; but the other he could not read and it might be good or it might contain some errors. As it turned out the young man sent for could interpret but not read. So it was read by four Moors, among them, at Gama's request, Monçaide. Together they interpreted it to the Zamorin, to the effect that 'as soon as it was known to the King of Portugal that the King of Calicut was a christian, he was desirous to cultivate a trade and friendship with him, for the convenience of lading spice in his ports; for which, in exchange, the commodities of Portugal should be sent, or else gold and silver should his majesty choose that, referring it to the captain-major his ambassador to amplify his message'.

Apparently well pleased, the Zamorin asked what kind of merchandise was to be found in Portugal. Gama said that there was much corn, cloth, iron, bronze and many other things. Had he any merchandise with him? Small quantitities as samples, said Gama, offering to fetch them and to leave four or five men behind in the meantime. No, the Zamorin said, there was no need to leave men behind. Gama and his men had better return to their ships. If the Portuguese stayed in the city, there might be words between them and the Moors, and words might lead to injuries, which would displease him. Gama should take all his people with him, tie up his ships securely, land his merchandise and sell it to the best advantage. The Catual would conduct them to their lodging.

Content with the outcome of the day's events, they stayed that night in the city, as it was already late. The next morning Gama was again brought a saddleless horse, which he again rejected. Instead he asked for 'a horse of the country', meaning a palanquin, which was provided by a wealthy merchant from Gujerat who lived nearby. Gama then set off for Pandarani to find the ships, trailed once again by a horde of onlookers. His followers on foot were again soon left behind; after being overtaken by the Catual, hurrying on to join the captain-major, they lost their way and wandered inland, where eventually they were found and put on the right road by one of the Catual's men.

Arriving at Pandarani after sunset, they found Gama with the Catual and a crowd of others in a rest-house, 'of which there are many along the road so that travellers and wayfarers may find protection against the rain'. Gama asked at once for a boat to ferry them all to the ships. Nothing was further from the intention of the Catual and his band. It was too late, he said, and too dark. They must wait till the next day. Black looks and an energetic answer came from Gama: either they had a boat or he would go back to the Zamorin to complain that he was being detained. No detention, no detention: he could leave at once, he could have thirty boats if he wished, countered the Catual.

They were led off along the beach to look for boats. Wary of what these men might be up to, Gama sent off three of his own in advance, giving them instructions that, if they found any of their people waiting with the ships' boats, they should tell them to hide. These three found nothing and were missed by the rest, who were led in the opposite direction. No boats were found that night: orders had been given to keep them all hidden. Late at night the Portuguese were given shelter in a Moor's house and a search party was put out for the missing three. At the end of the weary day the captain ordered fowls and rice and they ate together, tired out and oppressed by uncertainty.

In the morning Gama was more cheerful: he thought that perhaps the Catual had meant well in dissuading them from trying to leave in the dark. His companions, remembering how things went in Calicut, were more reticent, and their doubts seemed justified. When Gama again asked for boats, he was told to order the ships closer in to shore.

He replied that it was not possible: any such order sent to his brother would tell him they were being held prisoners and be his sign to sail for Portugal.

Why did they not beach their ships as was the custom on that shore in winter? Why lie always with yards hoisted as though prepared for some evil?

These were not like the ships of Malabar: they had keels, could not be beached.

No order to the ships: no boats.

If there were no boats, Gama repeated, he would go back and protest to the Zamorin, who had sent him back to his ships. If the ruler wanted after all to hold him in the country, he would stay with pleasure.

Go and complain as soon as you like but make your own way: the Catual's words seemed a signal. A group of Nairs, swords drawn, filed into the room and the doors were shut. Still 'fear restrained him from laying violent hands on da Gama'.

To the imprisoned Portuguese the Catual gave a new command: bring ashore the ships' sails and rudders.

Gama laughed at him. He had leave to go aboard without conditions; he would accept none from them. They could do with him what they liked but he would give up nothing. Every detail of the injuries done to him would be reported to the Zamorin.

Without answer the Catual left them. 'The captain and we others', the eye-witness recorded, 'were very downhearted though outwardly we pretended not to notice what they did.' And another account says, 'but although both he and his men put the best face upon it they were under great fear'.

Gama sent a message to the Catual asking that at least his men should be let go: otherwise they would die of hunger there.

But answer came that 'if we died of hunger we must bear it: he cared nothing for that'.

And their fears were doubled. Not without reason: for the penalty for those condemned by the Zamorin was to have a sharp stake driven up through the anus into the body and out between the shoulder-blades.

At this bleak time one of the three missing men got through to them, with news of Coelho: since the night before, he had been waiting down shore in hiding for them. By some means unrecorded, this man made his way back to Coelho with Gama's orders to go at once to the ships and prepare against surprise. As they drew away from shore they were seen and chased by armed canoes; but they got safely away.

Thus frustrated the Catual sent word again to Gama: he should send a letter to his brother to bring the ships within the roadstead.

Willingly, said Gama, but his brother would not do it; and, even were he ready to obey, those with him, not wishing to die, would not allow it. 'The captain did not wish the ships to come within the roadstead for it seemed to him—as to us—that once inside they could easily be captured, after which they would first kill him and then us others, as we were already in their power.'

They passed an anxious day. They had water but no food. Any man wanting to relieve himself was marched to a nearby thicket by a Nair, who stood over him sword in hand. More guards were put on at dusk. By then the prisoners had been confined to a small tiled court and were closely surrounded. The number of armed men, not only swordsmen but also bowmen and men with two-edged battle-axes, was increased to 200, sleeping by turns so that there was a permanent watch. Looking at their situation, at the apparent increasing anger of their gaolers, the Portuguese suspected that the following day they might be separated. But 'this did not prevent our making a good supper that night'.

One account says that the Catual provided the food and insisted on joining them at their meal. However anxious he was to earn such bribes as he may have received, he clearly was not sure how far he could go; very probably he was also getting equivocal orders from his master. For the next day he came back smiling with a new proposal. Gama should order his goods to be unloaded: it was the custom that all ships should land both goods and men so soon as they arrived, not returning aboard till all was sold. Once the goods were ashore the captain-major could go to his ship.

Gama consented to send for the goods: but the Catual must provide the boats to ferry them; for his brother certainly would not send ships' boats. This the Catual agreed, 'hoping', one malicious chronicler says, 'to get all the goods for himself'. Two men were sent with a letter from Gama to let Paulo know the terms of the agreement. They were detained but otherwise well treated, he wrote: Paulo should send ashore a part of the cargo. If they were still held, he should then—on the assumption that on the Zamorin's orders their detention was being used to gain time for a naval attack on the ships—sail at once for Portugal to report to King Emanuel and advise the sending of a strong fleet, both for rescue and to secure the trade of the rich land that they had discovered.

Paulo's answer was typical and spirited. He sent the goods at once and with them a message for his brother: he certainly would not leave without him and, if he were not released at once, would bombard the port. However, the Catual kept the bargain. Leaving behind as factor his purser, Diogos Dias, with the purser of the *Berrio*, Alvarez de Braga, Gama and the rest of the group rejoined the ships.

In their seven days ashore they had had one triumphal progress, two royal audiences, four days of imprisonment, and a dozen or more threats and provocations. Throughout all this the rest—'we others'— clearly had secure confidence in the courage and resolution of their chief. 'We rejoiced greatly and rendered thanks for having extracted us from the hands of people who had no more sense than beasts, for we knew well that once the captain was on board those who had been landed would have nothing to fear.

'When he was gotten on board he resolved not to go ashore any more, nor send more goods, till he understood those which had been already landed were sold. This was a great vexation to the Moors, who saw him now out of their reach; yet, to do him what hurt they could they began to undervalue his merchandises and hinder the sale.'

The captain-major, keeping a close eye on what went on ashore, prepared a message for the Zamorin.

Trade

Five days Gama waited quietly. Each day he sent messengers ashore for news; Monçaide came often to the ships. Provocation was the policy of the Moors: they spread word that the goods from Portugal were of poor quality, not worth the buying. Those Portuguese who landed were jeered on their way. Men spat on the ground as they passed, and shouted 'Portugal! Portugal!' in their faces and behind their backs. Their backs felt none too safe as they went to and fro to keep contact with Diogo Dias. Gama's orders forbidding any answer, retaliation or brawling were faithfully obeyed: but that was usual. There were no incidents; at least none are recorded.

At the end of the five days Gama sent a formal complaint to the Zamorin. At his audience, his message said, he had been given leave to rejoin his ships with all his men, and to land his goods and sell them; the Catual and factor had been commanded to see this was done. But what had happened? He had been stopped on the way by the Zamorin's own servants, by the man who was supposed to see his command carried out. He had been denied boats; he had been held under guard against his will and kept short of food. When he had at last landed his goods, as he had been ordered, the Moors cried them down, obstructing his free trade and insulting his men. He looked to what the Zamorin would order; he placed no value on his merchandise, but he and his ships were at the ruler's service.

In answer, the Zamorin professed great displeasure at this treatment: he gave assurance that those responsible would be punished, and that he would send down merchants to buy goods. His second promise he carried out: next day seven or eight merchants of Gujerat did visit the storehouse, conducted by a Nair guard from the Zamorin. But of punishing the Catual or restraining the Moors there was no sign. As for the Gujeratis, they stayed a week in the place but did not buy. They ran everything down: perhaps with reason, for possibly the stuff was not up to much; or perhaps making common cause with the Moors, who were no longer visiting the house themselves.

Gama suspected a plot; furthermore, Pandarani seemed to him altogether too much out of the way for good trade; so he asked leave to transfer his goods to the Calicut market. This was not only granted at once, but in addition the Zamorin sent at his own cost enough slaves to carry everything to Calicut, and proclaimed nothing belonging to the King of Portugal was to be burdened with expense while in his country.

On St John the Baptist's day the file of bearers wound off to Calicut, taking the merchandise to the factory provided by the Zamorin. Gama sent Diogo Dias again as factor, with Alvaro de Braga, the interpreter Fernan Martins, and three or four others.

During the days which followed this transfer Gama sent all the Portuguese in turn to visit the town. Each day each ship was to send a man ashore, so that each should have the chance both to see the place and to trade. These groups became a familiar sight on the road down the coast, and also welcome: the Malabar people along the way took them into their houses, giving them shelter from the rain, and food and lodging at night.

The local people, both fishermen and small traders, came out to the ships in growing numbers, bartering mainly fish for bread of Portuguese baking. Gama encouraged these visits, making sure there was always a welcome aboard for the 'christians'. Many brought with them 'their sons and little children and the captain ordered that they should be fed'. This was policy, 'done for the sake of establishing relations of peace and amity, and to induce them to speak well of us and not evil'. In the sixteenth century, as today, food was short in India. 'So great was the number of visitors that sometimes it was night before we could get rid of them; and this was due to the dense population of the country and the scarcity of food. It even happened that when some of our men mending a sail had biscuits with them to eat old and young fell upon them, took the pieces out of their hands, and left them nothing.'

In their dealings in Calicut the men found prices disappointing, much below their hopes. Fine shirts brought in cash a tenth of their cost in Portugal. But they sold all they could, however poor the price, in order to take home the things of the country, 'if only for samples'. They bought principally cloves, cinnamon and precious stones. They were dealing in the main with the common people, under the shadows of the malice of the chief merchants. In Calicut itself there was not the same simple curiosity and friendship as in the villages on the way. 'Having bought what they desired they came back to the ships, without anyone speaking to them.'

Nearly three weeks passed in this way. From time to time small quantities of pepper and other spices were sent aboard by Dias, results of meagre trading. Gama and his commanders stayed in the ships—a policy decided among themselves in council and backed by the advice of the 'Moor of Tunis'. Monçaide constantly warned that the Zamorin was fickle and greedy, much influenced by the Moorish merchants. They also discussed in council how much longer to stay. By early August they had decided to prepare for the passage home, 'the season for returning from the Indies being come', as they believed, though in fact the north-east monsoon was not due until about three months later.

On about 10 August, when they had been eighty days on the Malabar coast and thirteen months away from Lisbon, Gama sent word to Dias to put together a present of amber, coral, silks, scarves and other things and take it to the Zamorin with a message from his commander. He was to say that the Portuguese ambassador wished to leave and to ask that the Zamorin send with him an ambassador to the King of Portugal. The Portuguese would leave a factor in Calicut, with a clerk and some staff, to be in charge of the merchandise until the coming of the next fleet. On behalf of his sovereign, and in return for his present, Gama requested from the Zamorin a bahar (about two centners) of cinnamon, one of cloves and samples of such other spices as he thought proper; for these the factor would pay should he so wish it.

Four days passed with Dias waiting at the palace gate, refused an audience. Suddenly he was called in before a Zamorin black in looks and cold in speech. What might he be wanting? Dias, in some trepidation, gave his message and offered the gift. What he had brought, he was told, should have been sent to the palace factor; the Zamorin did not wish to see it. As for the captain-major's request to leave, first he must pay the Zamorin harbour dues of 600 xerafins (about 1,700 grams of gold), the custom of that country; then he might go. Dias undertook to take this answer to his chief. Leaving the palace he was followed by a file of Nairs, and felt rather pleased by what he took as a mark of honour. He learnt his mistake when he arrived at his lodging. A guard was set at the door; others with the only-too-familiar naked blades were posted inside, to keep watch on him and his staff.

Once again the Portuguese ashore were prisoners—this time by direct order of the Zamorin. It was 13 August. During that day a proclamation was cried through the town banning all boats from approaching the ships.

In spite of this Monçaide put out to visit Gama. He reported that the Zamorin was once more much influenced by the Moors' somewhat contradictory stories that the Portuguese were thieves; that if they were allowed to trade with Calicut there would be no more ships from Mecca, Cambay or Hormuz; and that Portuguese trade would be of no profit to him, because their goods were worthless. Moreover, he said, rich bribes had been offered for the capture and murder of the Portuguese. It seems that some others also ignored, or had not heard, the proclamation, for 'we were told by two christians that if the captains went ashore their heads would be cut off, as this was the way the king dealt with those who came to his country without giving him gold'.

His guards failed to prevent Dias from getting a messenger out. Perhaps the Nairs were not, after all, very vigilant, or (just possibly) were susceptible to bribes; perhaps Calicut merchant houses had many courts and nooks helpful to concealment; or perhaps it was just very dark and, as usual, raining. However it was managed, a young negro was given money and got out, directed to search along the coast for someone to take him to the flagship. In a fisherman's village at the edge of the city he found a boatman willing to risk taking him off in the dark for three fanoes (silver pieces, each valued at about a quarter of a gram of gold). Without sound, unseen, he sailed up the dozen miles of coast, put his passenger aboard and at once drew back into the night.

No boats came out to the fleet the following day; but on the day after that four young men came out in a pinnace, offering precious stones for sale. Gama thought they were probably spies but entertained them and sent them back carrying a letter to his impounded men. Their visit encouraged others; the ban was ignored; and within twenty-four hours traffic out to the fleet was as thick as ever, with many merchants and onlookers every day. All were welcomed, entertained with food and drink and allowed to leave without any hint of difficulty.

So for five days visits were encouraged. On the fifth day, Sunday 19 August, a party of about twenty-five came visiting which, as the watchful Gama noticed, included six leading citizens of Malabar. He locked them up with a dozen of their followers. The rest were packed off in the pinnace with a message to the Zamorin's factor: our men for yours. The news soon travelled, soon reached the captives' relatives, soon brought a crowd to the gates of the factory. By argument or by weight of numbers, they released Dias and his men and took them without hurt to the factor's house. The Zamorin played dumb. The factor was ordered to see about sending them back without fuss; but he did nothing.

For four days Gama sat quietly waiting for some response. On the 23rd, watchers from the shore could have seen that on all three ships sails were being untied and shaken loose. A fisherman arrived at the beach with a letter in the speech of Malabar. They were leaving for Portugal that day, it said; they would come back in due course. Then the people of Malabar would learn whether they were thieves. The fleet sailed out from Pandarani. Head winds turned them. That afternoon they anchored about twelve miles west of Calicut.

Then Gama began to build up suspense. On the 24th he moved the fleet in towards Calicut, but contrary tide and wind prevented him from crossing the shoals in front of the city; so he anchored within sight. On the 25th he took the ships out to sea, anchoring that evening just within sight of land. The next morning, while they waited for a breeze, a searching fishing-boat found them, bringing a message to say that Diogo Dias and his party were at the palace and would be delivered aboard if Gama released those whom he held. Gama suspected a plot; he feared that Dias had been killed and that they were being tricked into staying while the Zamorin armed and the Mecca fleet made towards them. He turned the messengers away, opening the gun-ports and threatening to shoot them out of the sea unless they went back at once to bring Dias and his men, or at least a letter from them; if Dias were not given up, the hostages would have no heads. By this time a breeze had got up, and Gama used it to sail along the coast and to anchor out of sight of the city.

In city and palace, turmoil and confusion reigned. Clamour rang from the stricken families: among those held were Nairs whose religion would prevent them from eating among their unclean captors; they would quickly die if not freed. The Moors saw with anger that they had pushed the Zamorin too far, and were soured by the gibes of Monçaide. The Zamorin was disengaging and changing direction. He had indeed called Dias to the palace, had received him with marked kindness, had asked why his commander had suddenly made off with some of his subjects, and had shown surprise when Dias said it was surely a reprisal for his own detention. Gama had done right, said the Zamorin; his factor had been wrong to demand unjustified imposts (the 600 xerafins!) from the Portuguese.

All the available accounts of what happened are Portuguese. The Zamorin's story has not been told. Through that distorting screen the elderly autocrat does seem to show a wavering and devious aspect—but with some reason, to be sure. Perceiving at once the threat to their monopoly, the merchants from Arabia and north Africa could not but try by every means they had to crush such interlopers —more especially since they were Portuguese, their most devoted and ruthless enemies. In their own accounts the Portuguese show that their intention was precisely that of destroying the trade of the Moors and ejecting them from the Arabian sea. This meant much, very much, to the Zamorin. But his standing between two worlds, the fame of Calicut as a free port, and the profit to him of trade, wherever it originated, were also important to him. Important, too, was his growing strength as the most influential and powerful ruler on the coasts of Malabar.

He had good reason to temporise, juggle and look several ways at once. As he soon learnt, he also had reason to fear the Portuguese and the mutual hatred of Portuguese and Moor. But at this moment he made a decision and kept to it. 'Go back to your ships', he said to Diogo Dias, 'you and the others with you; tell your captain to send me back the men he took; tell him that the pillar, which I understand him to say he desires to be erected on the land, shall be brought away by those who bring you back and put up; and, moreover, that you shall remain here with the merchandise.' He also gave a letter for the King of Portugal which Dias wrote down at his dictation upon a palm leaf with an iron pen, of which the content was:

Vasco da Gama, a gentlemen of your household, came to my country, of whose coming I was glad.

My country is rich in cinnamon, cloves, ginger, pepper and precious stones.

That which I ask of you in exchange is gold, silver, corals and scarlet cloth.

So it happened that on the morning of the 28th, the day after Gama's threat, the fleet at anchor was approached by seven well-filled pinnaces bringing with them Diogo Dias and his party. Avoiding direct contact, they transferred the Portuguese to the *S. Gabriel*'s longboat, which was on a line astern. They brought with them none of the merchandise, believing that Dias was to return as factor for the Portuguese. But once he had his men back the commander would not let them go. He had King Emanuel's pillar transferred to the Malabar boat; and he gave up the six leading hostages, who were Nairs, with some servants; but six he kept back—to be surrendered, he said, the next day, when the remaining merchandise was returned.

At early morning Monçaide got abroad, asking for protection: the Catual accused him of being a christian spy in service of the King of Portugal and had seized all his goods. The Moors had turned against him, said Monçaide—which was hardly surprising; he came to the Portuguese to save his life. He had done Gama good service and went with him to Portugal, where eventually he was baptised a christian.

Soon after, another seven crowded boats came out. Three of them had Portuguese striped cloth laid out on the benches—all that was left of the merchandise, they said. These three drew close to the flagship, while others hung back. The cloth would be returned, they said, if the detained Indians were put off in a boat. Suspecting trickery, Gama warned them off. At a council of the captains that evening it was agreed that they had achieved what they had been sent to do: they had made the discovery of the country which they had been sent to find, its spices and precious stones; and since 'it appeared impossible to establish cordial relations with the people it would be as well to depart'. They decided to take with them the men they still held, 'as on our return to Calicut they might be useful to us in establishing friendly relations'.

'We therefore set sail and left for Portugal, greatly rejoicing at our good fortune in having made so great a discovery.'

They rejoiced too soon: there was much still to endure.

Long way home

They set sail that day, 29 August, a hundred days from their first sighting Calicut. Gama set course north along the coast; why north is not explained. It may be that he thought it necessary to reach a higher latitude to catch the expected westward-blowing monsoon. Winds were light and variable. At noon next day, as they lay becalmed about four miles north of Calicut, a flotilla of some seventy oared boats crammed with armed men moved towards them. Once these came within range the ships' guns bombarded them; but the action was broken off almost at once by the onset of a violent offshore wind, which brought dense cloud, thunder, lightning and a sudden vertical downpour of rain. This thrust them out to sea.

For ten days the fleet worked north, tacking all the time with land and sea breezes, often forced to lay becalmed. On 10 September when off Cannanore, some eighty miles north of Calicut, Gama put ashore one of the hostages, to take to the Zamorin a letter written for him in Arabic by Monçaide. In this Gama excused himself for having carried away some of the hostages: he had done so to take with him witnessses to the discoveries he had made. He would have left his factor behind, he said, but he feared the Moors would kill him. He hoped that they would be able in the end to establish friendly relations to their mutual advantage. The Zamorin is said to have been 'much pleased' with this letter and to have read it to his wives and the relatives of the kidnapped men; but this smacks of Portuguese self-flattery—and the Zamorin, being a Nair, had no wives.

Fishermen came selling their catch during a calm day, clambering aboard the ships without fear. Four days later the fleet had made about a further fifty miles, reaching a small island, probably that known as Coconut island. There Gama set up a pillar dedicated to the Virgin Mary, after whom he named the island. During this halt many more boats brought fish and were rewarded by Gama with presents of shirts.

Another four days brought them 'to a hilly country, very beautiful and salubrious, close to which there were six small islands'. These were the Anjedivas, two and a half miles off the coast south of Goa, about 300 miles north of Calicut: it had taken twenty-one days to cover the distance. They anchored first off the coast of the mainland. To look for water and wood for the voyage across the Arabian sea, Gama took a boat ashore, where a young man showed them 'a spring of excellent water rising between two hills on the bank'. While the boats were plying for water next morning four men who brought gourds and cucumbers in a canoe asserted that there was cinnamon on that coast. Two of Gama's men sent to see came back carrying 'two big branches with their foliage' and with them came some twenty Indians bringing fowls, cow's milk and gourds. (These branches, which were taken back to Portugal, proved to be not true cinnamon but cassia.)

Little notice was taken of two vessels seen about nine miles off the coast the next morning—members of the crew were ashore cutting wood as they waited for the tide to take them up river to the spring; but, becoming suspicious later in the day, Gama sent some of the boats out to find whether the vessels were

Moorish or 'christian'. Going on board the flagship himself he ordered a man aloft: eight vessels were to be seen becalmed in the open sea about eighteen miles off. 'Sink them' was the order. And the opportunity to try this seemed to have come when a breeze got up soon after and the strangers downed helm to sail along the coast. 'When they were abreast of us, at a distance of a couple of leagues, and we thought they might discover us, we made for them.' One was disabled by damage to her steering gear and was abandoned, but her crew reached land safely in their boat. The rest ran for the mainland shore and beached before the Portuguese could come up with them. In the abandoned one they 'found nothing . . . but provisions, coconuts, four jars of palm sugar and arms, the rest being sand used as ballast'. Visiting gourd-sellers asserted that these ships had been sent against the Portuguese by the Zamorin.

Moving over the next day (24 September) to the largest of the Anjedivas, they found a sheltered anchorage in five fathoms with a bottom of mud and sand. Coelho, sent in search of a reported watering-place, came upon the ruins of 'a large stone church which had been roofed with straw'—so said 'the natives of the country', who there prayed 'to three black stones which stood in the middle'. Near the pagoda were water-tanks of hewn stone large enough to supply water for all the ships.

As the winds were still against them, Gama decided to clean and refit. In turn, the *Berrio* and *S. Gabriel* were careened on the beach in front of the pagoda: but not the *S. Raphael*, which seems to have been in no condition to stand the strain. Day by day more visitors came to the island; for the presence of the Portuguese was soon known all along the coast. First came fishermen and shore-dwellers selling food, soon also other less welcome. Such were two large galleys 'crowded with people' who 'rowed to the sound of drums and bagpipes and showed flags at the masthead', while five other boats stood off 'for their protection'. Said to be pirates by country people who were aboard the *S. Raphael* they were bombarded by Paulo da Gama without warning and chased for a short way by Coelho. As unwelcome were the dozen well-dressed men who came ashore from two small boats, carrying 'a bundle of sugar cane as a present for the captain-major and asking to be allowed to see the ships'. But 'the captain thought they were spies and grew angry'; and not liking the looks of him they made off. Unwelcome also was the appearance of a strange raft, covered with branches, which floated into the bay—the ruse of a corsair, so the villagers warned. A few rounds from the bombards split the raft apart: it consisted of seven or eight craft tied together, and carried armed men hidden below the branches. They were sent, the villagers said, by the noted pirate Timoja. (In later years he became an ally of the Portuguese, but this time he was chased off, less one of his boats seized by Coelho.)

Not unwelcome, as it turned out, was the arrival of a man who crossed to the island in a small boat. He spoke Venetian well. He wore a coat of linen which reached to his heels, a fine embroidered cap on his head, curved sword at his waist. So soon as landed he embraced Gama and the other captain as if they were old friends, making known that he was a christian from the west who had travelled to India in early youth, had become a moslem though still at heart a christian, and served a Moorish lord up the coast who could muster 40,000 horsemen.

At the house of his master (who was the governor of Goa), he said, news had been brought that men whose clothes covered them and who spoke a strange tongue had touched at Calicut. He knew, he said, that these must be Franks, and had begged his master's leave, so he said, to go and find these men, for a refusal would cause him to die of sorrow. His master gave him both leave and a commission: he should go to the Franks to tell them that they might have anything in his country which suited them, including ships and provisions, and that it would give him much pleasure were they to consent to stay permanently with him.

All these things the stranger said to the captain-major, using many words, and talking of many things. In the middle of this flow he asked the captain-major as a favour to give him a piece of cheese to be sent to his companions on shore: a signal that all had gone well. It seemed an odd request but the cheese was sent off and two soft loaves with it. The stranger prattled on, not noticing that sometimes he repeated himself; he seemed a man of wide knowledge, warm in goodwill to the Portuguese. Perhaps he seemed a shade too open and friendly, for Paulo da Gama went aside to some local Indians to ask what they knew of this man. 'Do not trust him; he is a soldier of a city named Goa, which is near here, and a Moor' was the answer, according to one report. In the words of Gama's eye-witness, 'they said he was a pirate who had come to attack us, and that his ships, with many people in them, had remained on the coast'.

Any doubt was cause enough to act. The stranger was seized, taken to the ship drawn up on the beach, and there scourged with whips 'to make him confess whether he was really a pirate, or for what purpose he had come to us'. After some of this he spoke: he knew well, he said, that all the country was hostile to the Portuguese; many armed men were hidden in the creeks around; but they were not yet ready to attack, waiting the coming 'of forty vessels which were being armed to pursue us'—when that was to be he knew not. Of himself he said no more than he had said before. He was not believed. Gama ordered him to be questioned. By one account he was 'hung up by the genitals and so hoisted up and let down by a pulley'. The eye-witness says 'he was questioned three or four times: we understood from his gestures'—apparently he could no longer speak— 'that he had come to see the ships, that he might know what sort of people we were, and how we were armed'. Gama ordered that he be taken below and treated 'till he was cured'. Many days later, when they were already

far out at sea sailing for Africa, the man spoke again, saying that he had in truth
been with the Sabayo of Goa, who hearing that the Portuguese were lost on the
coast, gathered a fleet to capture them. He had been sent to find out the strength
of the Portuguese and to try to persuade them to visit Goa; for the Sabayo,
hearing they were valiant, wished to seize them, and to enrol them in his forces.
The man said that his own name was Gaspar and that he was a Jew whose
parents, expelled from Poland, had settled in Alexandria, where he was born.
He was later baptised, became a retainer of Gama, took his name, and
served for many years as an interpreter on Portuguese expeditions.

After twelve days on the island, it seemed high time to get away. The
S. Gabriel and the *Berrio* had been refitted; the water-tanks were all full; and the
fleet was well supplied with fresh food. Gama decided to take what wind there
was and sail. It was 5 October. They left the India coast with nearly a fifth
fewer men than they had had on leaving Lisbon; thirty men had died, most of
them from scurvy.

Remembering their untroubled crossing of that gulf five months earlier their
hearts and hopes were set on a speedy passage to Africa, to the friendship of
Melinde. But they sailed before the start of the monsoon. Many days of calm,
many foul winds, many tempests held them, put them off course, threw them
violently about, straining the fabric of their much-enduring ships. Castanheda
wrote that 'they went always in cruel storms' but after that were 'again troubled
with great calms, which on the sea is very troublesome . . . with the heat, which
is more hurtful upon the sea than upon the land for that there is no covering to
defend the sun, whereon with the same men are stifled up as hath been seen in the
voyage towards the Indies.'

As the weeks piled up in the endless and hostile sea, the bodies of these men
could no longer resist. Scurvy took hold throughout the fleet. All became so
weak that none could look after another. They were at sea for three days less
than three months before they again saw land. Another thirty men died. In each
ship not more than seven or eight were able to work and those only slowly and
with difficulty. 'If this state of affairs had continued another fortnight there
would have been no men at all to navigate the ships.' 'We addressed vows and
petitions to the saints on behalf of our ships. We had come to such a pass that all
bonds of discipline had gone.'

'. . . *all bonds of discipline had gone*': here is Mocquet's picture of what those
words could mean. 'For the most part they died behind some chest, eyes and
feet gnawed by rats. . . . All that could be heard were cries of intense thirst.
Often having received a ration of water they would put it beside them to drink
when seized by thirst; then their companions would come and snatch the poor
dole of water from the miserable sick wretches when they were asleep. . . . Very
often thus deprived of water they died in misery for lack of a few drops, no one
willing to give a little water to save a life, not a father his son nor a brother his

brother. . . . Among us was the greatest confusion and chaos imaginable because of the great number of men vomiting, relieving themselves on each other. On every side only the cries of those assailed by thirst, hunger and pain, cursing the hour when they had come aboard.'

In all this travail the captains in council agreed that if a favourable wind made it possible they would go back to India. 'But it pleased God in his mercy to send us a wind which, in the course of six days carried us within sight of land; we rejoiced as much as if the land we saw had been Portugal, for with the help of God we hoped to recover our health there as we had done once before.'

It was night on 2 January 1499 when they came close to land; so they put about and lay to, uncertain where they were. They had no Moorish pilot on board and no one who knew that coast. As they scanned the land next morning, sailing cautiously closer in, it was said by some that they must be near the islands of Mozambique, for they were well known for the sickness which was afflicting the Portuguese. But soon they found themselves off a large town facing the sea, with houses several storeys high, big palaces at its centre and four towers round it. It was identified as Mayadoxo (Mogadishu). As they passed close in by the town Gama ordered all the guns to fire: whether this was a salute or an anti-Moorish demonstration is not clear. They sailed on by day but lay to at night, fearing to overshoot Melinde. On the third day a motionless calm was broken by a sudden violent thunderstorm, which tore the topsail ties of the S. Raphael. These took a day to mend; but by Monday 7 January the fleet at last dropped anchor off Melinde.

Without delay, the Sultan sent out a longboat with many people in it, carrying a present of sheep and a message of friendship and peace: the Portuguese had been expected for many days. Gama sent back an urgent request for oranges for the sick; but when they were brought next day these disappointed many hopes: for many were too ill to benefit from them; and numbers more died. Sheikh Wajeray showed his friendship in many ways, sending food out to the ships. His thought and help for them at this time of their great need, speeding their physical and spiritual recovery, much affected every man, not least the captain-major. By means of one of his Arabic speakers, Gama sent the sheikh a present and requested of him a tusk of ivory to take for the King of Portugal. He also asked for permission to put up a pillar on his land, as a sign of friendship. (It is not clear what had happened to the previous pillar.) The sheikh answered that, out of love for the King of Portugal, whom he desired to serve, he would do both; and he did. He sent too a young man from his court to carry his greetings to the King of Portugal.

After five days of good food, friendship and rest from the hardship of a passage through which all had lived with death, the Portuguese felt revived enough to move. They set off in the morning of 11 January, passed close before Mombasa the next day and on Sunday 13 January anchored at the shoals on which the *S. Raphael* had gone aground on the voyage out. There that ship was beached, everything in her was transferred to the *S. Gabriel* and the *Berrio*, and she was burnt. Gama no longer had enough men to sail all three ships. Paulo, a sick man, joined the flagship, there to be cared for by his brother with tender concern.

At this anchorage they spent fifteen days bartering for food with traders from Mtangata on the nearby coast and setting all to rights with the two remaining ships so far as they were able. On 27 January they set off; the next day they passed inside Zanzibar, keeping close to the coast; and on 1 February they anchored of S. George island at Mozambique. There, where they had said mass nearly eleven months before, they set up a pillar in a downpour of rain so heavy that they could not make a fire to melt the lead for fixing a cross on it.

No call was made on Mozambique itself. They sailed the next day, every thought set on a fast passage home. A month later, making an average of fifty-six sea-miles a day, they reached the Angra de S. Braz, Mussel Bay. There they rested for seven days, catching anchovies, seals and penguins, which they salted. On the eighth day they left; but some thirty miles out they ran into westerly gales so strong that they had to go back and endure a further week of frustration.

When at last there was a wind, it came sweet and true, carrying them round the Cape of Good Hope on 20 March 1499. Those of the crew who had survived so far had regained health, were 'quite robust, although at times nearly dead from the cold winds which we experienced. This feeling we attributed less to the cold than to the heat of the countries from which we had come.' But one man was ailing still; Paulo lay stricken by consumption in his brother's cabin.

For twenty-seven days a following wind carried the two ships up the coast of Africa, about ninety-five miles a day; carried them, they thought, to the neighbourhood of S. Thiago in the Cape Verde islands. In fact it would seem that they were near the Bizagos islands, off the Guinea coast. There at first the wind fell to a calm; but then plunging down from off shore came violent gusts, lightning, thunder and sheeting rain. They were enveloped in a tornado. They worked to windward as well as they could; and in the storm and the dark night which came with it the two ships were separated. When clear morning came, Gama could see no sign of the *Berrio*. Separated from his chief, Coelho sailed on alone on 25 April, to reach Lisbon on 10 July. But Gama made for S. Thiago. There he put Joan de Sá in command of the *S. Gabriel*. His thoughts at this time were only for his brother. He chartered a fast caravel, put Paulo aboard and sailed for the Azores, hoping for a quick passage to Lisbon by that route. How long he took to reach Terceira is not known. He landed there with his brother and asked the help of the monks of the monastery of San Francisco. But the next morning Paulo died. A certain Arthur Rodriguez, a man of Terceira, put out in his caravel that day, carrying to Lisbon the news of Vasco da Gama's coming. As for Gama, that man of iron, he stayed in Terceira to mourn his brother and to see to his burial in the monastery church. He made no haste to leave.

On precisely what day Vasco da Gama eventually arrived back in Portugal is not known for certain. It was somewhere at the end of August 1499, two years and two months from the time of his leaving. Joan de Sá had brought in the *S. Gabriel* some days earlier.

After landing Gama spent nine days alone at Restello in mourning for his brother. Not until 18 September did he at last make his official entry into Lisbon. He was received by the nobles of the court; the count of Borba and Bishop Calçadilha escorted him through thunderous crowds to the presence of the King, who, thanking him, addressed him as 'Dom' Vasco.

In thanksgiving to God for his great mercy in this adventure, King Emanuel ordered that on the shore at Restello, where the Navigator's vigil chapel stood, a splendid convent for S. Jeronimo should be built; the place he renamed Belém, or Bethlehem. In commemoration of the great discovery, he further ordered that a new gold coin, the *portuguez*, should be struck. (This coin was worth ten cruzados, or just over forty-six grams of gold.)

Of all the men who had started on this discovery, barely half came home to Portugal, to 'the shore of tears' from which they had sailed. Even so, many of those who returned strove for the honour of a place in the next fleet bound for India.

'With the help of God, who in His mercy thus ordained it'

'. . . as the principal motive of this enterprise has been, with our predecessors, the service of God our Lord, and our own advantage, it pleased Him in His mercy to speed them on their route . . . they did reach and discover India and other kingdoms and lordships bordering upon it; . . . they entered and navigated its sea, finding large cities, large edifices and rivers, and great populations, among whom is carried on all the trade in spices and precious stones, which are forwarded to Mecca, and thence to Cairo, whence they are dispersed throughout the world. . . .

'Your Highnesses may believe, in accordance with what we have learnt concerning the christian people whom those explorers reached, notwithstanding that they are not as yet strong in the faith or possessed of thorough knowledge of it, to do much in the service of God and the exaltation of the Holy Faith, once they should have been converted and fully fortified in it. And when they shall have thus been fortified in the faith there will be an opportunity for destroying the Moors of those parts. Moreover, we hope, with the help of God, that the great trade which now enriches the Moors of those parts . . . shall in consequence of our regulations be diverted to the natives and ships of our own kingdom, so that henceforth all Christendom, in this part of Europe, shall be able, in a large measure, to provide itself with these spices and precious stones. This, with the help of God, who in His mercy thus ordained it, will cause our designs and intentions to be pushed with more ardour as the war upon the Moors of the territories conquered by us in these parts. . . .

'We pray your Highnesses . . . to cause to be addressed to Him those praises which are His due.' (From a letter sent in July 1499 from King Emanuel to the King and Queen of Castile—Ravenstein's translation.)

'. . . letters had come from Portugal from a nuncio of the Venetian Signoria sent to that place on purpose to learn minutely the truth of the voyage to India begun by that king. . . . I can say for the profit that from one ducat they can make more than one hundred . . . and if this voyage should continue, since it now seems so easy to me to accomplish, the King of Portugal could call himself the King of Money, because all would convene to that country to obtain spices, and the money could accumulate greatly in Portugal with such profits as would follow each year from similar voyages. . . .

'. . . this news was held by the learned to be the worst which the Venetian Republic could have had. . . . there is no doubt that the Hungarians, Germans, Flemish and French, and those beyond the mountains, who formerly came to Venice to buy spices with their money, will all turn towards Lisbon, for it is nearer to all the countries and easier to reach. . . . the spices which come to Venice pass through all of Syria and through all the countries of the Sultan. And in each place they pay very large duties and similarly in the Venetian state they pay insufferable duties, presents and excises. . . .' (From the diary of Giralomo Priuli, written in July 1501—quoted by Greenlee.)

'It is impossible to procure the chart of the voyage because the king has placed a death penalty on anyone who gives it out.' (From a letter of Angelo Trevisan to Domenico Malipiero in Venice, 21 August 1501—quoted by Greenlee.)

Six

Admiral of the Seas of India

'The fleet entrusted to him, owing to the wisdom
and judgment exercised, has returned richly laden'

Cabral follows on

Gama lost a brother dear to him; on the other hand, he gained both fame and
fortune. At his homecoming, King Emanuel had addressed him as 'Dom', a
mark of nobility; before the end of the year he had granted him the town of
Sines, where he had been born, 'with all the revenues, privileges and tithes
pertaining thereto, as well as civil and criminal jurisdiction', subject to its
surrender by the Order of S. Thiago. Fifteen months later, with the Sines-grant
still hanging fire (which it did for years, without effect), there was a royal order
to the House of Mines for an annual payment of 1,000 cruzados in gold (rather
more than four and a half kilograms). A further annuity worth 770 cruzados
(over three and a half kilograms) was given a year later, in January 1502, 'freely
and irrevocably from this day in perpetuity' to him and his descendants. This
was only part of an extensive series of grants accorded in the same letters patent:
the title 'Dom' was confirmed and at the same time extended as hereditary to
Gama, his brother and his sister, with their heirs; he was appointed Admiral of
the Seas of India, with the honours, franchises and revenues due to the rank
'throughout the territories which shall be placed under the rule of the King'; he
was granted for himself and his descendants the privilege of sending to India
each year by royal vessels 200 cruzados of gold to buy merchandise free of
duty on import to Lisbon, apart from five per cent to the Order of Christ.
Together with the annuity he had already, his cash income thus became over
eight kilograms of gold. But Sines, with its rights and profits, still eluded him.

    Emanuel the Fortunate, of the greenish eyes and chestnut hair, whose arms
were so long that the fingers of his hands reached below his knees, had, and to

this day continues to have, the name of a mean, ungrateful man. However, in the long eulogy which opened the letters patent, the King stressed the super-abounding access of power and wealth brought to him by Vasco da Gama, who 'by himself, in this single voyage, discovered 1,550 leagues, in addition to a great gold mine and many wealthy towns and cities, having a great trade, and finally reached and discovered that India, which all those who have given descriptions of the world rank higher in wealth than any other country, which from all time had been coveted by the emperors and kings of the world.... This discovery ... he accomplished at a greater sacrifice of life and treasure, and at a greater peril to his own person, than suffered by those who preceded him. ... bearing in mind the great services yielded to ourselves and our kingdoms by this voyage and discovery ... desiring to recompense him for his services, as befits a prince when dealing with those who have so greatly and so well served him ... out of our royal and absolute power, without his having solicited it, nor any other person on his behalf, we grant him. ...'

These grants were made only a month before Gama left Lisbon on his second voyage to India. In the two-and-a-half-year interval much had happened. At some time—it was probably soon after he arrived home from India, but there is no record—he married into a noble family, taking for his wife Dona Catherina de Athayde. (Her father, Alvaro de Athayde, *alcaide-mor* [civil governor] of Alvor, had been a friend of John II, who died in his house.) It is probable that during this same period Gama settled in the old city of Evora, which may be where he had been at school.

Possibly also at this time (the document is dated October, without specifying the year), the King decreed that during Gama's lifetime he should have the right to take command of all fleets despatched to India, whatever their purpose: 'when he so wishes to take such captaincy we may not place in them nor appoint another captain-major but him'. But Gama did not exercise his right of command when within six months of his return the King commissioned a second, much stronger expedition for India. It is possible that he was then getting married; or perhaps he just did not want to go to sea again so soon. So the King's choice fell on a gentleman of his council, a member of the Order of Christ, a nobleman aged just over thirty, Pedro Alvarez Cabral.

This appointment was different in kind from that of Gama three years earlier, the mission being different in style and purpose from that which Gama had commanded. That had had as its prime object discovery; Cabral, by contrast, was given command of an expeditionary force both mercantile and military. No chronicler accords him any previous maritime experience, and, though this is not conclusive proof that he had had none, it certainly was not as a seaman that he was chosen. His mission was to subjugate, to gain riches, to establish posts, to exact tribute and to destroy infidels in the name of the 'King, by the Grace of God, of Portugal and the Algarves, both on this side the sea and beyond it in Africa, Lord of Guinea and of the Conquest, Navigation and Commerce of Ethiopia, Arabia, Persia and India'. His instructions ran to many pages, telling him in detail how he was to act in any of a wide range of circumstances.

Little was left to his own judgment; he went a commander shackled by the detail of bureaucrats. He carried a letter for the Zamorin; this bespoke friendship and trade but gave it as the King of Portugal's 'set purpose to follow the will of God rather than of men, and not to fail through any opposition to prosecute this enterprise and continue our navigation, trade and intercourse in these lands which the Lord God desires to be served newly by our hands, not wishing that our labours to serve him be in vain'. It was Cabral's mission, too, to gain leave to set up a factory (i.e. trading post) in Calicut. Should this be granted, he was in secret to press the Zamorin 'to prohibit the Moors from trading thither, or in any other of his ports and to promise on that condition to import from Portugal the same sorts of commodities, better and cheaper, than those the Moors brought'.

To carry through this task Cabral was given ten vessels, of which at least seven were ships of larger tonnage than those of Gama's fleet, the others being caravels. Thirteen vessels sailed, for Bartholomeu Dias took along another three caravels, being commissioned to set up a factory at Sofala, the 'gold port' on the east coast of Africa. Of Cabral's vessels one was owned by Bartolomeo Marchioni, a Florentine banker who in 1487 had provided letters of credit for Pero de Covilhan. 1,200 men were provided, many of them having been attracted by the stories of riches told by the survivors of Gama's fleet. Among them were eight Franciscan friars, eight chaplains and a head chaplain, three factors, the five Hindus brought to Lisbon by Gama, Gaspar da Gama and a 'new christian' astronomer, Master John, who apparently was sent by the King to take position readings in the south-west Atlantic. Among them, too, expressing the two faces of the mission, were both skilled gunners and merchants. Merchandise this time was given better thought: it included copper, vermilion, mercury, amber, coral, velvets, satins, woollens, with coin of Venice and of other countries known in the eastern trade.

Sailing from Belém on 8 March 1500 Cabral had with him detailed advice, apparently written by Gama, on handling the fleet and navigating the south Atlantic. They should 'make their course straight to the island of Santiago; and if at the time they arrive there they have enough water for four months they need not stop at that island, nor make delay, but when they have the wind behind them make their way towards the south. If they must vary then let it be in the south-west direction. So soon as they meet with a light wind they should take a circular course until they put the Cape of Good Hope directly east. From then on they are to navigate as the weather serves them and they gain more, because when they are in the said parallel, with the aid of our Lord, they will not

lack weather with which they may round the aforesaid cape. In this manner it
appears to him that the navigation will be the shortest and the ships more
secure from worms, and in this way even the food will be kept better and the
people will be healthier.'

As it turned out, they indeed did not lack weather, but it was not the
weather for which they hoped. An account written by an unnamed pilot in one
of Cabral's ships tells how the fleet dropped down from Lisbon to Restello
(where in the church of S. Mary of Belém the sovereign himself handed to
Cabral his royal standard), and then the next day, Monday 9 March, left early
with so good a following wind that five days later they passed the Canary
Islands, and in another six, on 22 March, made the Cape Verde islands—an
average of nearly 160 miles a day. The following day one of the ships was
missing, and she was never seen again. The rest made course south-west,
pressing on so well that by 24 April they had reached a most pleasant land, rich
in all sorts of fruit trees. Passing some 600 or 700 miles further west than Gama
they had found the coast of Brazil.

For long it was thought that Cabral found Brazil by mistake, through faulty
or over-cautious navigation. This may be so; but it seems more likely that his
instructions covered a look in that direction. For many years the Portuguese
had known well that there was land on the west of the south Atlantic. It was
not by chance that in negotiating the Treaty of Tordesillas, the Papal treaty
dividing between Portugal and Spain all newly discovered lands, the astute
John II secured a demarcation which gave Portugal the shoulder of South
America, Brazil. It is quite possible that unreported—perhaps intentionally
secret—voyages from Portugal had already found this coast, and that the need
for a publicly established 'discovery' was seen to have become pressing once
Columbus had made his own landfall in the west.

Whether by accident or by design Cabral 'discovered' Brazil for Portugal,
naming it Terra da Santa Cruz, and sent one of his ships hasting back with letters
to the King, uncertain still whether it was a vast island or a continent. He raised
on the shore a great cross of wood and left there two condemned men brought
along for just such an eventuality. These 'made such great lamentations that the
inhabitants were moved to compassion, showing by signs that they had pity for
them'. One of these men later went back to Portugal and was employed as an
interpreter for Brazil.

Historic though the discovery was ten days of Brazil were enough for
Cabral. On 2 May he left those shores, making a direct course for the Cape of
Good Hope—by their reckoning, 1,100 leagues away. Dismay seized them when
after a few days, prognostic of disaster, a comet with a very long tail appeared
and journeyed with them for nine or ten days. Disaster, when it came, was
sudden. Late in May, as the fleet lay in a calm, the sea innocent-seeming, the air
kindly and the ships lying with their sails spread, ready to catch the first hint

of breeze, a tornado struck them with such sudden fury that four ships were stove in and sank; the other seven were scattered, with yards broken, sails rent apart, and the sea so rough and wild that they were hurled up and down 'from sky to abyss' uncontrollably. Among the many men lost was the veteran Bartholomeu Dias, who in his life had done so much to shed light on this sea of darkness.

As suddenly the weather changed again; but for a time all were so terrified, so dazed by the first shock, that they dare not risk setting their sails to the wind. The fleet was scattered. High winds and seas came again, and drove them hard for many days. Two rounded the Cape of Good Hope without seeing it and remained unaware that they had passed it until in mid June they came up with Cabral and another ship on the east coast of Africa towards Sofala. (One ship, commanded by Diogo Dias, went too far east, found Madagascar, and continued north to Somaliland and the Red Sea, in what became one of the most extraordinary endurance feats of all time. Many men were lost from scurvy and from murdering Moors; the rest were saved by the feats of their gunner, lying sick on a pallet of straw as he plied his guns, sinking three Moorish boats. Three months later, the ship arrived at the Cape Verde islands with thirteen survivors, who were picked up there by Cabral on his voyage home.)

Now with four vessels, Cabral missed Sofala, but called at Mozambique; there he took on a pilot for Kilwa, about 500 miles north—where 'the houses are built marvellous high in the fashion of Spain, the traders are right rich in gold, silver and pearls, the people black, dressed in cloth of fine bombazine in silk'. Here 'Ibrahim, a man renowned among his people and rich with the trade of Sofala, reigned'. Ibrahim at first welcomed Cabral's visit, coming to meet him, on the day after he had dropped anchor, 'in a pinnace, accompanied with many attendants in boats, the streamers flying and trumpets sounding'. After hearing the text of King Emanuel's message, he consented to trade; but when next day Cabral's factor went to open business with him he was turned away. The goods were not suitable, said Ibrahim, and furthermore the purposes of the Portuguese were suspect: their design, he thought, was to take possession of his realm. Ibrahim had learnt that his visitors were christians, with whom he would have no traffic. During the three or four days for which Cabral hung on, trying to negotiate, his last two stragglers turned up, bringing the number of ships in his fleet to a total of six. But his arguments all failed. So far from treating Sheikh Ibrahim appeared to be arming, and strengthening the defences of his town against attack.

'Much irritated', on 30 July Cabral sailed for Melinde, where the Portuguese were greeted with benevolence and with quantities of capons, fowls, eggs and lemons, the best that they had ever seen, and saluted the city with all their ordnance. Cabral sent ashore Ayres Correa with a rich present for the ruler from Dom Emanuel. For five days there was feasting, entertainment and mutual greetings, and the fleet took on fresh food and water. Melinde was to the Portuguese a haven of friendship in a region heavy with mistrust and enmity.

But on 7 August Cabral sailed out for Malabar, setting his course more to the north than Gama had done. A fair wind took them to the Anjediva islands in fourteen days. For a fortnight the fleet rested there, taking on wood and water. The ships were careened in turn for cleaning, while watch was kept on the sea for ships from Mecca, 'to rob them were it possible'. Mass was said several times during these days and all confessed and took communion. But since no ships from Mecca came they sailed for Calicut; and there on 13 September many boats put out to meet them. Most of them had food to sell, but there was also one bearing the Catual, who brought greetings from the Zamorin.

Fair and friendly words were sent by the Zamorin; Cabral responded by putting ashore the five Hindus taken by Gama, richly habited in Portuguese fashion, and with them Gaspar. Gaspar the Zamorin received with favour; the others, being only low-caste fishermen, he would not see. The Zamorin offered assurances of friendship and a safe-conduct for the Portuguese commander. Cabral answered by calling for hostages. He has been criticised for arrogance; but he was following the letter of his instructions: he was not a free agent, not an independent commander. After some to-ing and fro-ing, five Brahmins were sent aboard. Cabral then landed in much ceremony, but in an atmosphere already soured, to the advantage of his Moorish opponents. For, as before, the Zamorin's action showed him in two minds: keen for richer trade, but cautious not to damage his profitable involvement with the Moors.

This time Emanuel had not neglected to provide sumptuous presents: a silver basin decorated in gold, a great covered vase of silver embossed, a silver decorated cup, two silver maces with chains for carrying them, four cushions of crimson velvet, a large piece of gold brocade, two pieces of fine decorated cloth and a large silver-gilt fountain. Apparently they pleased the Zamorin; so, it seemed, did King Emanuel's letter, written in Arabic, and Cabral's verbal message. These asked for friendship and for an agreement that would provide for establishing a factory in Calicut to sell goods from Europe, and for Portuguese ships to load spices in return. The Zamorin was affable: the King his master, Cabral was told, would be welcome to whatever the city afforded.

This cordiality was almost at once clouded by a series of ridiculous misunderstanding about the hostages, some of whom, alarmed by the noise and tumult of Cabral's return in pomp from his audience, jumped from the flagship into the water, were hauled out again and were put under hatches instead of being released as they should have been, since Cabral was safely back on board. Three days passed in exchanges of mutual incomprehension and growing suspicion—among the Portuguese, almost hysteria. Some more hostages plunged overboard and escaped. The last remaining one refused to eat—to avoid pollution, being a Brahmin—and was sent ashore by Cabral lest he should die. In reply the Zamorin returned two Portuguese. Then followed three days of silent immobility on both sides.

At length Cabral decided to send to the Zamorin for an answer. So touchy had the Portuguese become that only Ayres Correa would consent to risk his life ashore. And when he did, in spite of all the hysterics, affability reigned again. He would be pleased to have trade settled, the Zamorin said. After a time he gave Correa the use of a house as a factory, and provided an experienced Gujerati to advise him on trade practices and prices, and an interpreter. Trade started; but it went slowly. The Gujerati seemed to the Portuguese neglectful of his duties and probably in the pay of Moorish competitors; the Moors once more disparaged the Portuguese goods; and in the earlier days the Indians were nervous of visiting the factory. After a time complaints from Cabral induced the Zamorin to be more active in help. He gave Correa a more convenient place for his factory, by the water-side, with title deeds granting perpetual possession.

For several weeks trade improved. The Moorish merchants became alarmed at the competition. Not unnaturally, they demurred when, in a weak or greedy moment, the Zamorin granted the Portuguese priority of loading for their ships; and, not unnaturally, they tried to get round this. They devised a plan of provocation. Early in December Correa was warned that there was a danger that his warehouse would be attacked. But all seemed calm. The Portuguese went about the city quietly, and no one interfered with them.

At nightfall on 16 December some 3,000 people, led by Moors, surrounded the ten-foot walls of the Portuguese compound. 'Thieves! Thieves!' cried Correa's servant; but too late. While the Portuguese strove to defend the stout gates, Moors, Moplas and Hindus had ladders to the walls, ran over the roof, and shot down on them with arrows and darts. They were too many: the defenders had too few arms. Correa and his men tried to fight through to the beach. At the time of the attack they had numbered eighty; only thirty-six, most of them badly wounded, succeeded in reaching the water's edge and tumbling into the boats. The rest lay dead—Ayres Correa, a brave leader, among them.

It was a massacre. In his *Tohfut-ul-Mujahideen* the Moslem historian Zain al-Din puts responsibility on the Zamorin, who 'having resolved upon their destruction, attacked them and put to death sixty or seventy of their party'. The consequences of this were to prove far-reaching. In the immediate present, Cabral answered by seizing ten Moorish vessels, killing their inmates to the number of some 600, and burning the shells. Three elephants found in the cargoes were killed and salted down. Next day he bombarded the city; chased some ships to Pandarani but lost them as they beached; sailed south for Cochin, intercepting on the way two Moorish ships, which were looted of their rice and burnt.

At Cochin, by contrast, things went well. The ruler was gratified by their sharp treatment of the Zamorin and of Calicut: he was both inferior and hostile to them. He granted a site for a warehouse. Trade was welcomed and established. A permanently-manned warehouse was set up. During three months in Calicut. Cabral had succeeded in loading only two vessels; in two weeks at Cochin, he filled most of the other four, taking on pepper, cinnamon, benzoin, musk, porcelain and fine cottons. From Cochin, on about 9 January, he sailed north to Cannanore, where again he was well received by the king, a Brahmin. He loaded 400 quintals of cinnamon and the king sent him an ambassador to carry to the King of Portugal. On 16 January 1501 he set sail for Africa and for home, where he arrived on 31 July with six ships, having gathered up Diogo Dias at the Cape Verde islands, but having lost a ship on the coast of east Africa, through the insubordinate pride of Sancho de Toar.

Losses on the way to India had been great. There had been setbacks at Calicut. But the wealth of goods that Cabral brought back with him was many times greater than the cost of sending him—men's lives not being reckoned. 'They took on a heavy cargo at a price I fear to tell because they declare they have obtained a cantara of cinnamon for a ducat and less', Giovanni Maltio Cretico reported to the Signoria in Venice. There was much wealth to be had from setting up an Indian trade; but it was not to be had for the asking.

Who shall be master?

One thing was clear from Cabral's reports: these Brahmins, Nairs and so on were not christians. They were heathens: not, indeed, to be cast into the same dark pit as the irredeemable, infidel Moors; but heathens all the same, though possibly convertible. This fact must change the approach. It was plain that, at least in Calicut, defeat of the Moors was a prerequisite for annexing the trade—and also plain that it would be necessary to establish the strong name of the Portuguese on the east coast of Africa as well as in Malabar, and to show any who doubted who was master. For trade would flow from strength.

In this new approach the Portuguese were equipped with one strong force denied to their intended vassals—their religion. Islam it is true, had shown itself in its early generations a flaming sword, able to persuade peoples, kingdoms and empires to acknowledge Allah and his prophet. But, when established it often tolerated others, even acknowledged some worth in them. It was a strength of the christian church that it tolerated no other. Convinced that they alone enjoyed the way of salvation, christians were fortified to look upon those of other beliefs as men inferior and lost who, if they would not be converted even by force, were destined for destruction or, at least, slavery. For the greater part of Christendom there was the further power of the Bishop of Rome, who assumed the right to apportion the world between nations, bless their endeavours, redeem souls, and acquit men in advance of all sins, however monstrous—except only heresy. The power of faith is great. To be able to say 'in this sign shall I conquer' gave the strength to break through all barriers, overcome all obstacles.

To this strength kings, especially Iberian kings, turned constantly, not least Dom Emanuel. After Gama's first return, the King sent to Dom Jorge da Costa, the aged Cardinal Protector in Rome, an account of his great success, and asked him to hand it to the Holy Father and ask, as if it were his own thought, 'for a fresh expression of satisfaction with reference to a matter of such novelty and great and recent merit, so as to obtain His Holiness's renewed approval and declaration, in such form as may appear best to you, most Reverend Father, whom Our Lord hold in his keeping.'

Within a few weeks of Cabral's return, the King, in spite of doubts voiced in his council, settled that a new expedition must go, more numerous, more powerful and better armed. 'Very mindful of the great treachery which the King of Calicut had committed towards Pedro Alvarez Cabral', Dom Emanuel ordered large ships to be prepared for lading, ten in number, into which 'was put much beautiful artillery, with plenty of munitions and weapons, all in great abundance'. This new fleet he intended for Cabral's command. He also prepared a subsidiary flotilla of five vessels, probably caravels, commanded by Gama's uncle Vicente Sodre, whose task was to search the Indian Ocean for Moorish traders and destroy them.

At some point in the preparations command was transferred from Cabral to the Admiral of the Indian Seas. Each chronicler has a different reason: that Cabral was offended because Vicente Sodre was given an independent command; that he thought the fleet too small to do the job, or to suit his worth; that on reflection the King thought Cabral's efforts in Calicut showed him not the man for the job; that late in the day Gama exercised his right under grant from the King to ask for the command. Perhaps all or several of these reasons combined towards the decision.

Once Gama was appointed the semi-independent squadron of Sodre was placed under his command; and a further element was added. A squadron of five ships was commissioned under Estevan da Gama, the admiral's nephew. Its original purpose was to stay in Indian waters to safeguard Portuguese factors and warehouses, though later it was incorporated in Gama's main fleet. This squadron, commissioned after the main fleet, was to follow on after three months and meet Dom Vasco in the Arabian sea.

Probably all the commanders were present when the King attended a solemn mass in the cathedral of Lisbon on 30 January 1502. He there made an oration praising Gama's merits and achievements (one account says that a member of his court made the speech for him), received from the admiral his oath of fealty, gave him a ring from his own finger and presented to him the royal standard. When, on 10 February 1502, Dom Vasco sailed from Belém in his flagship, *S. Jeronimo*, he commanded ten ships and five caravels. He took with him the ambassadors from Cannanore and Cochin who had travelled to Portugal with Cabral, plus Gaspar da Gama and possibly Monçaide. His mission was diverse: he was admiral, ambassador, trader, avenger, destroyer. The fleet he commanded was both armada and argosy. He was to make far seaways safe for the subjects of his king, perilous for the infidel. He was to trade peacably with the heathen, pillage the Moors, and strike unmercifully any who had stood against or wronged his countrymen. His role as ambassador was significantly different from his first mission, three years before. Then he went expecting to treat with christian kings, offering equal friendship. This time he was aware he had to treat with heathens, who knew not the light of the world, each prince inferior to the humblest son of the christian kingdom of Portugal.

So far as is known Gama set the same course out as on his first voyage. While they were loading water and wood at Porto Palo in the Cape Verde islands by good chance a gold ship from S. Jorge de Mina put in, laden with gold and jewels. Gama had all these riches fetched out to impress the Malabar ambassadors; for the Venetian legate in Lisbon had fed them stories of the dire poverty of the Portuguese, saying that they were unable to send ships to sea without the aid of Venetian bankers. This had once been true: in earlier times Portuguese kings had raised money for exploration from Jewish financiers in Nuremberg, Antwerp, Florence and Genoa, as well as from Venice. By 1502 gold was flowing more richly into Lisbon than into any other town of Europe. There was not too much exaggeration in saying, as Gama did to the envoys of Cochin and Cannanore, that 'ordinarily twelve to fifteen ships brought gold in such quantity each year to Dom Emanuel'. It impressed them.

Two months later, when the fleet was safely round the Cape of Good Hope and some 1,300 miles up the east coast of Africa, Gama turned west for Sofala with four caravels, sending the main force on under Vicente Sodre, who made Mozambique, where he supervised the construction of a caravel from pre-cut timbers and spares brought out in cargo from Lisbon.

Sofala was already known to the Portuguese as a source of ivory and of Zimbabwe gold. Covilhan had reported on it. Ibn Majid wrote of a Portuguese ship being wrecked there in the year of the Hegira 900 (AD 1495–6); it is possible that Gama was on that voyage, if it took place. On Cabral's journey home the year before he had sent Sancho de Toar to Sofala with one small ship, some merchandise, and Gaspar da Gama to help him. Gama's loop west was a sequel to this. Toar had done good business (gold for beads), made good friends with the ruler and beguiled him into asking that the King of Portugal should 'send more ships'. Bringing those ships Gama also had orders to survey the city 'to see if there was a convenient place for building a fort' and to enquire into the supply of gold; for it was thought in Portugal that this was the region of the mines of Ophir. Little gold was to be had at this time, as traffic with the mines inland was broken by a local war; but things went well with the sheikh. When Gama left he had with him an agreement for setting up a trading post. As they sailed one caravel was lost on the shoals; but men and cargo were saved.

At Mozambique Gama found a change: a new and friendly ruler had replaced his old opponent of three years earlier. This successor, wrote Osorio, 'had conceived a great liking for the Portuguese and treated Gama in the most respectful manner'. The admiral was able to make a treaty with him, set up a factory, and leave the newly-built caravel as a guard for the interests of the Portuguese in those waters. It was intended to make Mozambique a principal supply port for ships on the way to and from India.

The admiral had quite different intentions concerning Kilwa, where the insolent Ibrahim had so disdainfully treated Cabral and put the Portuguese to shame. On 12 July he led his fleet into the harbour 'in order', in Gama's own words, 'to establish peace and amity with him'; but he 'treated me very discourteously, wherefore I armed myself, together with all my people, prepared to destroy him, and drew up my vessels before his house, and called upon him with far more rudeness than that with which he had met me'. Barros tells that the city was in terror at the salvoes of artillery which the admiral fired to frighten the people.

What happened then is vividly described by Thomé Lopes, the clerk in one of Estevan da Gama's ships; he was told all about it when they got to Melinde a few days later. The shots from the guns had such an effect that the sheikh 'was constrained to leave the town and withdraw to the admiral's ship, looking more dead than alive, even though he feared the admiral would give him a bloody head.

'But it turned out quite differently; for his lordship received him with great humanity, giving him to understand that he wanted to know nothing from him save on one point, namely, did he prefer peace or war. He must choose one or the other; he should answer frankly without dread or awe, while it was still in his power, his lordship said, promising to put him safe ashore again, as he had come aboard on the basis of faith, assurances and safe conduct. The King, in the face of so magnanimous a reception, an offer so much more liberal than he had expected, answered the lord admiral that he asked only peace with him. This his lordship granted but with the conditions that he would remain a vassal of the King of Portugal and pay a tribute of twenty pearls a year. The King thought the deal honest enough except that he doubted his ability to provide a tribute of the quality asked, namely a weight of one mithkal [4·4 grams] each pearl, something difficult to get hold of. But to discharge his obligations to the King more easily, as things were in a state that he had to find some way out or other, he asked the admiral instead of pearls to accept 1,500 gold pieces a year. The lord admiral found this offer most honest and reasonable, and graciously accepted it.'

The story is amplified by other accounts, which say that the sheikh went ashore ostensibly to find the money, leaving as hostage with Gama an elderly Moorish merchant named Muhammad Ankani. In fact, they say, the sheikh's intention was not to send the money. 'Ibrahim was a prince of great wickedness and injustice', according to Osorio; 'he had paved his way to the crown by the murder of his predecessor. His own perverse disposition made him distrustful of others; he was suspicious of everyone but especially of those whom he observed to be men of genius and abilities; he had for a considerable time very much hated Muhammad; this, however, he had concealed under an appearance of friendship. Now a favourable opportunity seemed to present itself for his getting rid of this obnoxious person; he therefore resolved not to pay the tribute, thinking that Gama, being provoked by this breach of faith, would sacrifice the hostage. Muhammad, having at last seen through this artifice, discovered the villainous behaviour of his master to Gama; and, having paid the tribute out of his own fortune, was then set at liberty.'

Gama was content to accept. The ruler had agreed vassalage; and he had the money. He sent Ibrahim a patent in the name of King Emanuel which said that the King accepted him as a vassal with the agreed tribute, promising to defend and protect him. He also sent ashore a standard of the royal arms of Portugal which 'was placed in sight of our ships on a tower of the King's houses'. Before sailing from Kilwa he left written instructions for any Portuguese who might visit the port, describing his agreement with Ibrahim and commanding 'those arriving in these parts where I am that you should not delay here but continue on your way immediately to Melinde, and if you do not find me there go on to Anjediva, and if you do not reach me there follow on the way to Cannanore, and keep watch day and night in order that you do not pass me by.'

Sailing on Gama was forced by adverse winds and tides to pass Melinde without putting in. The nearest anchorage he could find was some thirty miles beyond; and from there a fair wind carried him across to the Anjedivas. Thomé Lopes reports that the Sheikh Wajeray had sent the admiral a letter which could be got to him only by wading through water up to the waist, because in that country there were a great many vicious and malignant animals. When Estevan da Gama's flotilla put in, the sheikh, through an interpreter, dictated to Lopes a second letter for Gama, and this was on its way the next day; for, in spite of the great welcome they received, Estevan's ships stayed only thirty-six hours and then hurried on to catch up with the admiral.

Estevan's ships made the passage in fifteen and a half days, reaching the Anjediva islands on 20 August. Before showing themselves, they fired off guns, at which the admiral sent out three ships and two caravels to repel what he thought to be a Moorish attack. The new arrivals ran up a Portuguese standard;

mutual recognition brought jubilation and trumpets. With the exception of
one ship, commanded by Ruy Mendes de Brito, the whole of Gama's fleet had
joined him. To their surprise the newcomers found their fellows in poor health.
'They were all low in spirit or ill, had been badly knocked by the excessive heat
(they had dug trenches in an effort to keep the sick cooler), and were amazed to
see us so much fitter than they were, who were all decaying, misshapen, with
their gums growing over their teeth, so greatly distorted that numbers, unable
to eat, died.'

Another report says that, when the main fleet arrived at Anjediva thus
afflicted with scurvy, 300 sick were put ashore. During the newcomers' stay on
the island Indians came often from the mainland selling fresh fish, lemons, and
several other fruits 'of such great goodness that however much you ate of them
even to excess they did not harm the stomach or cause any ill'. During this time,
also, a new mast was stepped in one of the ships damaged by high winds in the
Arabian sea. This apparently was done on the mainland; for 'two elephants did
us great service bringing a new one down from the hills. It is a wonderful thing
how this animal, whose nature is endowed with such perfect kindness and
understanding above all other creatures, understands all that is said to it and
does everything it is told to do.'

By 26 August the crews were again fit enough for the admiral to order the
fleet to sea. A single ship was sent out well in advance to look out for ships from
Mecca. An advance group of two ships and two caravels was also sent to scout
towards Cannanore. During the following days Gama stationed the whole fleet in
echelon out from the coast north of Cannanore in order to trap any Moorish
ships sailing for Malabar ports.

'These are the ships which bring spices to these lands', wrote a sailor in the
fleet, 'and we wished to destroy them and thus the King of Portugal would
alone have the spices there brought together.'

Gama was also concerned with revenge. While the fleet had been at the
Anjedivas, the Zamorin had sent a letter complaining about the way the
Portuguese had treated Calicut and proposing peace. Gama answered 'that he
had not yet inflicted on Calicut an injury equal to that which had been committed by the killing and robbery of the Portuguese, and until he had compensation for that he would fulfil the order of his King, Dom Emanuel'.

Gama's trap soon produced a victim. 'Following our ways and commerce
through the sea', Lopes wrote, 'flitting here and there to overtake some prey
among those of Mecca, we fell in with a great ship returning to Calicut from
the Mecca pilgrimage, carrying 240 men, not counting women, children and
lesser trash. Face to face they seemed little inferior to us; but once they had
felt a few rounds from the guns they thought of nothing but saving their lives,
which they held very dear on account of their great riches. For there were ten
or a dozen big Calicut merchants and among them a certain great and well-

disposed personage, factor to the Sultan of Mecca, who owned this ship and four others.'

She was the great dhow *Meri*, of which the various accounts say either that she belonged to one of the principal merchants, or that she was a ship of the Sultan's fleet. All agree, however, that she was a large, safe ship laden with much wealth. The admiral could not get close with the *S. Jeronimo*, as the wind had dropped. With his factor, Diogo Fernandes Correa, and two clerks he crossed by longboat to Gil Matoso's ship, which was standing guard. There he questioned the dhow's captain and the principal merchants about their merchandise and about how much capital they had brought to lay out in spices. 'Speaking lightly, without putting much pressure on them', he told them to go back to their ship and bring him such smaller things as they had brought for their trading. When they came back with gold coins, wrought silver, brocades and silks worth perhaps 12,000 cruzados, the admiral told the factor to collect it all; and he sent the Moors back to their ship, saying that he would send them away next day as it had grown very late. So it seemed to them that by supple submission they had ransomed themselves.

By the next morning, with the aid of the night breeze, the rest of the fleet had gathered close round the prize. Gama crossed over to her with Diogo Fernandes, clerks and guard; had all the merchandise brought on deck into the keeping of the factor; stood by to see it done; and, calling the *S. Jeronimo* alongside, ordered the goods to be transferred to the flagship. But during this manoeuvre a member of his crew was crushed between the sides of the ships and killed, 'which so grieved the admiral that he removed his ship and ordered Estevan da Gama and the factor Diogo Fernandes Correa to take the Moorish ship further out to sea, so as not to be in the way of our ships, and after they had discharged all the cargo which it carried, to burn it'—so writes the official historian, Barros.

It was done. Transfer of the cargo, and of such arms as were found, took many hours; when all was finished the hatches were fastened down, and the ship was fired in many places. The Portuguese ship drew back for safety from the flames. But the Moors broke through the hatches with arms that they had hidden and with stones. They overcame the fire. There was no longer any question of submission. Their assailants, taking things easy, moved back with their torches but were driven off with volleys of stones hurled down on them from the high deck of the dhow. Seeing the Portuguese loading their guns the victims crowded the rails, holding up great collars of gold and silver with other jewels and riches, calling out and offering all the remaining wealth for their lives, the women beside them holding up their children begging pity and succour. But, seeing that all was hopeless, and their death decided, they threw the treasure into the sea. They piled mattresses, sails and clothes to form breast-works for defence. Ruy Mende de Brito, with Thomé Lopes aboard, sailed his

small caravel up to support the boats. Fire from his forward guns made a great
hole near the mast. At the crash many Portuguese sprang, without body armour,
from their castle on to the dhow, thinking that they were taking on unarmed
men. They were met, in a fury of hate and despair, with stones, clubs, knives
and arrows; the Moors broke this attack, hurled some into the sea, threw others
back into their ship and jumped down after them into the caravel. Hours long
the fight wavered through the dhow, from dhow to caravel, from waist to
poop; the Portuguese were too few, and were overwhelmed. Some jumped
into the sea; many lay in the waist unable to move.

For a short time the Moors held the caravel; but they had to give up towards
nightfall when another ship sailed up to the dhow from the other side, firing her
guns. All during the next day and for three days after this unequal battle
dragged on, as ships and caravels crowded against the dhow, and the dhow,
though reduced to a smoking hulk, remained under control, its people indomi-
table, beating out and dowsing each fire started. But one of them at length
gave in, swam to the Portuguese and put a plan to the admiral, who gave his
approval. That night a boat party succeeded in fixing a cable to the helm of the
dhow, which, unable to steer, at last was overwhelmed by the firebrands poured
into it. Of all those in it, only twenty children were spared, to be taken back to
the monastery at Belém and saved for christianity.

Thomé Lopes, himself a spirited combatant, could not withhold his admiration: 'what courageous and noble people they were; though already worn out
and we being far stronger and more numerous than they, we found them so
sturdy, skilful, tireless, of such superb courage, when one was pierced by an
arrow he would tear it out of his body and throw it back at us, fresh and ready
for battle as ever, not changing colour, not losing heart'.

On the way to Cannanore four more ships were chased, but these escaped
in the high wind by running on shore. When the fleet dropped anchor off the
city on 18 October royal messengers delivered greetings from the ruler with
many graceful compliments, saying that he greatly desired to speak with the
admiral. To provide a proper place for this ceremony, he ordered that next day
a wooden pier should be built out over the water.

Trade and terror

By the morning of 20 October all was ready. In a caravel, the poop of which was
covered with crimson velvet, the Admiral of the Seas of India, Ambassador of
the Lord of Guinea and of the Conquest, Navigation and Commerce of India,
attended by the most splendid of his staff, with his standard bearer, with tabors
and trumpets, with guards bearing lances, crossbows and other arms, himself
clothed in a fine silk gown and decorated with several massive gold chains, was

ferried towards the shore. His ship was moored at one end of the new pier. To the other end the ruler of Cannanore came, in a procession with elephants and attended by 400 Nairs. Most of his train he left on shore as he stepped into a small lodge at the landward end of the pier to refresh himself, accompanied by two servants fluttering a banner over his head.

At length he walked up to meet the admiral. By agreement each was attended by thirty men. As they met they joined hands the one from the pier, the other from the caravel; for, the admiral had said, his king had expressly forbidden him to set foot on land. They exchanged greetings through inter-preters, while the two attendants with the banner continued to wave it, and two others, each with a banner showing a white hawk, danced before them. Ever courteous and open-handed, the ambassador–admiral with his own hand passed across vases of silver richly gilt, and himself received a number of precious stones from the ruler.

So Thomé Lopes, who was there, describes it. Later writers, collating other accounts, say that Gama sent ashore as presents to the ruler two chairs of state and that he landed on the pier, where the ruler warmly greeted him and, to please him, though it was 'contrary to his custom', sat on one of the chairs while Gama sat beside him on the other. There was an exchange of presents, accompanied by much ceremony, music and discharge of ordnance.

From these polite and magnificent exchanges Gama turned to business: settlement of an agreed price for spices and other goods. Agreement flowed less readily than kind messages and presents. An old man in his seventies, poor in health, the ruler said he could not deal with the details himself. He would give orders throughout the country that goods must be supplied at reasonable prices; and to settle the trade for his brother the King of Portugal he would send to the admiral his own factor and some of the principal merchants. But little progress was made with these when they came.

While he waited for agreement to be reached, Gama busied himself with another message to the Zamorin at Calicut. He gave grim details of what had happened to the dhow *Meri*, how many lives had been forfeit and in what way. These men were killed, he explained, as payment on account for the forty or more Portuguese massacred in Calicut. This action was an example to show how the Portuguese took compensation for injury done to them—an example only: more would be done when they came to the city of Calicut, and that very soon. Probably Gama's message was sharpened by a note received at this time from Cabral's factor in Cochin. He reported that the Zamorin had written to the ruler of Cochin abusing and reproaching him, and warning him that twenty great ships had arrived from Portugal and were seizing and sacking all the vessels that they met, to the great injury and loss of the whole country. Only one remedy would serve, he said: all on the Malabar coast should refuse to supply any further spices to the Portuguese at any price. He had wished to summon all the people of India to take up arms against the christians; but this the Moors had opposed, saying that they had not the force for an armed resistance to Portuguese power. He asked his dear brother the ruler of Cochin not to supply any spices to the Portuguese, and to support this instruction among all the other lordships under his suzerainty. The ruler of Cochin had refused. He answered that he had made an alliance with the Portuguese and that he would not deliberately break it; in any case, he had found them to be men of faith and truth and he did very well out of trading in spices with them.

Two Moors and two Hindus came from the ruler of Cannanore to negotiate prices and terms of trade. Spices, they said, belonged to the merchants who traded in them; they alone set prices, not the ruler, whose interest was only in the duties to be paid. Gama was insisting that the Portuguese be charged the same prices as those 'given to the Moors of Mecca' and that these be controlled by royal mandate. As his talks with these merchants led nowhere, he sent word to the ruler to ask for his agreement to the Mecca terms. The answer came that he should go on to Cochin—whatever prices he got there would be fixed for Cannanore. Gama's rejoinder was sharp. Since the Moors in Cannanore had such great power over the ruler's will as to make him change it, he would indeed sail at once to Cochin. For at Cochin there was a king of much good faith, 'who took more account of the Portuguese than of the Moors'. As for the Moors of Cannanore, he would treat them as he did those of Calicut: their safe-conducts and navigation permits were cancelled; for those who disturbed the peace did not deserve that others should keep it with them.

Before morning he sailed, leaving a single caravel to pick up the Portuguese still ashore, including the factor Rodriguez who had been left there by Cabral. The passage south to Calicut was enlivened by an encounter with three big ships. These, being closer in shore, were chased by eight ships' boats—led by an Italian captain, John de Bonagracia from the *Julia*, who boarded one and astonished the others with some fine shots from the bombard. All this was seen from shore by the ships' owner, a great lord of the country. With seven or eight brave men he took canoe out to the flagship, where he assured the admiral that, as a vassal of Cannanore, he would not have had the hardihood to venture out but for his faith in the agreement between Portugal and his king. He gave Gama a present of fowls, figs, rice and lemons, which the admiral received graciously, granting him and his vessels safe conduct. This he did out of respect for the ruler of Cochin, to whom the merchant was related.

This passage to Calicut, a matter of only three days, saw also a brisk passage of messengers north and south. From Cannanore came a servant of Rodriguez the factor there to say that the ruler had accepted Gama's conditions: he was sending a written mandate by the hand of Vicente Sodre. Rumour reported that the ruler had settled things with the merchants by agreeing to make up to them out of the excise he received any difference in prices.

From Calicut the Zamorin, with rising alarm, sent one envoy after another offering to treat for peace and friendship. Of these the last arrived when the fleet was within ten miles of Calicut. It rejected the admiral's demand for payment for Portuguese goods lost during the attack on the warehouse in Calicut. This had been provoked by outrages committed by the Portuguese, the Zamorin said; Gama should rest content with what he had captured from the *Meri*, of far greater value than Cabral's loss. A balance-sheet of losses, damage and death on either side would, he stressed, show that the Zamorin had been the greater sufferer. Yet, in spite of the outcry of his people, he asked no compensation for the evils they had suffered from the Portuguese; for he desired peace and friendship with the King of Portugal. For these reasons the admiral should not dwell on past matters but be content to come to the city of Calicut where he would find the spices he wanted.

In an earlier message Gama had demanded that the Zamorin expel from his kingdom all the Moors of Cairo and Mecca. The ancient enmity between the Moors and christians meant, he said, that there could be no stable peace so long as the Moorish riff-raff stayed in Calicut. To expel them was patently impossible, the Zamorin wrote. There were more than 4,000 families of Moors living in the city, not as foreigners but as natives and he received much profit from them. If the admiral would establish peace and trade without laying down impossible conditions he would be happy to make an agreement.

Gama sent to say that he would bring his own answer. Within hours, on 29 October, his fleet was anchored near the city—a city whose face had changed since he had seen it last. For after Cabral's bombardments the Zamorin had set a stockade of thick palm trunks along the shore. Apparently this did not impede the use of the beach. Several fishing boats sailed out to the fleet within hours of its arrival. All were seized and their occupants were herded below. So too was a small trader setting out from Calicut with coconuts and honey.

Perhaps further annoyed by this, the Zamorin sent out another messenger to say that if the admiral really wanted peace he would not refuse it provided there was open behaviour without perfidy. If that were accepted, what had been taken from the Portuguese in the city of Calicut would be restored and this would be done in good faith. But this was subject to the precondition that Gama compensate for all the loss and damage caused in the country by the christians, that everything taken from the dhow *Meri* be restored, and that since Calicut had ever been a free port open to the trade of all, there should be no more talk of ejecting the Moors nor any hindrance to them in their traffic. With these conditions the admiral must be content if he wanted peace with him. If these were not acceptable to him he could be off, and take to the high seas without hope or pretence of ever returning to Calicut, or to India.

It is hardly surprising that Gama's answer to this was 'wonderfully rough and haughty'. A lieutenant-general for Emanuel, King of Portugal, he wrote, his status was greater and more honourable than all the realm of Calicut. His king could make such a ruler as the Zamorin out of a drum. He would keep him under such strict control that he would have no desire from one day's end to the next to drink or eat. The Zamorin could have until midday the next day to concede the demands made on him or expect war in the name of the King of Portugal, exalted and puissant by sea and on land, rich in gold and silver, able with ease to send men and ships enough to carry out war against the kingdom of Calicut and destroy it.

Orders were promptly given to the fleet. The same day, being Sunday, the admiral himself made a close reconnaissance in his pinnace, studying every detail in shore. As a result, towards nightfall, all the smaller vessels were moved in and stationed bows-on to the beach so that they could use their largest guns to the best advantage. The biggest ships, such as the flagship, *S. Jeronimo,* and the *Esmeralda, Lionarda* and *Flor de la Mar,* were stationed further off. The prisoners who had been taken from the fishing boats and the honey trader were shared out among the inshore ships.

During the night the watching Portuguese could see lanterns and torches on the beach and people digging ditches and building breastworks for artillery there. When day came the ships pressed in closer. The admiral stood by an hour-glass on the flagship poop. The Zamorin kept silence, influenced to do so by the Moors, it is said. At noon, at the turn of the hour-glass, a gun was fired in the flagship. At once from the yards of the inshore vessels thirty-four prisoners were hanging by the neck—a sight which drew to the beach a multitude of people weeping, shouting and cursing. Another gun signal brought a cannonade from the whole fleet, catching all these people in the open. There were a few answering shots; but the Calicut guns were of little power and were worked with little skill. Throughout the remainder of the day the ships' guns played on the city, not with great damage to the wattle houses, which the shots passed clean through, but doing much harm to the palm trees and bringing terror to the people.

At nightfall the hanging bodies were hauled down. Their feet, hands and heads were cut off. The mutilated carcasses were thrown into the sea to float ashore. Feet, hands and heads were piled in a canoe. With them, set at the top of a lance, was a large notice written in the vernacular, saying 'I came to this port with fine goods, to sell, to buy, to pay your customs. Here are the customs of this land. I now send you as a king this present: if at this hour you wish for our friendship you have these heads to pay for what you have taken in your port under your protection and security and to pay for the powder and shot which you have caused to be expended here. If this is done we shall straightway be friends.' The admiral ordered a cease-fire so that when this fine sight reached the shore no one should be kept away from seeing it.

'We took great pleasure', Lopes the clerk writes, 'watching these poor people running here and there in trouble and despair. As we were not far from there we kept a good guard during the night because of the murmuring and riot among the people of the city, hearing the tears, lamentations and keening which they made over the hanged bodies which the fleet had thrown into the sea. But none kept watch at the breastworks or visited them with lanterns, for they feared we might fire suddenly on the city—which in fact at daybreak we again began to greet with fine shot from our cannon.'

This bombardment was kept up till noon of the second day, with special attention to the houses of the nobility, the wealthy and the merchants.

The next day, Tuesday 3 November, Gama led out the fleet for Cochin, leaving behind him six ships and a caravel, under command of Vicente Sodre, to blockade Calicut, with orders to take any craft that tried to get in and keep in any that tried to leave. First to greet the admiral in the roads at Cochin was Gil Barbosa, who had been left there as factor by Cabral. Accounts of the Portuguese blockade had already reached the Cochin Moors from their fellows in Calicut; things were bad there it seemed. Apart from the pillage of ships, no food was allowed in and no fishing boats were allowed out. In Cochin it was a different story. The ruler had treated the Portuguese well; spices were readily available; and good trade was possible.

Barbosa was very soon followed by the ruler's emissary bringing greetings, thanks for the release of the three ships above Calicut, and promises that the Portuguese should have their fill of spices. The smaller ships were moved in closer to prepare for loading. Bargaining for spices and other goods started two days later, directly between the ships' captains and clerks and the merchants, mainly Moorish. At the same time there was a frequent exchange of messengers between admiral and ruler. They treated mainly of prices and terms of trade. Sometimes sharper questions came up, among them an urgent request from the ruler—he was known to the Portuguese as Trimumpara, a confused abbreviation of his true name, Itiramamarnetim Qullunirana Coul Trimumpate—that a ship which he expected from Calicut should be allowed in and not be waylaid. The port is yours, was Gama's answer. His fleet was there under orders from the King of Portugal to serve the King of Cochin. This ship and all others from Calicut would be treated as his, though they were the greatest enemies of the Portuguese.

Gama's reply opened the way to a direct meeting with Trimumpara, and not before time. Some four or five days of direct dealing with the Moors had brought the Portuguese captains no firm prices and no concluded bargains. They were getting restless, suspecting another Cannanore.

Thus it was that, with all the state of an ambassador and a commander, Gama, in a caravel gorgeously dressed, escorted by pinnaces dressed also, and heralded with trumpets, drums and peals from the bombards, met Trimumpara on a pier. As at Cannanore, fine presents were exchanged, with mutual cour-

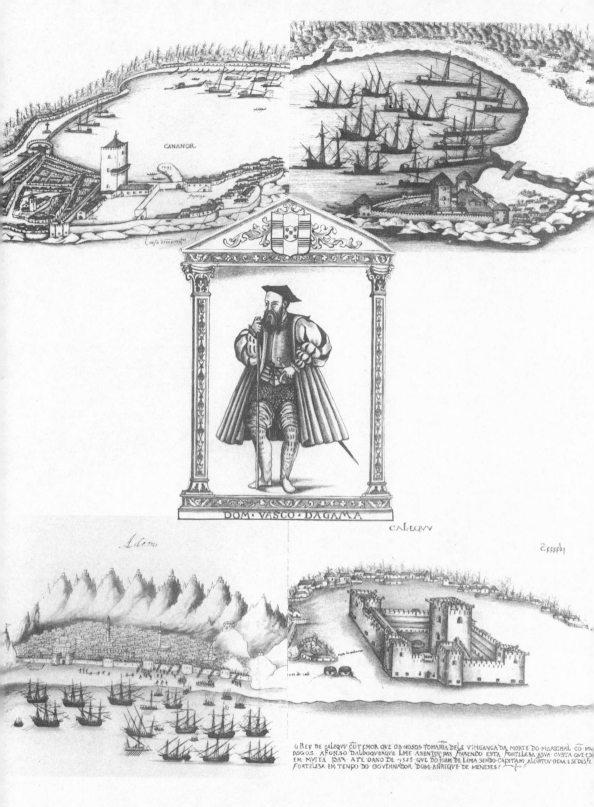

CANANOR

DOM · VASCO · DAGAMA

CALEQVV

Adem

Č FFFFbj

O REY DE CALEQVV COT EMOR QVE OS NOSOS TOMARIA DELE VINGANGA DA MORTE DO MARICHAL CO MV
ROGOS AFONSO DALBOQVERQVE LHE ASENTOV PAS FASENDO ESTA FORTELESA ASVA CVSTA QVE ES
EM MVITA PAS ATE OANO DE 1525 QVE DO JOAM DE LIMA SENDO CAPITAM ALEVATOV GEM E SEDESFE
FORTELESA EM TENPO DO GOVERNADOR DOM ANRIQVE DE MENESES

By the time da Gama was Viceroy of India, the Portuguese through his achievements as navigator and administrator were bringing to Europe unprecedented treasure and all the spices of the Orient from all ports shown in these contemporary drawings from *Lendas da India* by Gaspar Correa who was in Goa when da Gama was Viceroy.

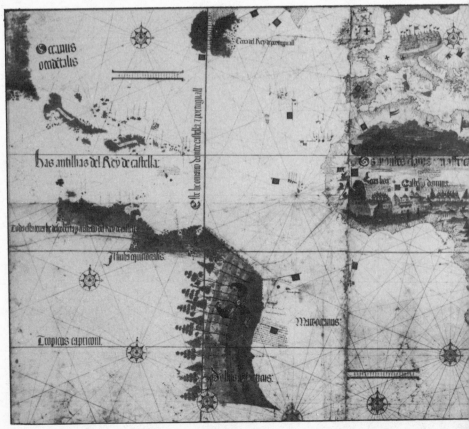

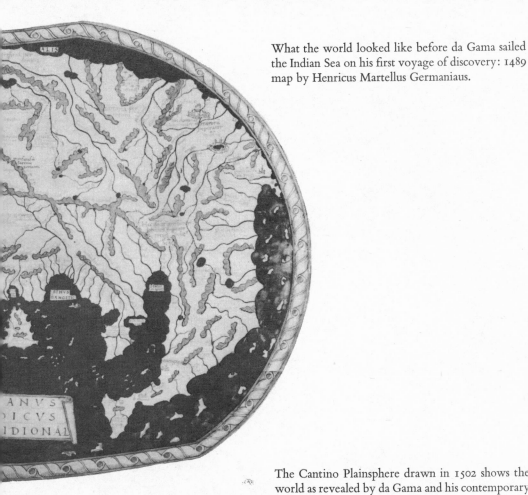

What the world looked like before da Gama sailed the Indian Sea on his first voyage of discovery: 1489 map by Henricus Martellus Germaniaus.

The Cantino Plainsphere drawn in 1502 shows the world as revealed by da Gama and his contemporary Portuguese discoverers.

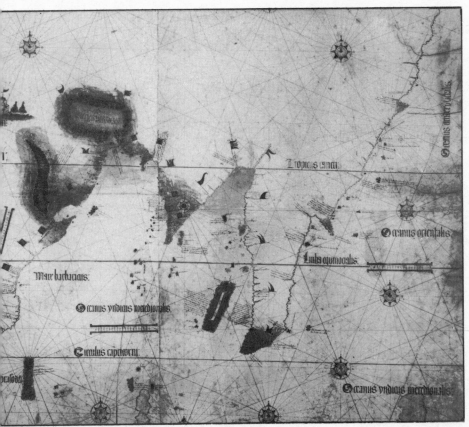

Nutmeg tree   from: Cristoval Acosta
Tractada de las drogas y medicinas de las Indias
Orientales, con sus plantas 1578.)

Clove tree

Some of the exotic trees, plants, spic
fruits (eg coconut and date, palms, ba
figs, areca) of the East which the Port

Avellana

Palm

ght back thus transforming the flora,
tation and horticulture of Europe
choten's Itinerario 1598).

Pepper

Linschoten's picture of Goa Market shows how quickly the Portuguese imported their own urbanity and ways of life into their colonies and how the Malabar people adopted some of these.

The Dutch de Bry brothers' European fantasy reconstructions of Malabar life. In the village above (15) the women, animals and houses are recognisably European though amusingly orientalised.

In Cochin on the Malabar coast (the flourishing centre of the pepper trade), the King of Cochin rides his royal elephant attended by his guard of elegant Nairs, who were the celebrated warrior caste and whose arms here are the product of the artist's eclectic imagination. On the right the renascence native figure sports a fashionable European hat, as was often the case.

A page from the famous navigator's manual, João de Castro's *Roteiro*. Vasco da Gama sailed to India as Viceroy in just such a splendid fleet of *naus* and caravels.

tesies and blandishments; and once again Gama was led to suspect evasion. Trimumpara was understood to be saying, as the ruler of Cannanore had done before him, that it was up to the merchants, not him, to fix prices.

The meeting thus ended in adjournment instead of agreement; but the next day things took a new turn. Trimumpara put out to the flagship without 'the pontificate and magnificence of the day before', bringing with him no more than five or six of his Nairs. When he got aboard he said that he had noticed Gama to be less than satisfied. Perhaps he had seemed difficult to satisfy and unwilling to make concessions; so he had come to put himself in the admiral's power. An act without precedent, such trust made its mark with Gama. 'He thought all proceeded from the goodness of God; and he thanked the King; and they settled the prices of the spices and made written agreements concerning them.'

The improvement seemed to be general. The day after, three of the Portuguese ships arrived from Calicut, and with them a pinnace bringing an ambassador from the ruler of Cannanore, who invited Gama to send ships to load there at Cochin prices. Lest the admiral doubt his word he also sent hostages. Much encouraged Gama sent off two caravels at once, the hostages with them, answering the ruler that he put trust in his royal word. About this time, too, Barros and others report, came a group from Cranganor, a princedom down the coast from Cochin. They brought letters from several lordships offering obedience to the King of Portugal—in reality hoping for a protective alliance.

With a generous offering of fowls and fruits these men also brought with them a sceptre-like staff covered in red, with at each end a silver head from which hung clusters of small silver bells. This, sent as a sign of faith and obedience, was the rod of justice of their city, and had never before been rendered up in this way. For the first time the Portuguese were in the presence of genuine Indian christians, Nestorians of St Thomas, who claimed to number 30,000 in that region, with five bishops, many priests and, as a place of pilgrimage, the sepulchre of St Thomas. They complained that the infidels around pressed upon them and proposed that the Portuguese build in their parts a fortress, which would be a key to lock up and hold subject all India. All of which obeisances the admiral received with kind words, gifts of wheat, wine, silks and other things, and promises to carry their words to his sovereign.

Correa also says that in those days an embassy came from the Queen of Coulam (Quilon) offering pepper and seeking the Portuguese trade. This opening of a possible new market Gama examined in council with his captains: it seemed a valuable resource should things go wrong at Cochin. Gama thanked the queen's envoys, saying that he would tell his king of her good offers, but that he could not accept of his own authority, since he had pledged his word to the King of Cochin, who was good and true in fulfilling all agreements. As he could do nothing without the goodwill of the King of Cochin, he asked the queen to send her message to him and seek his assent. This answer gained him credit for honest dealing; for she made her application to Trimumpara, telling him what Gama had said.

Trimumpara and the queen were kin, on good terms, their ministers and merchants related and friendly; but Trimumpara saw in this request potential loss of trade and of river dues on pepper if the Portuguese shipped direct from Coulam what otherwise would come through his own territory. He tried to reach some secret terms with Gama for keeping the queen out of things, which was not at all to the mind of the admiral. By negotiating openly in the presence of both groups of envoys, hers and his, Gama so steered the conference that Trimumpara could not but agree to let Coulam into the trade. It was settled that ships should go to Coulam only with the consent of Trimumpara, but settled in such a way that he could not refuse. So a trade agreement was made between Coulam and Portugal; and according to this account two ships were sent at once to load.

At this busy time things were also stirring at Calicut, both openly and secretly. Openly there came one day to Gama a respected Brahmin, perhaps eluding Sodre, perhaps granted safe conduct by him. He was 'a holy man of great authority and eminence' whose commission it was to carry out the special mandates of the Zamorin. With him were one of his sons and two other notables. He came as a mediator, he said. The Zamorin invited Gama to go to Calicut to compose their differences and agree perpetual peace, with an irrevocable regulation of trade and a settlement of what was owed to the King of Portugal. The Brahmin placed his own person as surety in Gama's hands. Moreover he gave the admiral many rich jewels, which he said were valued in India at 3,000 carats. This treasure Gama at once had converted into twenty quintals of cinnamon which were loaded without delay.

At about this time, secret messengers carried letters to Trimumpara once more urging the Zamorin's resentment of his disloyalty and the danger to all India from dealing with the pirate Portuguese, whom he pressed to turn out. Money talks, was Trimumpara's answer; they brought him such profitable trade that he would no more turn them out than the Zamorin would send away the Moors from Calicut. In his answer to this the Zamorin became less diplomatic and more direct, threatening reprisal. But Trimumpara held his ground. He also kept all this to himself, saying nothing to Gama at that time.

To the Brahmin Gama gave consent, after consulting with his captains and deciding against their advice. Leaving the rest of the ships to their loading, and Dom Luis Coutinho as commander in his absence, Gama sent ahead a caravel to warn Sodre and sailed early in January for Calicut in the *Flor de la Mar*. No sooner had he left than the Moorish merchants broke off dealings, refusing to supply any more goods. The admiral could get all he needed at Calicut they said; furthermore there was no profit for them in the stipulated price. After three or four days of this obstruction Coutinho went ashore to try to negotiate.

Nothing moved them—not gold, nor silver, nor precious stones. He decided to rejoin Gama to concert their plans. Leaving some of the ships to hang on in Cochin he set out that night for Cannanore. The dull life of those who were left behind was at one point enlivened when three men who sold them a cow were impaled alive by order of Trimumpara. Coutinho passed Calicut in the evening of 13 January. Seeing no sign of the *Flor de la Mar*, he did not stop; and four days later he reached Cannanore, confident that by that time the admiral had achieved a treaty.

Far from it. Coutinho found Sodre's squadron, and the other ships that had reached Cannanore, with lateens apeak, yards squared, standards raised, gabions strengthened with stones, the men drawn up, as though for battle against a thousand sail; all were ready to give a good account of themselves at Calicut. The spirits of all were strengthened by the arrival of new force and by Coutinho's report that things had seemed quiet at Calicut as they passed. For there had been considerable excitement there.

On arriving in the Calicut roads, ten days earlier, the admiral had dropped anchor close in shore. The Brahmin was sent ashore in the admiral's barge with messages for the Zamorin; signals were decided upon; and the admiral agreed to wait for him till nightfall. The Brahmin was seen to be met at landing by royal attendants, who escorted him to the palace. Nothing more was heard or seen from the palace throughout the day. When evening came without news Gama's signal of a single gunshot brought a splendid figure hurrying from the palace to give the admiral assurances that all was to be settled as he wished: all was prepared, listed, ready for delivery to him in the morning. The Zamorin asked him to send a representative ashore to receive them. Not the meanest manservant in his employ would he lower himself to send, Gama blazed out. He owed the Zamorin nothing. Everything that the Zamorin owed should be delivered into his ships without question. Begging Gama to be patient till the morning, for certainly the Zamorin intended that all should be well, the messenger gave renewed assurances and left.

Shortly afterwards the ship's lookouts noticed a small boat sailing close to the *Flor de la Mar*. Those in it seemed to be fishermen, but on a closer view were clearly seen to be something much rougher than that. In line behind them came two further craft. A message was sent to call the admiral from his cabin. Suddenly from another side seven or eight pinnaces, apparently fishermen, were seen rowing towards the ship. As suddenly they opened fire with shot and with arrows, backed up by their fellows from the other side—so close up that the crew could not bring the guns to bear, with such fierce fire that no one dared show himself above the rails.

Apart from their crossbows, the only resource available to the Portuguese, once they had pulled themselves together, was rocks and stones, which they hurled into the boats. The Moors set fire to a pinnace tied alongside the ship but this Gama himself cut adrift, so that it floated away. A string of canoes head to tail made out from the beach in support, adding to the curtain of arrows, darts and shot. 'Cut the cable and shake out the sails!' was the order. That took time, for the anchor had been bent to a chain as a precaution against its being severed by the Moors. At length, however, after much hot work, the ship was freed; her sails filled and with an offshore breeze she pulled away. Even so canoes and pinnaces hung on until Sodre with two caravels came up.

Gama sent the Brahmin's companions across to the caravels with orders to string them up and sail about in front of the city so that all might see. Thereafter their bodies were sent ashore with the message, 'Vile man, you sent to call for me and I came. You have done me the greatest evil in your power. Revenge and punishment shall be as you deserve. When I return to this place I shall pay your dues but not with money.' Then he sailed for Cannanore.

With the ruler of Cannanore the terms of trade were working out. Gama wrapped them up with a written treaty. Portugal was to have a trading post, for which the ruler provided buildings. Spices were to be sold at a settled price. Cannanore and Cochin were to defend each other. Cannanore would give aid to none against Trimumpara. Gama was to leave twenty-four men to run the post. With all this agreed and the available spices loaded the fleet sailed south again for Cochin, finding, when they arrived, that loading had restarted—though whether through pressure from Trimumpara or through the persuasions of the Portuguese is not clear (perhaps through both). In a last meeting the king and the admiral confirmed their agreements. Trimumpara at last revealed to Gama the Zamorin's provocations and his answers, saying that he would risk his kingdom to serve the King of Portugal. That king, Gama said, would ever be grateful for such friendship and loyalty. In his sovereign's name he promised Trimumpara succour and support against his enemies. As for Calicut, such fierce war would be carried against the Zamorin that he would have enough to do to defend himself: he would have neither time nor strength to go against others. These things he deliberately said in the presence of those Nairs around Trimumpara who were friendly to the Moors and disliked the grant of trade to Portugal.

With his ships gathered together and laden, and with two trading posts established, Gama was ready to set out from Cochin on his way home. News came, however, that at Calicut the Zamorin had collected a fleet of many vessels to intercept him, thinking that heavy with cargo his ships would be easily overcome. Trimumpara counselled caution and a change of course. But Gama signalled Sodre to join him and led his ships out, setting course for the Zamorin's fleet.

They met near Pandarani. Thirty-three vessels came out from Calicut, with a host of armed pinnaces and canoes. Gama ordered the caravels to lead the attack. These fast craft, firing their screw-guns from the bow, caused havoc and confusion. Moorish ships broke formation, turning towards the shore. The admiral turned the flagship to lead the fleet among them. But high seas favoured the lighter vessels. At the first onset the leading caravels had closed on two of the Moorish ships, whose crews threw themselves into the sea. Taking to their boats the Portuguese hunted them with javelin and lance, killing without pity. In the plunder of these ships they found porcelain, silver vessels, other precious goods and a monstrous image of gold weighing some forty pounds, clothed in a gold mantle, and having for its eyes two valuable emeralds and in its breast a large ruby 'which gave as great a light as if it had been fire'. Gama called off all chase to ensure that none of the heavy ships ran on shoals. The two prizes were burnt.

At length, after a short stay at Cannanore to replenish stores of water, fresh food and fruit, on 28 February 1503 the main fleet set out to cross the Arabian sea. Gama left behind the squadron of six caravels under Vicente Sodre. His uncle was commissioned to guard the trading posts of Cochin and Cannanore and to intercept Moorish ships either off the Malabar coast or at the strait of Bab-el-Mandeb at the foot of the Red Sea, according to the state of the monsoons. So for the first time a standing European naval force was stationed in the Indian Ocean. The policy of the King of Portugal had developed from simple trade (filled out by plunder) to the assertion of command.

With his ships heavy loaded and long at sea Gama decided to set course direct for Mozambique, sailing on a south-westerly course from Cannanore. As a few days later they made their way through the Laccadive islands Sodre was already busy with his squadron, holding up a Calicut spice ship off Coulam.

Aided by the north-east monsoon, which in late February blows strong, Gama's fleet was carried across the Arabian sea in about fifteen days. On 15 March, not far from Mogadishu, a hilly island was sighted—too far off to tell whether it was inhabited. Beyond it were several more all beautifully situated and well wooded. Later they were told at Mozambique that the two largest islands in the group were rich in cattle, ginger and cinnamon, with sweet water. But the admiral had allowed no landing there and had hurried the fleet on.

No halt or landing is reported before Mozambique, which was reached on 12 April. There a short break was allowed for repairs and victualling. Water was the great need after seven weeks at sea; but there was none fresh to be had from the usual points. In this emergency Gama set his men digging deep wells. Eventually, and much to everyone's joy (not least that of the people of Mozambique), spring water was discovered.

After six days they sailed, leaving two ships which were still being repaired to follow on. But within a few days they had to turn back because the *Lionarda* and the *Flor de la Mar* were both damaged and leaking on all sides. By 1 May all were back in Mozambique. This time there was a more general and thorough overhaul. All set off again three weeks later—but to little effect. Hostile winds and currents frustrated them. In the Mozambique Channel the southern monsoon blows strong from south-south-west in May and June: the weather is fine with few storms, seas are heavy and winds strong to gale force—troublesome for heavy-laden and weary vessels. At the beginning of June they were once more at Mozambique; once more the *Lionarda* was starting at the seams. In the night, during a sudden storm, she had struck against Ruy de Brito's ship, whose forward castle was smashed.

This meant two more weeks of work, of fume and fret, and of shortening rations. Bread ran out on some ships. Millet could be bought while they were at Mozambique; but a bushel cost a ducat (3·4 grams of gold). They made soup from biscuit crumbs, 'which we found bitter as gall, all the more since it was mixed with water punking like a dead dog, which gave it its own sauce and spice; all the same, for better or worse, we were glad to fill ourselves up with it.'

High winds and storms from the south-west baffled them for many days as at length they beat down again round Cape Corrientes. At least the current, the great Agulhas flood, was with them. In early July the leading ships met two of Albuquerque's on their way to India. During one of these storms, as they neared the Cape of Good Hope, Estevan da Gama lost touch with the fleet. By late July the main body was clear and sailing north in the south Atlantic. They passed near an island without a single tree but covered with vegetation so that it resembled green water—'never before discovered' says Lopes; but it was probably St Helena, the first recorded sighting of which was by Joan da Nova in 1501. Pressing on well, they 'saw again the North Star' on 12 August. No stop was made at the Cape Verde islands; none at the Azores.

On a day at the beginning of September in 1503 three boats from Holland tied up at Lisbon, and so too did two caravels from La Mina and two bringing carpets from Oran; all eyes, though, were on the *Annunciada* from the Levant, one of the most beautiful vessels in Europe. But towards evening, the tide running full, watchers saw a greater sight—nine slow, unlovely ships, stained and scarred, with worn and mended sails, making their way into the Tagus. There can be little doubt that they were dressed with flags, their trumpets sounding; and little doubt that they had already been sighted from Cascais and Estoril. For on the shore before which the Admiral of the Seas of India dropped anchor a great crowd thronged; many relatives and friends were there; and there was the captain of the guard with horses, to take Gama and his captains to the King. He received them at the cathedral of Lisbon, where the Bishop of Guarda led them all, King and adventurers and lookers-on, in prayers of praise and thanksgiving. Then, so sanctified, Vasco da Gama and his captains kissed their sovereign's hand. Gama presented him a great silver basin containing the tribute from Kilwa—1,500 mithkals of gold, a weight of 6,600 grams. Just six days later Estevan da Gama arrived—no mean feat, since his mainmast had been broken.

To Gama King Emanuel allotted a further annuity of 1,000 cruzados, saying 'Vasco da Gama has faithfully guarded the royal interests, both in making war upon the Moors of Mecca, and in peacable negotiations with the kings of those countries. The fleet entrusted to him, owing to the wisdom and judgment exercised, has returned richly laden. On these grounds he is entitled to some recompense.'

From the great weight of Kilwa gold King Emanuel caused to be made a tabernacle for the Host as a gift to the church of the monastery of Belém, then rising fast. A symbol of thanksgiving to God for his great mercies in opening to Portugal the wealth of India, it was symbolic, too, of how that wealth was used in this 'monopolistic mercantile monarchy', as Magalhaes-Godinho describes it.

'He caused the Franks to prosper'

'God, when he would make trial of His servants, caused the Franks to prosper; establishing them in the greater part of the seaports of this part of the world. . . . Furthermore they have found their way to the Chinese empire, carrying on trade in all the intermediate and other ports, in all of which the commercial interests of the Mahommedans have been in consequence consigned to ruin; the traders of that religion having been at the mercy of the Franks, and, of necessity, subservient to them; the faithful, indeed, having been prevented from carrying any trade but that for which they have neither turn nor inclination, whilst the traffic that was most congenial to their pursuits, and afforded the largest return, was interdicted them, as the Franks have rendered it impossible that any others should compete with them in it.' (Zain Al-Din in *Tohfut-ul-Mujahideen—* Rowlandson's translation.)

Seven

Viceroy

> 'Many persons went to him with offerings
> such as is customary to make to governors
> when they are newly arrived; he would not
> take anything from christian or Moor, and
> still less from this city, which we all look
> upon as extraordinary, as it is the custom
> for all to be accepted.' (From a letter sent
> to King John III by the Chamber of
> Goa, 23 September 1524, reported by
> Barros.)

Creation of an empire

Vasco da Gama brought to Lisbon from his second voyage 30,000 quintals of spices, fifteen times as much as Cabral had landed. In his negotiations with Trimumpara at Cochin in 1503 he had established the price of pepper at 2·5 cruzados (11·5 grams of gold) a quintal, free-on-board—a price held steady for a generation. In 1500 it had been 4·5 cruzados (20·7 grams of gold). Taking the gold content of a Venetian ducat as 3·4 grams, these prices work out at six ducats a quintal in 1500, and 3·4 ducats a quintal in 1503. The market price of pepper at Alexandria in 1498 was from sixty-one to eighty-one ducats a sporta, equivalent to twenty to twenty-seven ducats a quintal; at Cairo in 1501 it was about thirty-three ducats a quintal. A quintal of ginger cost about 2·2 ducats at Malabar in 1500, at Cairo twelve, at Alexandria nine. Fifteen years later the Malabar price was less than two ducats: at Cairo it was thirty-five.

Gama also brought back with him agreements for established trading-posts or bases at Sofala, Kilwa, Mozambique, Cannanore and Cochin. His combination of trade and terror had proved the worth of the eastern enterprise, showing that the volume of trade that could be expected was potentially far greater than that of the existing trade through the Red Sea to Venice, which could be expected to suffer from the favourable prices he had secured. He had brought about the founding of an empire.

That empire was based on the mastery of the sea and the power of gold. The Indian Ocean became for a time Portuguese water, as the rush for the trade and riches of the east gathered speed. Within six years there was a Portuguese station in Malaya; in fifteen years stations at Tidore and Ternate on Halmahera in the Moluccas.

How to handle things in the Indian Ocean was being decided in Lisbon even before Gama arrived home. The King in council reached three decisions. To shut up the mouth of the Red Sea a squadron of three ships would be sent to cruise at the strait of Bab-el-Mendeb. Spices were to be loaded in Malabar, supported by naval forces to protect the trading stations during the navigation season and to prevent any merchantmen from leaving for Mecca; two squadrons each of three ships would provide this, under command of the cousins Albuquerque—Afonso and Francisco. A fort was to be built, also by the Albuquerques, as protection for the trading-post at Cochin when there was no naval presence in those waters.

This third decision showed a just appreciation of the problems. At the very time when Gama was passing up the Tagus to Lisbon, in September 1503, Francisco de Albuquerque with seven ships arrived at Cochin to find Trimumpara and the Portuguese from the trading-post penned up in the holy island of Vaipim, the land occupied by vassal lords under the Zamorin's control and much of Cochin itself burnt down.

Within weeks of Gama's leaving the Zamorin had called on Trimumpara to hand over to him the Portuguese; and at his denial had invaded. Vicente Sodre refused to help the defence; for being the sea commander, he thought that land war was not his concern and certainly not profitable. He chose to make sail with his squadron for Bab-el-Mendeb there to plunder among the merchantmen of Mecca. Several ships of Gujerat and Calicut fell to him; but he and another, ignoring all weather warnings from local navigators, foundered in a sudden storm. His other four ships survived, made back for the Malabar coast and met Francisco de Albuquerque on their way, which is how he came to Cochin with a strength of seven. Soon Afonso also arrived with his three; and soon after that Trimumpara was restored, his errant vassals were punished, war was carried to the lands of Calicut, and a fort was built, with Duarte Pacheco Pereira installed there to command and to trade.

Trade was poor that season. Supplies of spices to Cochin had been interrupted by the war. There was enough only for the three ships of Francisco. Afonso set off for Coulam, where he loaded his three ships and set up a third trading-post. With their ships the cousins set off for Lisbon leaving Pacheco with a wooden fort, 150 men, a ship and two caravels. None thought that he would survive; as the monsoon bore the homing fleet steadily across the ocean, those aboard prayed for the souls of their companions. Their fears were not misplaced. Within weeks, some 50,000 troops, nearly 300 boats, nearly 400 cannon, and many elephants had been brought to bear in an all-out attempt to invest the city and destroy the fort. All were frustrated by the able defence and audacity in leadership of a remarkable man. From January to September 1504 Pacheco with his small force foiled every effort of the Zamorin's forces. He earned the name the 'Lusitanian Achilles', and laid bare the military and naval weakness of Calicut when faced by the superior equipment and aggressive ardour of the Portuguese. Pacheco, who later wrote the brilliant geographical survey of the coats of Africa known as *Esmeraldo de situ orbis*, was rewarded by Trimumpara with a 'coat of arms': an escutcheon gules, to represent the blood he had shed, charged with five crowns to represent the five princes he had overthrown in battle.

The lessons taught by experiences such as these were soon applied in the councils at Lisbon. Spices involved war, conquest, the destruction of a long-established trade-net dominated by Moors. A presence was necessary, and more than that, an authority. That authority was to be provided by a viceroy, with a fleet in being as a permanent force. In March 1505 Dom Francisco de Almeida, with fourteen ships and six caravels (six more to follow in two months), sailed off to represent King Emanuel in the Indian seas. His preparations had been made with the help and counsel of Gama, 'who was the principal person in all the affairs of India'. Correa adds that Almeida had great abundance of stores and munitions, 'according to the very full minutes which D. Vasco da Gama gave with respect to all, for he directed and ordained everything'.

Almeida's operational mandate was a direct extension of Gama's practice. Forts were to be built at Sofala and Kilwa—to safeguard the trade in gold; at the Anjediva islands—to secure a supply-base and support other strong points in India; and at Cochin, Cannanore and Coulam—to keep a watch over the sea-lanes. Should the King of Cochin die, the town should be annexed to the Portuguese Crown, if this were possible without reproach or censure. A fort should be set up at or near the entrance to the Red Sea, to prevent spices from reaching the Mameluke empire and to foster trading and religious relations with Prester John. Peace should be negotiated with Calicut on the basis of full reparations for past injuries and expulsion of all 'moslems of Mecca'; otherwise total war, even fishing should be prevented. Squadrons should be sent to Cambay in Gujerat and Hormuz in Persia with orders to seize all Moorish vessels, to persuade these kingdoms to acknowledge the sovereignty of Portugal and pay tribute: they must break off all trade with Aden and Mecca, thereafter selling their goods to the Portuguese and taking from them what formerly came from the Levant. The viceroy would ensure the loading of vessels, with all buying of spices reserved to the King's factors, and should see that prices were kept stable. To extend the Portuguese interest the viceroy should send ships to Ceylon, Pegu (Burma), Malacca and other places. Diplomatic relations should be established with the Hindu empire of Vijayanagar.

Thus plans were laid to bring the Indian Ocean, from the Cape of Good Hope to Cape Comorin, under the control of Portugal: to create not a land empire but a supremacy of the sea. Their navigating skill, superior technology, powerful guns, vigorous audacity, and consciousness of their spiritual mission were among the factors which brought the Portuguese success in this lucrative crusade. Equally they gained from the antagonisms and diversity of the nations of India. Moslem and Hindu still disputed for leadership and power.

Everywhere from the Red Sea to farthest Asia, seaborne trade was mainly in the hands of moslems. Along the seaboard this was a unifying influence; it furnished the Portuguese with a single main antagonist. But within India there was confusion and rivalry. In the small area of Malabar, the divisions between Calicut, Cannanore, Cochin and Coulam served the purposes of the Portuguese. Equally they gained from the strength of the Hindu empire to which these kingdoms were tributary, Vijayanagar. This powerful state covered nearly all southern India below sixteen degrees north. Gujerat, Ahmednagar and Bijapur, the moslem states to the north and west, could not combine against the Portuguese; for their main concern in the power struggles was Vijayanagar, whose fighting men were numbered in hundreds of thousands and whose resources were immense. Divisions among their opponents, though mainly moslem, also gave the Portuguese advantage as they penetrated among the warring sultanates of the seas of Andaman, southern China, Java and the Celebes: their jealousies, perhaps also their geographical dispersion, frustrated combination. Within six years of Almeida's sailing from Lisbon, Portugal was in control of Malacca.

Wise advice on conciliating Vijayanagar was given by Timoja, that pirate who had had a brush with Gama in the Anjediva islands. He was part freebooter, part servant of the Hindu rajah of Honawar, who paid tribute to Vijayanagar. With his fast flotilla of darting single-masted galleys he lived by raiding Moorish traders. Many times the Portuguese were glad to have his help—as when he supported Almeida's successor, Afonso de Albuquerque, in the taking of Goa.

Governor-general, not viceroy—a difference of name only, however—the astounding Albuquerque was the man who settled the main lines along which the Portuguese empire in the east developed. He extended Almeida's policy of fleet plus forts to include naval bases. He was fifty-six when he became governor. During six years he seized Malacca, the great entrepôt of farther Asia; laid hands on Hormuz, gateway to the Persian Gulf, 'vast emporium of the world'; and established Goa as the territorial power-base of the Portuguese in Asia. Also he forced the Zamorin to accept a Portuguese fort in Calicut. He failed only in his efforts to lay hands on Aden and close up the Red Sea.

Portugal's further advances in Asia during the first quarter of the sixteenth century grew from what Albuquerque achieved. Ceylon was brought under control in 1518. Missions in the Moluccas and in Sumatra were operating three years later.

As a means to control the trade in the Arabian sea the Portuguese introduced passes. Zain Al-Din tells how 'after the Franks had established themselves in Cochin and Cannanore, and had settled in those towns, the inhabitants, with all their dependants, became subject to those foreigners, engaged in the arts of navigation, and in maritime employments, making voyages of trade under the protection of passes from the Franks; every vessel, however small, being provided with a distinct pass, and this with a view to the general security of all. And upon each of these passes a certain fee was fixed, on the payment of which the pass was delivered to the master of the vessel, when about to proceed on his journey. . . . to enforce its payment, if they fell in with any vessel in which this their letter of marque, or pass, was not to be found, [the Franks] would invariably make a seizue both of the ship, its crew, and its cargo.'

Goa was the centre of strategic policy, created by Albuquerque because armadas sent from Lisbon could not provide the ever-present power necessary for dominating the seas of Arabia and India. Almeida had defeated the Egyptian fleet in 1509. A far greater threat was the strength of the Turks: 'powerful, they have much artillery: and know how to build ships like our own', Albuquerque wrote; 'they are well furnished with arquebusiers and bombardiers, with master-gunners as skilful as ours, naval architects who can rival our best work, smiths, carpenters, caulkers as good as any we have.' Goa was to be the place for building, repairing, supplying and manning ships; for hospitals and stores; and for administration of all forts and trading-posts under the command of govern-general or viceroy.

To populate this colony, Albuquerque, through financial inducements to soldiers, craftsmen and clerks from Portugal, and compulsory baptisms of women prisoners, Brahmin and moslem, encouraged intermarriage of Portuguese and Indians. This policy became normal practice in Portuguese settlements overseas. Many paid posts were open only to married men. The object was to create a cadre of craftsmen, shopkeepers, farmers, clerks and government officials; but the prime result was a class of idlers too proud themselves to work, who used slaves to carry out the tasks they would not do themselves and whose wives were happy to buy their clothes and trinkets with money brought in to them through the benevolence of their prettier slave-girls.

Trade was controlled by the Crown. The Crown alone had the right to equip and send ships to India. All imports and sales of spices, silks and shellac, all exports of gold, silver, copper and coral, and all trade between Goa and the other main posts were Crown monopolies, handled mainly by merchants and bankers. Officers, officials and sailors were for the most part paid not in cash but in permits to buy and import spices to be carried free in the King's ships; if they wished they could sell these permits for cash. It was a system inviting abuse and speculation, an invitation which governors, captains and officials sent out for a three-year tour were generally happy to accept.

Within twenty-five years of Gama's first descent on Malabar the gains to the Crown from this trade were remarkable. Each year a cargo fleet was sent home with merchandise to the average value in each ship of 20,000 cruzados, rising to 50,000 by 1510. Gold and silver coins formed a large part of what was sent, for, as Joan de Nova found out in 1502 at Cochin, the Indians expected payment in cash not in goods. Bar silver and copper, plus lead, mercury and coral, were also sent. Though later, to satisfy the needs of the Portuguese settlers and officials, it became necessary to send other goods, these were the essentials. In return came principally spices and drugs (especially pepper), but also precious stones, dyes, amber, civet and other rarities. What this meant is suggested by the figures for one year: in 1512 half a dozen ships brought back to Lisbon cargo worth 1,300,000 cruzados, equivalent to nearly six metric tonnes of gold. How the Crown benefited is shown by comparison. In the quarter century up to 1500, the Crown's principal foreign income was from the Guinea gold mines: in 1476, 38,200 cruzados; in 1486, 133,000; and in 1497, 181,000. Income from India was in 1507 250,000 cruzados; in 1515, 334,000; and in 1520, 703,000. Net profit to the Crown from the spice monopoly was nearly ninety per cent. In 1515 profit from the spice trade was as great as all ecclesiastical revenues in Portugal. Five years later overseas trade represented nearly seven-tenths of the total resources of Portugal.

Gama himself benefited from this great and growing influx of riches. However well deserved may have been Dom Emanuel's name for stinting his servants, as the years went by he did well by his admiral—partly by giving him other people's property, it is true; but that was a habit of feudal monarchs. It is also true that Gama himself was ever ready to remind the King of his due, or what he felt was his due. He looked both for cash and for credit, the credit of land-ownership and a patent of nobility. His first voyage had brought him valuable pensions and trading rights, the hereditary title of 'Dom', and high rank; it had also brought him promise of the town of Sines, its revenues, privileges and tithes, but this proved elusive. Four months after he landed from his second voyage he and his heirs were awarded 1,000 cruzados a year in perpetuity.

At Sines, however, things continued to hang fire. The town belonged to the Order of S. Thiago, whose master was John II's bastard son Dom Jorge, Duke of Coimbra—in his father's day a patron to Gama. A dispensation to sanction the arrangement was made by the Pope; but the Order would not move. So, after waiting another two years, Gama did. He took his family to the little port, founded a new church, began to build himself a manor-house and behaved as though confirmed in his authority. But what might do in the colonies would not pass at home. The local governor kept quiet; but the Order through its Grand Master complained to the King; and the Grand Master was blood royal. So it was that in the spring of 1507 Gama received, at the hands of an uncle who chanced to be bursar to the Order, a letter from the King. It charged him on pain of a fine of fifty cruzados, and at risk of incurring 'the punishment deserved by those who refuse obedience to the orders of the King their Lord', within thirty days to remove himself, his wife and his whole household from the town of Sines never to return to it but by permission of the Master of the Order; under the same penalty he was to stop building his house.

Within the due time he moved to Evora, where he decorated the outside of his house with murals showing Hindus, Indian beasts and trees and plants of Malabar, in scrollwork said to be gilded with gold leaf brought from Asia. At this time the Venetian ambassador made a note that Gama's income reached about 4,000 cruzados a year; in all Portugal only six noblemen and seven bishops received more. For ten years the admiral lived in Evora, quietly or unquietly, content or, more probably, not content.

He was perhaps the most famous man in Portugal yet very little is known of his life in the twenty years after his second voyage. With Catherine de Athayde he raised a daughter and six sons, each of whom became a sea captain or a military commander. Emanuel may have consulted him on Indian affairs; but he never employed him at sea again though he did make certain further grants. In 1503 Gama was relieved of freight charges on merchandise from India; in 1515 he was granted leave to hunt in the royal preserves of Niza and to send with the India fleet a person to attend to his business; in the same year he and all the members of his house were freed from any property or excise taxes, wherever he might reside or own property.

After ten years discontent got the upper hand. In 1518 the admiral, by this time nearing sixty, made a formal complaint to the King that though there had been many promises he had not been given the title of count; and he asked permission to leave the kingdom and settle elsewhere. Perhaps he was thinking of following the example of Magellan, who had moved to Spain the year before and engaged himself to serve King Charles in the far east; though, indeed, Gama had a poor opinion of Magellan, for reasons unknown. It is probable that Dom Emanuel at least suspected what was in Gama's mind, for on 17 August 1518 he wrote to him, 'Friend Admiral, we order you to remain in our kingdom up to the end of December of the present year and we hope by that time you will have seen the error you are about to commit and desire to serve us as is seeming and not take the extreme course you propose. But if by that time you are still minded to go we shall not hinder your departure, with your wife, your sons and your movable property.'

Emanuel soon found the way to hinder this departure. He arranged for Gama to surrender to the Duke of Braganza 1,000 cruzados of his pension and a payment of 4,000 cruzados in return for receiving from the duke the town of Vidigueira, with all revenues and privileges, civil and criminal jurisdiction, ecclesiastical patronage and all the seignory, which carried with it the title of count. This was all signed and delivered in Evora in early November. In December, also at Evora, the King conferred upon Vasco da Gama the title of Count of Vidigueira, with all prerogatives, rights, graces, privileges, liberties and franchises enjoyed by the counts of the kingdom by usage and ancient custom.

Emanuel died in 1521. In December that year Dom Vasco da Gama, Count of Vidigueira, Admiral of the Seas of India, was present when John III took the oath as King. Then, it would seem, he returned to Evora or Vidigueira, to continue what, in the absence of any information at all, may be called his retirement. It was not long, however, before events in Goa and Malabar called him out again to India.

'If your brother had sold fortresses he would not have his head where it now is'

Albuquerque was succeeded as governor-general by men weak, grasping, or criminal; sometimes all three. He died at the end of 1515. Within ten years inherent weaknesses in the system of government—absolute monarchy and absolute bureaucracy—began to show in India. One such weakness was Portugal's great shortage of men—the reason for Albuquerque's stock-breeding approach to population and for the falling quality of those sent out as rankers from Lisbon: they were increasingly recruited by release from prison. A second was Portugal's poverty in merchants. State power centred on the Crown made speed and energy possible in opening the sea-route to India and founding an empire; but it could not handle the results. The abundant riches resulting from this activity were used by the King, the nobility and the Church for investment in property and for aesthetic purposes, but not for investment in marketable goods and to finance further profitable ventures. Even from the early days of the empire, when precious metals and foreign purchases made Portugal the richest country in Europe in terms of money or bullion, the capital required for new expeditions and so on was usually supplied by the Marchiones, Welsers, Fuggers and their like. Moreover, the trade in spices soon began to find its way into the hands of merchants in Antwerp and Bristol, and Jewish traders scattered all over Europe (they had been expelled from Portugal).

Most immediate in its effect was the third weakneess; the system of appointments and of payments. All top and many middle-ranking appointments were made for three years only. Pay was low, legitimate profits of office were high; the illegitimate were almost without limit. There was no continuity of government or stewardship. Each subordinate captain treated his command as a personal possession. Loyalty became a rare virtue. The coming of a new governor or viceroy meant new appointments in the government machine, places for relations, friends and dependants. Some were rewarded not by direct appointments but by reversions. Reversions could be sold for ready money or given as the dowry of a married woman or be lost by gambling. What all this led to is shown by Dom Garcia de Novonha's declaration, when he became viceroy in 1538, that he intended to gather the fruits of fifty years' service. As a start he offered every vacant office to the highest bidder.

Novonha's ways were foreshadowed by Lopo Soares de Albergaria: he began well by auctioning for his own gain the private property of the dead Albuquerque, whom he succeeded. Under his lax rule Portuguese began to trade on their own, ignoring the royal prerogative; in a short time some of them (including some of the captains of the fleet) developed into pirates. There exists a letter sent to King Emanuel in 1513 by Duarte Barbosa, telling how, in response to the excesses and cruelty of the local commander, Diogo Correa, the people of Cannanore had revolted. Next came Diogo Lopes de Sequiera, who had been an opponent of Albuquerque; he proved a talkative and boastful man. Most of his military and naval adventures went awry, his enemies foreknowing his plans. His only success as governor was in securing great riches for himself, both fairly and fraudulently—the bulk he succeeded in taking back to Portugal. Even more fraudulent and rapacious was Dom Duarte de Menezes, who, in the year Dom Emanuel died, distinguished himself by accepting some 100,000 cruzados for putting a Persian vizier in power at Hormuz (his brother Dom Luiz de Menezes had recently displaced the vizier, at a much smaller cost). He freely sold licences to privateers to plunder on the coasts of the Arabian Sea.

Their still remarkable vigour and rapacity was carrying the Portuguese ever further east. But these achievements were being undermined by misrule, indiscipline and blind self-interest. Near the end of Dom Duarte's time as governor the mainland behind Goa was occupied by Moors. Duarte was then at Goa with a force got together to settle some troubles at Hormuz. Goa's citizens appealed to him to help throw the invaders out before they became too many. 'He answered that he could not do it' the Chamber of Goa wrote to John III, 'as he was on a voyage; and that even if Goa should be lost, he would not desist from going to Hormuz. . . . His brother, Dom Luiz de Menezes, was also at that time in this city, and he went to winter in Cochin, and carried away all the men whom he could.' So the Moors 'increased in numbers and got possession of the country'.

Along the long ocean lanes to Lisbon, ill news travelled slowly; and the many tales, accusations, vindications and counter-charges confused the picture seen at the India House and in Montemór. But a picture did slowly form—and this in turn forced a decision. At the end of February 1524, at Evora, before witnesses,

Vasco da Gama, Count of Vidigueira, Admiral of the Seas of India, swore fealty to John III on his appointment as Viceroy of India. He was already sixty-four years old. So far as is known, he had not had a command or been to sea for twenty years. There must have been strong reasons for bringing this man out of retirement and sending him half across the world endowed with the 'complete power of justice and revenue like the King's self over all persons who might be found beyond the Cape of Good Hope'—a man described by Gaspar Correa, who was among those who greeted him when he reached Goa, as 'very disdainful, ready to anger, very rash, much feared and respected, very knowing and experienced in all matters'.

Among those reasons, no doubt, were complaints such as those from Goa concerning injuries said to have been done by their captain, Francisco Pereira, 'such as putting many of the citizens into prison in irons without reason and without charge or inquiry held upon them . . . ordering their houses to be taken from some of the inhabitants to lodge other persons in them . . . ordering all the provisions to cross the wharves in order to lade his ships and again sell them in the city . . . putting in prison the ordinary judges who by election are appointed . . . he ordered the solicitor of the city to be put in prison in irons for requiring what his office made requisite . . . fines of the market . . . he did not choose should be conveyed to the Chamber, by which the city suffered loss.'

With 3,000 men in nine large ships and five caravels the admiral sailed from Lisbon on 9 April 1524. There is no record what size these ships were but certainly they were far larger than those with which he had set out in 1497. By the end of the reign of King Emanuel ships of 500 tons were usual; during the next ten years they were reaching 800 tons. Two of Gama's sons were with him on this voyage, Estevan and Paulo, the one to be captain-major at sea (sixteen years later he was governor of India), the other to go on to Malacca. Many noblemen were in his train, 'very brilliant soldiery, and as captains, men of high family, the greater number of whom had been brought up in the labours of Indian affairs'. Among them were three future governors of India; but more important for the immediate future of Indian affairs was Afonso Mexia, clerk of the King's Chamber, who as overseer of the treasury was called by Whiteway 'one of the ablest and most honest officials that ever worked in Portuguese India'.

Some warning of the admiral's outlook on discipline was given by a fleet order published at Belém before sailing, concerning the evil of bringing women aboard, 'both on account of their souls and on account of plots and brawls'. Proclaimed on shore, and posted at the foot of the mainmast on each ship, this order directed that any woman found in the ships after sailing should be publicly scourged; if she were a married woman with her husband, he was to be sent back to Portugal in irons; if she were a slave, she was to be confiscated for the ransom of captives; and any captain who found a woman in his ship and did not give her up would lose his commission. Captains, it appears, were more impressed by this than were some of their crew—or, at least, one captain was. For when the fleet put in to Mozambique for repairs three women were found in one of the ships. Delivered up by the captain, they were locked below by the admiral, to receive their punishment when the fleet had arrived in India.

From Mozambique they had bad weather: three caravels were totally lost in violent storms; a ship went aground on the Melinde shoals. In one caravel the crew mutinied: master and pilot killed the commander, Mosen Gaspar, a Majorcan, 'a man of narrow understanding, not conducting himself well with the people'; then they seized the vessel and went off pirating towards Bab-el-Mandeb. Eventually the fleet approached the coast of India, towards Dabul as they thought. As they lay becalmed in the early hours of dark, out of sight of land, without warning and without breath of wind, all the sea was thrown into chopping waves, smashing against the ships and throwing them about. 'They pitched so violently that the men could not stand upright; the chests were thrown from one end of the ship to the other.' This trembling of the sea came on with violence, died off, came on again, 'each time during the space of a credo'. 'The whole lasted for about an hour in which the water made a great boiling up, one sea struggling with another.' When the seas fell, rain suddenly flooded down, without wind or warning.

General fear led the masters to strike their sails. Thinking they had run on shoals the pilots ordered leads to be cast but found no bottom. Boats were lowered. But Gama, when he saw the fears of the crew, called out to them 'Friends, be glad and rejoice, for the sea trembles at us. Have no fear, for this is an earthquake.' Through it all there was no damage, nor any loss of life but that of one man who threw himself into the sea, thinking the ship grounded on a shoal.

This earthquake weighed on the spirits of the sailors, many among whom were by then affected by scurvy. A Moorish ship seized soon afterwards had also felt it. As the Moors told Gama that they were only days south of Diu, he ordered course to be set in that direction. But, though they sailed on, without storm, for a full six days, still they saw no land. There ran through many of the crews a new terror born of the earthquake: it seemed that the land had been swallowed up and that they were condemned for ever to wander on the sea. Their minds had been prepared for this by astrological forecasts, known from before they left Lisbon, that the conjunction of the planets in that year of 1524 foretold an almost general deluge. These divinations had so panicked the wealthy of Lisbon and other coastal parts that they had laid up for themselves great store of biscuits at places in the hills.

So thanksgiving was unusually heartfelt when the next day land was sighted. That day, 15 September, they anchored; but not at Diu. The twice three days' sail was explained: they had arrived at Chaul. To the local commander, who at once visited the flagship, Gama published his commissions, in accordance with the King's decree; and from that moment he took the title of viceroy, having at last reached India. He celebrated his office by entertaining the commanders and the captains of the fleet. As viceroy he made great state. He was attended by two men carrying silver maces, a major-domo, two pages with gold chains, equerries and body servants 'very well clothed and cared for'. He had with him rich silver vessels, Flanders tapestries and brocade cloths for the table. At table they brought him 'large dishes, as if to the King, with his napkin-bearer bringing him the ewer, and all the forms of precedence of a king'.

When eventually the viceroy went ashore he had a guard of 200 men with gilt pikes, clothed in his livery; but he did not land at Chaul nor did he allow anyone ashore there but the auditor-general and the secretary of Cochin. These took with them in his name the various appointments specified in his commission, among them that of Christovan de Sousa as captain of the fortress of Chaul, and an order to be published in the fortress summoning all soldiers who were not married or who did not belong to the local garrison to board ship at once and follow the viceroy. To de Sousa Gama gave written orders that, should Dom Duarte de Menezes, the governor whom he was deposing, arrive at Chaul, he should not be allowed ashore; he should not be allowed rations for more than four days; and any orders he might give should not be obeyed, for 'the King was very indignant with him for his evil deeds'.

Three days were enough for this; on 18 September the fleet sailed. Five days later they arrived at Goa. 'The city gave him a great reception with festivities and a rich canopy, and a harangue, and they bore him in procession to the cathedral; and they conveyed him with rejoicing to the fortress, which Francisco Pereira had kept in very good order.' He confirmed to the Chamber of Goa all their privileges and liberties of the city; and they were amazed, as later they reported to King John, that the count refused all offerings such as it was customary to make. At the fortress the viceroy said to Pereira, who received him into it, 'Senhor Francisco Pereira, I should wish to find all your affairs so kept in as good order as these buildings.'

Barbed words: the next day he made Dom Henrique de Menezes governor and arranged to receive the complaints of the citizens against the displaced Pereira, having brought with him a number of written charges made through certified enquiries. The viceroy himself questioned each person who brought a complaint, and he ordered Pereira to recompense all those who had suffered loss through him. Pereira protested to Gama that he was being robbed of his property simply upon the oath of the claimant. Correa gives the viceroy's answer: 'When you took what was not yours why did you not choose that it should be judged by means of the administration of justice? It is not well that you should meet with justice since you did not observe it; but to discharge your conscience I will order it proclaimed that whosoever you may owe money or property to may come without fear to demand it, and it shall be paid to him: and I will not hear of criminal matters until the fit time for it.' It is noteworthy that this 'bold man who conducted himself so ill with the people' had nevertheless during his command built a new hospital ('a great comfort to the sick with the good management which it has'), a stone quarry at the strand gate ('a very good work') and other public works. Such combination of good achievements with malversation was not unusual. Some startling bandits were also effective commanders and administrators.

At about this time the Moorish vessel that had been seized on the way to Chaul was brought in under command of Tristam de Athayde, Gama's brother-in-law. This happened just after Gama had posted an order forbidding the hospital to take in any sick person who was not afflicted with sores or wounds. When great protests were reported to him from the sick who were landed from the ships, he answered that he knew a remedy to give them an immediate cure. And he posted another order that in three days the cargo of the Moorish ship, which contained gold to the value of 60,000 cruzados and some 200,000 cruzados' worth of other goods, would be sold at auction, the proceeds to be paid out in shares.

Everyone crowded to this pay-out. To their cost, many from the hospital joined with them: they found themselves barred from going back by order of the viceroy. Gama followed this up by forbidding anyone wounded in a brawl to be taken to hospital—for they brawled 'only on account of women'. Orders great and small for tightening discipline poured out from the old man, who worked throughout the day. He took no siesta and kept open office 'with no porter at the door'. He stopped all shore-leave and placed the auditor-general on guard over the ships at the bar. All men due for service were to go to Cochin to be enrolled, or lose their pay.

A simple listing of some of the orders made by Gama shows him going on from one abuse to another, leaving the Goan community panting in his wake, and often trembling. On pain of death and loss of property, no one was to navigate without the viceroy's licence. Shipowners were to make their contracts and shipments with the King's factor, and were not to sail unless their papers were in order. Any man trading with the property of a King's officer was to lose his ship and all his property to the King and be banished for ever to Portugal. No married man was to receive pay and rations unless serving in war or with the fleet. No seafaring man was to wear a cloak except to go to church on Sunday or a saint's day; if he wore one at any other time, the constables were to take him, seize his cloak, and put him 'at the pump-break for a day in disgrace'. Every man drawing pay as a matchlock man was to wear his match fastened to his arm. If men-at-arms kept slaves, these were to be able-bodied men capable of all work: they would not be allowed 'to embark pages dressed out like dolls on board the King's ships' but grown-up slaves going with the fleet would receive the King's rations.

On pain of death and confiscation of property, any who had guns of the King's artillery were to deliver them to the magazine. If this were done within a month, there would be no penalty, even though the pieces had been stolen; but thereafter there would be due process of the law. It seems there had been a regular traffic in guns between officers and traders, who sold off the powder and ball. 'Much artillery was gathered in.' On condition of a 'return to the service of God and the King' within three months, pardon was offered to any person who had fled from justice into India before the viceroy's coming. General permission was given for any man who did not wish to stay in India to go back to Portugal, provided he had no debts to the King or to justice.

On the other hand the viceroy made enquiry into embezzlements and robberies of the King's revenue by officers. He ordered that strict accounts be exacted from all of them, for he 'was very zealous for the King's revenue and used to say that men came to India poor and enriched themselves'. He was 'very ill-disposed towards those of the King's officers who were rich'. His handling of appointments was typical. He examined personally anyone who claimed an appointment from the King, checking both past performance and actual capability; any who failed his tests he refused to commission. Every applicant for a clerk's post he at once asked to write in his presence: no good writing, no job. 'If a man wrote badly and begged for a clerkship,' he would say, 'it was only for the purpose of evil-doing.' Correa comments, 'he did not give appointments except to very official men'. He refused to give any posts as reward for services rendered: men's services, he said, should be recompensed not with positions from which they could gain money, but with favours and honours— to which end he had authority to grant pensions, increase allowances, and so on.

Of all the punishments which Gama ordered imposed during his term as viceroy, the one that caused the greatest excitement and scandal was that decreed for the three women found in a ship at Mozambique. Soon after the fleet arrived at Goa the crier called through the town, 'The justice of the King our sovereign! It orders these women to be flogged because they had no fear of his justice and crossed over to India in spite of his prohibition.' Remonstrances came fast, from gentry, bishop, friars, Brothers of Mercy. Some of the charitably minded joined together to offer as ransom 3,000 gold pardoes (nearly the same as cruzados). 'The viceroy would not listen at all.'

Carrying a crucifix, a procession of Brothers of Mercy and Franciscan friars came next day to beg that the women be given up to them. Gama sent word that they should take the crucifix back to the altar before he would hear them. When they had done this, he saw them, and said that such a thing must never happen again: to march to his house with a crucifix through the crowded streets was a kind of conspiracy, designed to show him cruel and pitiless. As for their pleas, he swore he would not pardon for anything in the world, but would execute strict justice on all who came before him. In the next world, the Lord would have mercy on those who deserved it. So the women were flogged; and the people, much scandalized, 'judged the viceroy to be a cruel man; but seeing such great firmness in carrying out his will they felt great fear and were wary, and reformed many evils which existed in India, especially among the gentlemen who were very dissolute and evil-doers'.

All this activity Gama carried through in about four weeks. Then he turned his attention to Cochin, still the chief trading-centre for spices. He gave orders to the new captain of Goa, Dom Henrique, not to allow the deposed governor to land (should he turn up), nor obey him in any respect. Leaving the main fleet to sail out at sea, he sailed close in shore in a newly built galiot—a small pursuit craft with sails and oars—with six large open galleys in support. For company he took a few servants, 'who were not gentlemen, for he always rid himself of those, and preferred the lascars [Indian seamen], who conducted themselves after the manner of good soldiers'. Things were not good on this coast. To counteract Portuguese mastery at sea Moorish traders were using fast light open galleys to pass from place to place through the lines of backwaters at the river mouths, described by an Englishman in the middle of the nineteenth century as 'the wonderful chain of inland navigation'. (Chisholm Anstey quoted by Stanley.)

As he moved down the coast Gama met one who suffered from these activities: Francisco de Mendonça, in command of eight ships guarding the coast. Of these the Moors 'took little account; for they were swift, the Portuguese large and heavy, and they dealt with our vessels like a light horseman'. So it came about that the traders of Calicut 'had factors in the rivers of Mangalor and Cacanor, who sold the plunder which they took and gave them cargo of rice which they carried off to Calicut'. As an immediate answer Gama sent in a force of six smaller vessels to close up the river mouths; one report says that with these craft Jeronimo de Sousa destroyed more than forty light galleys that had been collected there by order of the Zamorin to intercept Portuguese provision ships from Cannanore.

At Cannanore, it seems, Gama went back to his flagship. Spending only three days in that town, to settle in a new commander, and passing by Calicut at night, without a stop, he sailed on to Cochin. Delayed by light wind at Cranganor, which with a good wind is half a day's sail short of Cochin, he was met by one of Portugal's more remarkable civil servants in Malabar, Dr Pedro Nunes, comptroller of the treasury. When news of the viceroy's coming reached Cochin, he took a large boat 'with an awning and dressed out', to land the viceroy in 'if he was so pleased'. Gama received him with great honour. He had been much commended by the King, with good reason: during his six years in office he had transformed the quality of pepper supplied to the Crown.

For years consignments had been showing losses of thirty or forty per cent, being damp, green and adulterated with sand and grit by the factors, 'from which they made their profit'. Those arriving from Nunes showed a loss of only seven or eight per cent—normal wastage in transit.

That night Nunes stayed on board the flagship to provide Gama with a long account of 'the affairs of the governor and of all India'. He spoke highly of the governor's brother, Dom Luiz de Menezes, especially 'of the manner in which he had reproved the governor's faults, so that they were not on good terms together'. Dom Luiz himself set out next day to search for the viceroy, who was standing well out to sea with the land breeze. He sailed in his newly refitted galleon, well equipped with artillery of heavy calibre, with awnings and flags, taking with him many fidalgos and much food. As he sailed up to the stern of the flagship he dipped his captain-major's standard in salute. He was answered with trumpets and kettledrums, and with his gentlemen attending was received at the ship's side by the viceroy with many courtesies.

With the coming of the sea breeze that evening they put in to Cochin. Though they dropped anchor after dark their arrival was 'a wonderful sight to see'; for the viceroy's ship made a a salute with much artillery, after which all the fleet fired salutes and 'could be seen by the glare of the artillery fire'. The light was strong enough for Gama to notice at the harbour bar a ship whose captain, Vicente Gil, had broken orders by leaving the fleet and stealing ahead to Cochin so as to get the first trade and the best prices.

This delinquency could not be seen to at once. First had to come the official landing, the civic welcome, the ceremonies at the church, and the meeting with the ruler, who came upon his elephant to greet the viceroy. All of this Gama carried through with the proper circumstances, dignity and courtesies. Then he went without pause to his residence in the fortress and once more to work. Vicente Gil very soon found himself in prison, and was fined 300 cruzados as well. His pilot and master each had to pay a hundred, the money being allocated to the upkeep of the hospital.

With the Moors in the backwaters much on his mind Gama inspected some newly built sharp-prowed rowing boats, rejected them, and sent for a Master Vyne, a shipwright of Genoa, whom he had brought with him from Europe to build galleys. He challenged Master Vyne to build him rowing boats faster than those of the Malabars. 'Sir, I will build you brigantines which would catch a mosquito for you', said the Genoese; and in twenty days he had produced two of Levantine design. To every Portuguese who would row in one, Gama offered monthly pay and rations, a share of all goods above deck in any vessel that was seized, double shares of all other prizes distributed, and freedom from any other service. As a result, he had his pick of the best. Each rower had under his bench a breastplate, a steel helmet, a lance, a shield and two pots of powder.

As in Goa, Gama's vigorous justice soon spread alarm among officers and

officials. He enunciated a number of principles. He would give captaincies only
to men who had shown themselves good soldiers in war: the honours of war
were to go to those who had won them with their right arms. Any guilty
official of justice or revenue would be subject not to civil but to criminal
penalties. He was specially severe with captains of forts, who went in fear of
him. 'If he found them in fault he would chasten them and execute them', or
send them back to Portugal to be dealt with by the King. For, if the captains
were bad, he said, the officers of the fortresses would be so also, and the officers
of justice and revenue too, to the destruction of the people. Indeed, he said, the
injuries committed by the Moors sprang from the captain's robberies of them.
No one should escape to Portugal from the consequences of his crimes in India;
by chastising the great he would make the small afraid. By the same token, if he
found a man aggrieved or injured by the great, or by an unjust sentence, he
would give redresss and punish the wrongdoer. Any gentleman who sheltered
a malefactor and refused to give him up would be sent in irons to the King.
Anyone who contrived the escape of a malefactor would be punished in his
stead.

While absorbed with all his efforts to root out corruption and restore respect
for the law Gama still gave personal attention to the trading side of his commission—the preparation of cargo, the refitting of ships. Morning and evening
every day he visited the shore and the warehouses. 'Thus in everything he
shewed himself a strict minister of the service of the King and the good of the
people, for the service of God and the good of India.'

The most troublesome task which Gama had in establishing his authority
as viceroy was that of disciplining the governor whom he had superseded. In
his stay of above a year in Hormuz, Dom Duarte de Menezes had had a profitable time, what with his brokers compelling traders to buy his good at high
prices; bribes that the chief minister took from the people 'to give to him to
keep him in good humour'; intercepting part of the tribute payable to the King;
and taking profits from captured Moorish traders. About the time that Gama
was leaving Goa for Cochin Dom Duarte collected his goods and his fleet, left
Hormuz, called at Muskat and sailed for India, arriving at Chaul in late October.
De Sousa sent out refreshments to him and a note stating that the viceroy had
ordered that he should not land but go on. Dom Henrique in Goa gave him
the same treatment. So, after a few days' trading, he moved in leisurely fashion
down coast to Baticala, where he started buying goods. His second in command,
Hector da Silveira, grew tired of these delays, which were a tactic to avoid the
viceroy, and eventually took the greater part of the fleet down to Cochin.

At length, in early November, the deposed governor anchored at the bar
of Cochin. Word was sent to him from Gama to transfer to the *Castello*, then
loading, to go in her as a prisoner on parole to the King in Lisbon. Dom Duarte
argued, transferred his baggage to a different ship, the *S. Jorge*, and there took

up quarters. He was dragging things out, believing the viceroy to be ill and hoping that he would soon die. Ill or not, Gama acted with energy. He ordered out from the building-yards two galleons, and instructed that next morning they were to go, charged with artillery and with gunners, into the river. In them he sent the chief constable and the auditor-general with orders that the ships were to anchor on either side of the *S. Jorge*, near the stern. That done, the auditor with two notaries was to take a boat alongside and call upon Dom Duarte in the King's name to leave the ship at once and go to the *Castello*. If he did not obey an official protest was to be written out and witnessed. The viceroy's order was to be repeated three times. If Dom Duarte did not obey the crew was to be summoned to leave the ship, because she was to be sunk. When all was done, they were to go back to the galleons and sink the ship.

During this time Dom Luiz, who had shown his clear disapproval of his brother's doings, tried to smooth things for him. Correa records how Dom Luiz begged Gama as a favour not to be so rigorous with his brother, who, after all, 'had not sold any of the King's fortresses'. Gama is said to have answered, 'Senhor Dom Luiz, if your brother had sold fortresses he would not have got his head where it now is, for I would have ordered it to be cut off. You should not have said that to me. Your brother never annoyed me for me to feel hatred towards him . . . I act thus because I am your servant and the King our sovereign is your friend. With respect to your brother I was going to advise him, and to you as a brother I also give the advice, that for the future he pay great obedience to the commands of the King, since up to this time he has observed them so ill in the governance of India that he is the scandal of Portugal.'

This grew into a dispute. After much contention Gama went to the door, saying 'Senhor Dom Luiz, go in peace, I have told you many truths; you little believe me, you think you have all the reason on your side and that I am the one mistaken; you show yourself unthankful for what I could do and which I do not do because I see you stand in my way.'

Dom Luiz wanted to speak again, but taking off his square cap the viceroy said, 'Sir, do me the favour to let there be no more today'; and he turned his back on him.

An enraged Dom Luiz went out. As he passed through the hall many heard him say, 'You do not choose to hear me. I trust in God a time will come in which I shall not choose to hear you. I will go to my brother and whatever happens to him shall happen to me.' And with his followers he went to his lodging.

His words came quickly to Gama who responded promptly. As Dom Luiz was sitting down at his table to dine with his associates Lopo Vaz de Sampayo, captain of the fortress, came to him. Without going in to the hall he called from the door, 'Senhor Dom Luiz, the viceroy commands that you should go with me to embark at once; and he stands at the window waiting until you go aboard.'

'I am amazed he did not send bailiffs to carry me off: all that he commands shall be done.' Those at the table rose to go with him but they were forbidden to leave the house.

With two servants Dom Luiz went to the shore and took a boat out to the *S. Jorge*. Up till that time he had kept clear of his brother. At the ship's side he found the auditor calling out the viceroy's orders, interrupted him, went aboard, and prevailed on his brother to submit to fortune, taking him off to the *Castello*. There Afonso Mexia, the new comptroller, arrived from Gama to call in various monies received by Dom Duarte but owing to the Crown. Prevaricating about this, protesting that he would give his account to the King, Duarte also decided to have his treasure buried, in case the viceroy had a search made to take it from him. He entrusted a chest full of rich gold stuffs, pearls and jewellery 'worth a large price' to the vicar-general. This old accomplice, with another confidential priest, went at night 'in a boat of black Malabar men' to a beach outside the town. They sent away the boat, buried the chest in the sand and marked the place with an ox-skull; afterwards they took a bearing on the monastery of St Antony, 'but not very exactly as it was night'. Next morning the vicar-general took a stroll on the beach to take his bearings more exactly and made marks on the wall with a javelin. But the scheme went wrong. Probably someone walking on the beach kicked the skull; for when the priest went down at night to probe he could not find the chest. For that night and many nights more the two reverend men searched about the beach, until at last they met success—'for God did not choose so great a treasure should be lost'.

Though he prevaricated for so long as he could, hoping all the time for the viceroy's death so that 'he should remain in his government', Duarte had finally to accept that he was a prisoner, not to leave the ship except by order of the King of Portugal. He sailed soon afterwards, his brother with him in a different ship. On the way home through the south Atlantic they were separated. Luiz was captured and killed by pirates. Duarte reached the coast of the Algarve, buried his treasure on the beach near Faro, landed his goods at Sesimbra, and ordered the ship to go on to Lisbon; but a storm drove the ship on shore with cables broken 'or, as some said, cut at night in order that it might be supposed Dom Duarte's money was lost there'. For losing his ship Duarte was shut up in prison in Torres Vedras for many years. Though eventually released to be captain of Tangiers it is said that he never found his chest—nor did the King.

Dealing with Dom Duarte did not deflect Gama from his many other tasks. He sent groups of armed vessels along the coast to control marauders and smugglers and to the Maldive islands against Moors who were interrupting supplies for the fleet. Preparing ships to patrol the coast he found that, as at Goa, he had to call in artillery from the merchants. Learning that in the division of the prize ship at Goa the factor of the fleet and the factor and clerks ashore had contrived a share-out among themselves he had them arrested and brought to Cochin to 'learn by what devices they had enriched themselves'.

'He went on examining diligently into other evils', Correa writes, 'so that without any doubt he put India into a very straight road for the King's service and for the good of the people and, above all, very strict justice, which had become much perverted.' His health was failing. He suffered 'great pains in the neck, which had got awry, and some boils came to the surface at the nape of the neck, but very hard; they would not ripen for all the remedies that were applied; nothing availed and they gave him such great torment that they did not allow him to turn his face in any direction.'

He was affected, too, by great fits of irritation. With 'the heavy cares which he felt on account of the many things which he had got to do his illness was doubled'. He took to his bed and gave all the necessary orders 'with great travail of spirit, which caused him to be overtaken by mortal illness, with such pains as deprived him of speech'. It seems probable that he was afflicted by deep intractable carbuncles and that either these or the treatment of them brought on septicaemia. Even in this condition he kept control over official life. At this time the cinnamon ships arrived from Ceylon. He pressed the transfer of the cargo to the Lisbon argosy, by then almost fully loaded, sent off at once a fast ship with his letters and reports for the King, and turned his attention to the captain of Ceylon, against whom were many charges of evil living—'fond of divisions, reckless in doing evil'. When this man's ship reached the bar the auditor-general met him to take from him a signed pledge that he would not leave the ship without orders from the viceroy. 'If he would not give such a pledge the auditor was to bring him as a prisoner and shut him up in irons in the fortress and collect the depositions which came from Ceylon; and this was done.'

Near to death, Gama moved from the fortress into the house of a wealthy merchant, Diogo Pereira. He called in the captain of Cochin, Lopo Vaz de Sampaya; the comptroller, Afonso Mexia; and with them the secretary of the government, to make a record. From them all he took an oath that they would carry out exactly and in full whatever he had ordered, until such time as the next governor might direct otherwise. To this oath each signed his name. Gama then made a written instruction that the captain and comptroller should not alter or countermand anything he had done, but see that in all matters of justice and revenue everything would be carried out as he had ordered it. At his death, when the letter of succession was opened, they were to hand everything to the new governor, with a box of papers to be delivered to them by his son Dom Estevan and belonging to the King. Everything to be done at the handover of power was set down in detail.

In his will he directed that his sons should take all his servants and all his goods to Portugal, selling nothing; that any of his servants who wished to stay in India should be allowed to do so and be paid everything due to them for their services; that all his clothes and 'household furniture of silk' should go to the churches and hospital; and that his bones should be carried to Portugal. To each of the women flogged at Goa he left 100,000 reals (250 cruzados), 'to be given them with much secrecy'.

His mind clear to the last Vasco da Gama died at three o'clock in the morning of Christmas Eve 1524. His death was not announced until dusk; 'and soon after all the people of the city came together in the court of the church and each one shewed what he felt'. Dressed in silk clothes, over them a mantle of the Order of Christ, and with a dark barret-cap, a sword and a gilded belt, and gilt spurs on dark buskins, his body was placed, uncovered, on the bier of the Brotherhood of Mercy and carried by gentlemen of that order to the monastery of St Antony. He was buried there in the principal chapel. Not till fifteen years later was his body taken to Portugal, to the church at Vidigueira.

All his great mass of work as viceroy—reform, restitution, retribution, reorganisation—he had accomplished in less than four months: between 15 September and 24 December 1524.

'They first set on Foot the Navigation of the Ocean'

'Of all the great Events that have happened in the World of late Ages, those which concern the Voyages and Discoveries, made by the *Europeans* in the fifteenth and sixteenth Centuries, do justly challenge the Preference. . . . In the Merit and Glory of these Achievements, the *Portugueze*, without all Controversy are intitled to the first and principal Share . . . it must be confessed, that they first set on Foot the Navigation of the Ocean, and put it into the Heads of other Nations, to go on the Discovery of distant Regions.

'Other Nations were so far from being as early as the *Portugueze* in Attempts of this Kind, that these latter had been carrying on their Enterprizes, near fourscore Years, before any of their Neighbours seem to have thought of foreign Discoveries . . . the several Events showed, that the Designs were the Results of solid Reasoning, and formed on the most rational Grounds.' (Thomas Astley, *A New General Collection of Voyages and Travels.*)

Envoi

Such is the story of Vasco da Gama, his part in finding the direct sea-route to India and the times and conditions which made it possible. For most of the fifteenth century the Portuguese were leaders in seamanship and navigation, chief adventurers in what the seafarers of his time called the 'ocean sea'; for most of the sixteenth century they dominated the Indian Ocean and the eastern trade with Europe. Then they were overtaken by others, mainly Dutch and English adventurers, and later French. Eventually Brazil—and Angola and Mozambique —became more important to them than India.

Writers on Portugal, India and Gama have shown a marked tendency to involve themselves in moral—and even genetical—judgment in the effort to explain the 'Portuguese failure'. The Portuguese, it seems, were ferocious, avaricious, treacherous, sanctimonious. But is not that the essential nature of colonial conquest whether it is in Malabar, Ireland, Zululand, Damaraland, Congo, Malaya or Vietnam? It only grows larger in scale as the centuries pass, more bestial and more ingenious. The Portuguese have been criticised as corrupt and disloyal administrators: that is a general failing in which colonial officials are easily tempted, a fault inherent in the nature of empire. But there are also instances of able and incorruptible administrators, among them Albuquerque and—outstandingly—Gama.

But the Portuguese tolerated, indeed encouraged, mixed marriage—even married their own slaves in Portugal! Miscegenation undermined the virility, injured the national character and physique! A man who marries a slave, still treating her as such, is indeed himself enslaved. So in fact mixed 'marriages' in Malabar—commonly little more than enforced and legalised concubinage involving compulsory baptism—often had disastrous results, moral, social and economic: but the origin of these disasters was social and economic, not racial or genetic.

It is said that Portugal's great problem was lack of men. There is some truth in that; but a similar weakness did not hold back the Dutch, who supplanted the Portuguese in the Far East. When, in the course of a single generation, great wealth poured into Portugal the greater part went to three groups: the King and his household, the nobility and the Church. All three used these new resources to create handsome buildings, extend their estates, commission works of art and compete in the luxury of living. Unfortunately the 'mercantile monopolistic monarchy' lacked the financial skills—and perhaps the will—to make the new wealth breed. Portugal was relatively poor in merchants; some of the best had been lost with the expulsion of the Jews between 1497 and 1525. Such skills were to be found more in Antwerp, Amsterdam and Bristol than in Lisbon. Scarcely two or three generations were needed for the chief profits on the eastern trade to find their way into the hands of north European entrepreneurs, many of whom opened agencies in Lisbon. For similar reasons the corruption which permeated the Portuguese eastern colonies was more destructive of enterprise than was the systematised corruption in the British East India Company.

It was nothing inherent in the character of the Portuguese that caused their troubles. To see that it is only necessary to look at the immense vitality of dour old Vasco da Gama, his audacity, perseverance, self-sacrifice and endurance, his scientific spirit, forethought and ability to organise—attributes to be found in many others of the Portuguese heroic age. Telling the story of the discoveries to which Gama's forms the climax one is forced in the end, in spite of the cruelties, jealousies and other failings into, perhaps reluctant, admiration.

The narrative of *Sail the Indian Sea* has been based on the surviving eye-witness reports: the anonymous *Roteiro* of the first voyage written by a member of the crew of the *S. Raphael* (said by some, not very convincingly, to have been the soldier, Alvaro Velho); for the second voyage, the *Navigation* written by the clerk Thomé Lopes, who sailed in Estevan da Gama's flotilla, and the short and inaccurate account known as *Calcoen*, apparently written by a Flemish pilot; and for the third voyage the relevant passage in the *Lendas da India* of Gaspar Correa, who was serving in Goa when Gama arrived as Viceroy. These accounts I have amplified from the work of the sixteenth-century historians whose texts were based on contemporary documents, state papers and personal knowledge: Joan de Barros, Fernan Lopes de Castanheda, Jeronymo Osorio, Gomes Eannes de Azurara, Duarte Pacheco Pereira and Duarte Barbosa. I have also used with discretion the much criticised earlier passages of Correa's *Lendas*: he has been magisterially reproved by Ravenstein and others for his jumble of truth and fiction but he is sometimes confirmed by other writers (such as Castanheda and Osorio) who cannot have seen his text.

My method has been strict use of the facts and descriptions given by eye-witnesses, preferring them when they differ from the historians. Where the eye-witnesses leave gaps or are vague I have brought in mainly Barros, Castanheda and Osorio. The narratives, particularly the first voyage *Roteiro*, often have little to say on such topics as weather and conditions of the voyage. Arriving in Malabar with the monsoon the fleet must have experienced constant rain—during June, July and August rainfall commonly reaches eighty inches— but it is hardly mentioned in the *Roteiro*. There is scarcely a word about the days in the south Atlantic. I have had to use other sixteenth- and seventeenth-century descriptions, such as those of Linschoten and Mocquet, in an attempt to show some of the realities of life at sea.

For the history of Portugal in the fifteenth and sixteenth centuries, and the earlier background, my main aids have been the *History of Portugal* by Antonio de Oliveira Marques; *L'Economie de l'empire portugais aux XVe et XVIe siècles* by Vitorino de Magalhaes-Godinho; *L'Expansion européenne du XIIIe au XVe siècle* by Pierre Chaunu; *The Perfect Prince* by Elaine Sanceau; for the Portuguese in Malabar most useful have been K. M. Pannikar's *Malabar and the Portuguese*, Zain Al-Din's *Tohfut-ul-mujahideen*, Duarte Barbosa's *Account of the Countries Bordering on the Indian Ocean*, Garcia da Orta's *Colloquies on the Simples and Drugs of India*, R. S. Whiteway's *The Rise of Portuguese Power in India 1497-1550*, F. C. Danvers' *The Portuguese in India*, Edgar Prestage's *Portuguese Pioneers*, K. G. Jayne's classic *Vasco do Gama and his Successors 1460-1580*; for navigation most help has come from Pacheco's *Esmeraldo di Situ Orbis*, G. Ferrand's *L'Astronomie nautique arabe*, J. Bensaude's *L'Astronomie nautique au Portugal à l'époque des grandes découvertes*, D. W. Waters' mighty work *The Art of Navigation in Elizabethan and early Stuart Times* and 'Science and the Techniques of Navigation in the Renaissance' from *Art, Science and History in the Renaissance* by C. S. Singleton, E. R. G. Taylor's *The Haven Finding Art*, B. Penrose's *Travel and Discovery in the Renaissance 1420-1620*, S. E. Morison's *Admiral of the Ocean Sea*, the Admiralty's *African Pilot* and *Indian Pilot*, and several reprints in the splendid series published by the Junta de Investigacões do Ultramar-Lisboa, in particular *The navigational theory of the Arabs in the fifteenth and sixteenth centuries* by G. R. Tibbetts, *How did the navigator determine the speed of his ship and the distance run* by E. Crone, *The Iberian bases of the English art of Navigation in the Sixteenth Century* by D. W. Waters and *O navio S. Gabriel e as naus manuelinas* by J. M. Barata. Two exceptionally useful books have been, in their different ways, Armando Cortesão's *The Mystery of Vasco da Gama* and Thomas Astley's evergreen *A New General Collection of Voyages and Travels*. Apart from one quotation I have made no use of the *Lusiad* of Camões. It is essentially the epic poem of Portugal, with Gama as a personification rather than a person. Anyone writing in English on such a theme must be grateful for the rich series of translations and reprints published by the Hakluyt Society. The many other publications I have consulted are shown in the bibliography on page 161.

Many people have helped me with advice and information. I offer my particular thanks to Commander D. W. Waters RN (whose percipient remark I quote on page 16), Professor Luis de Albuquerque, Frank Allen, Prakash

Datta, K. K. Elliott, Helder Macedo, Derek Weber, and the staff of the British Library, the London Library, the National Maritime Museum Greenwich, the Portuguese Embassy London and the Royal Geographical Society. Errors and omissions which in spite of their help still mar the text are mine. The enjoyment has been mine as well.

Bibliography

The publications listed are those which have been referred to in preparing this book.

AA, Pieter Vander (Boekverkooper), *De Doorlugtige Scheeps-Togten der Portugysen na Oost-Indien*, Leiden 1727.

Abdur Razzek, *see* Major.

Acosta, Cristoval, *Tractada de las drogas y medicinas de las Indias Orientaleis, con sus plantas*, Burgos 1578.

Acosta, J. de, *The Natural & Moral History of the Indies*, Tr. C. R. Markham, Hakluyt Society, London 1880

Admiralty, Lord Commissioners of, *Africa Pilot*, London 1915–20; *India, West of, Pilot*, London 1919–22.

Africanus, *see* Leo, Joannes.

Alaux, J. P., *Vasco da Gama*, Paris 1931.

Albuquerque, A. d', *The Commentaries of the great Afonso Dalbuquerque*, Tr. W. de G. Birch, Hakluyt Society, London 1875–83.

Albuquerque, L. de, *Um roteiro primitivo do Cabo da Boa Esperança até Moçambique*, Coimbra 1970.

Alvarez, F., *Narrative of the Portuguese Embassy to Abyssania*, Tr. and ed. Lord Stanley of Alderney, Hakluyt Society, London 1881.

Anon, *A Journal of the First Voyage of Vasco da Gama 1497–1499*, Tr. and ed. E. G. Ravenstein, Hakluyt Society, London 1898.

Anon, *The Periplus of the Erythrean Sea: Travel and trade in the Indian Ocean by a Merchant in the first century*, Tr. and ed. W. H. Schiff, New York 1912.

Anon, *Calcoen: A Dutch Narrative of the Second Voyage of Vasco da Gama*, Tr. J. B. Berjeau, London 1874.

Astley, T., *A New General Collection of Voyages and Travels*, London 1745–7.

Azurara, G., *The Chronicle of the Discovery and Conquest of Guinea*, Tr. C. R. Beazley and E. Prestage, Hakluyt Society, London 1896–99.

Barata, J. M., *O navio S. Gabriel e as naus manuelinas*, Coimbra 1970.

Barbosa, D., *An Account of the Countries Bordering the Indian Ocean*, Tr. M. L. Dames, Hakluyt Society, London 1918.

Barros, J. de, *Decadas da Asia*, Lisbon 1778.

Barros, J. de, *Die Asia des João de Barros in Wortgetreuer Übertragung*, Tr. E. Feust, Nuremberg 1844.

Bell, C., *Portugal and the Quest of the Indies*, London 1971.

Bensaude, J., *L'Astronomie nautique au Portugal à l'époque des grandes découvertes*, Berne 1912.

Bensaude, J., *Histoire de la Science nautique portugaise*, Geneva 1917.

Bensaude, J., *Lacunes et surprise de l'Histoire des Découvertes maritimes*, 1e Partie, Coimbra 1930.

Bensaude, J., *Les Légendes allemandes sur l'Histoire des Découvertes portugaises*, Geneva 1917-20.

Bigourdan, M. G., *L'Astronomie. Évolution des idées et des méthodes*, Paris 1911.

Bittner, M. and Tomaschek, W., *Die topographischer Capitel des indischen Seespiegels Mohît*, Vienna 1897.

Boxer, C. R., 'Portuguese Roteiros 1500-1700', *The Mariner's Mirror*, vol. XX, No. 2, April 1934, pp. 171-86, London.

Boxer, C. R., *see also* Brito, G. de.

Braun, G. and Hogenberg, F., *Civitatis Orbis Terrarum*, Cologne 1572-1618.

Brito, G. de, *The Tragic History of the Sea 1589-1622*, Tr. C. R. Boxer, Hakluyt Society, London 1959.

Brownlee, W., *The First Ships Round the World*, Cambridge 1974.

Bry, Johann Theodor de and Johann Israel de, *India Orientalis*, Part II 1598, Part III 1599, Part IV 1600, Leiden.

Burton, R. F., *First Steps in East Africa*, London 1856.

Cadamosto, *see* Crone, G. R.

Cabral, *see* Greenlee, W. B.

Cameron, I., *Lodestone and Evening Star*, London 1965.

Camões, L. de, *The Lusiad*, Tr. W. J. Mickle, London 1798.

Carr Laughton, L. G., 'The Way of a Ship', *The Mariner's Mirror*, XIV, 2, 1928, 132-48.

Castanheda, F. L. de, *The first book of the historie of the discoveries of the East Indies*, Tr. Nic Litchfield, London 1582.

Chaunu, P., *L'Expansion européenne du XIIIe au XVe siècle*, Paris 1969.

Congreve, H., 'A brief notice of some contrivances practised by the native mariners of the Coromandel coast', *Madras Journal of Literature and Science*, vol. XVI, pp. 101-4, Madras 1850 (reproduced in Ferrand, G., 1928).

Cooper, P., 'Buccaneering Medicine', *M & B Pharmaceutical Bulletin*, vol. VII, No. 12, December 1958, pp. 134-7.

Correa, G., *Lendas da India*, Lisbon 1858-64.

Correa, G., *The Three Voyages of Vasco da Gama and his Viceroyalty*, Tr. and ed. the Hon. E. S. Stanley, Hakluyt Society, London 1869.

Cortes, M., *The Art of Navigation*, Tr. R. Eden, London 1584.

Crotesão, A., *The Mystery of Vasco da Gama*, Coimbra 1973

Cortesão, A., *The Suma Orientalis of Tomé Pires and the book of Francis Rodrigues*, Hakluyt Society, London 1944.

Cortesão, A. and Texeira da Mota, A., *Portugaliae Monumenta Cartographica*, Lisbon 1960.

Crone, E., *How did the navigator determine the speed of his ship and the distance run?* Coimbra 1969.

Crone, G. R., *The Discovery of the East*, London 1972.

Crone, G. R., *The Voyages of Cadomosto*, Hakluyt Society, London 1937.

Culver, H. B., *The Book of Old Ships*, New York 1935.

Danvers, F. C., *The Portuguese in India*, London 1894.

Ferrand, G., *Instructions nautiques et routiers arabes et portugaises des XVe et XVIe siècles*, Tome III, *Introduction à l'astronomie nautique arabe*, Paris 1928.

Filgueiras, O. L. and Barroca, A., *O Caique do Algarve a Caravela Portuguesa*, Coimbra 1973.

Firishta, A., *History of the Rise of the Mohamedan Power in India till the year 1612*, Tr. J. Briggs, London 1829.

Galvano, A., *The Discoveries of the World*, Ed. Vice-Admiral Bethune, Hakluyt Society, London 1862.

Gibb, H. A. R., *The Travels of Ibn Batuta AD 1325-1354*, Hakluyt Society, Cambridge 1958-62.

Greenlee, W. B., *The Voyage of Pedro Alvarez Cabral to Brazil and India*, Hakluyt Society, London 1938.

Hacke, W., *A Description of the Sea Coasts Ports Bays harbours Rivers etc of Monomotapee Soffala Mozambique etc*, Manuscript maps, Wapping? 1690?

Harrisse, H., *Document Inédit Concernant Vasco da Gama*, Paris 1889.

Hart, H. H., *Sea Road to the Indies*, London 1952.

Hawkins, R., *Observations*, London 1622, Argonaut Press reprint, Ed. J. A. Williamson, London 1933.

'History of Discovery and Exploration': *The Search Begins* and *Eastern Islands, Southern Seas*, Ed. anon, both London 1973.

Huemmerich, Fr., *Vasco da Gama und die Entdeckung des Seewegs nach Ost-Indien*, Munich 1898.

Ibn Batuta, *see* Gibb, H. A. R.

Jayne, K. G., *Vasco da Gama and his Successors*, London 1910.

Kamal, Yusuf, *Monumenta Cartographica Africae et Aegypti*, Leiden 1926–53.

Landstrom, B., *The Ship*, London 1961.

Landstrom, B., *The Quest for India*, London 1964.

Leo, Johannes, Africanus, *Description de l'Afrique Tierce Partie du Monde*, Tr. J. Temporal, Lyon 1556.

Leo, Johannes, Africanus, *The History and Description of Africa*, Tr. J. Pory, Ed. R. Brown, Hakluyt Society, London 1896.

Linschoten, J. Huygen von, *Itinerario. Voyages ofte Schipvaert*, Amsterdam 1604–5.

Linschoten, J. Huygen von, *His discours of Voyages into ye Easte and West Indies*, Tr. W.P., London 1598.

Linschoten, J. Huygen van, *The Voyage of John Huygen van Linschoten*, Ed. A. C. Burnell and P. A. Tiele, Hakluyt Society, London 1885.

Lopes, D., *A Report of the Kingdom of Congo*, Tr. M. Hutchinson, London 1881.

Lopes, T., *see* Schefer, C.

Magalhaes-Godinho, V. de, *L'Economie de l'empire portugais aux XVe et XVIe siècles*, Paris 1969.

Major, R. H., *India in the Fifteenth Century*, Hakluyt Society, London 1857.

Mariner's Mirror, The, Note on the *Santa Maria* of Columbus, XVI, 2, 1930, 187–95.

Markham, C., 'The History of the Gradual Development of the Groundwork of Geographical Science', *The Geographical Journal*, vol. XLVI, No. 3, September 1915, p. 177.

Medina, P. de, *Regimiento de Navegacion*, Seville 1563.

Miller, C., *Mappae Arabicae*, Stuttgart 1926–31.

Mocquet, J., *Voyages en Afrique, Asie, Indes Orientales et Occidentales*, Rouen 1665.

Mocquet, J., *Travels and voyages into Africa, Asia and America, the East and West Indies*, Tr. N. Pullen, London 1696.

Morison, S. E., *Admiral of the Ocean Sea*, Boston 1942.

Nordenskiöld, A. E., *Periplus: an essay on the early history of charts and sailing directions*, Tr. F. A. Bather, Stockholm 1897.

Oliveira Marques, A. de, *History of Portugal*, New York 1972.

Orta, G. de, *Colloquies on the Simples and Drugs of India*, Tr. C. Markham, London 1913.

Osorio de Fonseca, Jeronymo (Bishop of Sylves), *De Rebus Emanuelis Regis Lusitaniaei n Victissimi Virtute et Auspicio*, Lisbon(?) 1576.

Osorio de Fonseca, Jeronymo (Bishop of Sylves), *The History of the Portuguese during the Reign of Emanuel*, Tr. J. Gibbs, London 1752.

Pacheco Pereira, D., *Esmeraldo di Situ Orbis*, Tr. G. H. T. Kimble, Hakluyt Society, London 1937.

Panikkar, K. M., *Malabar and the Portuguese*, Bombay 1929.

Penrose, B., *Travel and Discovery in the Renaissance 1420–1620*, Cambridge, Mass. 1952.

Pinkerton, J. A., *A General Collection of the best and most interesting Voyages*, London 1808–14.

Plischke, H., *Vasco da Gama – Der Weg nach Ostindien*, Leipzig 1924.

Prestage, E., *The Portuguese Pioneers*, London 1933.

Prinsep, J., 'Note of the nautical instruments of the Arabs', *Journal of the Asiatic Society of Bengal*, December 1836, p. 784.

Purchas, S., *Hakluytus Postumus or Purchas his Pilgrimes* (Maclehose reprint), Glasgow 1905–7

Pyrand de Laval, F., *Voyage to the East Indies, the Maldives, the Moluccas and Brazil*, Tr. A. Gray and H. C. P. Bell, Hakluyt Society, London 1887.

Ravenstein, E. G., *see* Anon.

Renault, G., *The Caravels of Christ*, London 1959.

Roberts, G., *Atlas of Discovery*, London 1973.

Rodriguez, F., *see* Cortesão, A.

Sanceau, E., *The Perfect Prince*, Oporto 1959.

Schefer, C., *Navigations de Vasque de Gamme*, Paris 1898.

Sidi 'Ali, *see* Bittner, M.

Taylor, E. R. G., *The Haven Finding Art*, London 1956.

Tibbets, G. R., *Arab Navigation in the Indian Ocean before the Coming of the Portuguese* [Oriental Translation Fund New Series, vol. XLII], London 1971.

Tibbets, G. R., *The navigational theory of the Arabs in the fifteenth and sixteenth centuries*, Coimbra 1969.

Unger, R. W., 'Four Dordrecht Ships of the fifteenth century', *The Mariner's Mirror*, vol. VXI, No. 2, May 1975, pp. 109–16.

Varthema, L. di, *Travels*, Tr. J. W. Jones and C. P. Badger, Hakluyt Society, London 1863.

Vespuccius, Albericus, *The Voyage from Lisbon to India 1505–6*, Tr. C. H. Coote, London 1894.

Waters, D. W., *The Art of Navigation in Elizabethan & early Stuart Times*, London 1958.

Waters, D. W., *The Iberian Bases of the English Art of Navigation in the Sixteenth Century*, Coimbra 1970.

Waters, D. W., 'Science and Techniques of Navigation in the Renaissance' in *Art, Science and History in the Renaissance*, Ed. C. S. Singleton, Baltimore 1968.

Whiteway, R. S., *The Rise of Portuguese Power in India 1497–1550*, London 1899.

Williamson, J. A., *The Cabot Voyage and the Bristol Discovery under Henry VII*, Hakluyt Society, London 1962.

Zain Al-Din, *Tohfut-ul-mujahideen*, Tr. M. J. Rowlandson, London 1833.

Index

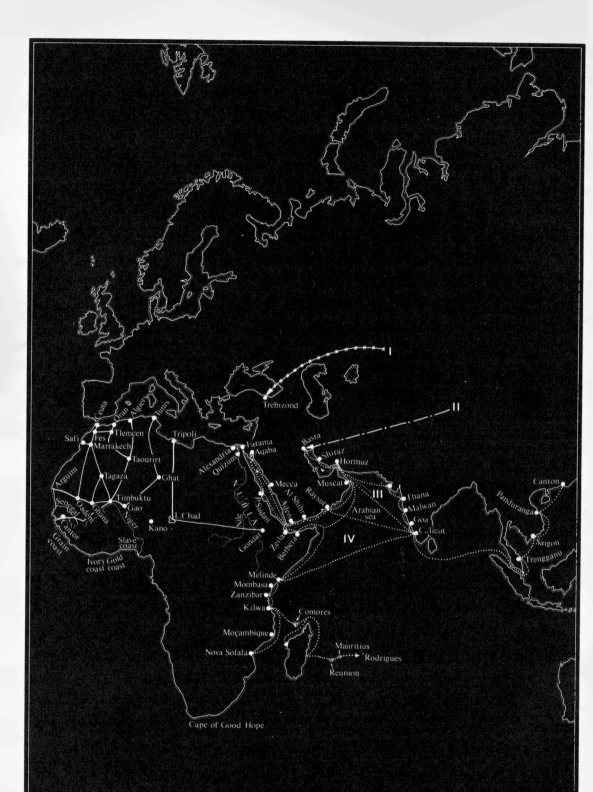

Moorish trade routes
before da Gama

.... Moorish trade routes

———— Caravan routes

I ✶✶✶✶✶ Old northern caravan route

II —·—·— Caravan route from Turkestan

III ———— Old sea route with long portage

IV ———— Sea route with shortest portage